IMAGINE A
COUNTRY

IMAGINE A COUNTRY

IDEAS FOR A BETTER FUTURE

This edition includes new contributors

EDITED BY

VAL McDERMID
& JO SHARP

CANONGATE

This paperback edition published in 2022 by Canongate Books

First published in Great Britain, the USA and Canada in 2020, 2022
by Canongate Books Ltd,
14 High Street, Edinburgh EH1 1TE

canongate.co.uk

1

Contributions copyright © individual contributors
Edited by Val McDermid and Jo Sharp

British Library Cataloguing-in-Publication Data
A catalogue record for this book is available on
request from the British Library

ISBN 978 1 83885 764 6

Typeset in Bembo by
Palimpsest Book Production Ltd, Falkirk, Stirlingshire

Printed and bound in Great Britain by
Clays Ltd, Elcograf S.p.A.

'Work as if you live in the early days of a better nation.'

Alasdair Gray
(28 December 1934–29 December 2019)

CONTENTS

INTRODUCTION TO
NEW EDITION

B ack in August 2019, when we sat late into the night drinking red wine and planting the seed of this book, we couldn't have imagined what sort of a world it would emerge into. *Imagine A Country* was published in March 2020, days before the first COVID-19 lockdown in the UK. Our plans for events across the country to discuss the book, to share our hopes for the future, to debate the way our country should be travelling, were derailed. We had to abandon a celebratory launch with a big get-together of contributors when the Aye Write festival had to be cancelled, and we were all forced to take events online. While we were excited by the discussion in the virtual events we did – and recognised their vastly more inclusive nature – we missed the spontaneity of discussion in person.

The pandemic has made the arguments of many of the chapters in this collection so much more urgent. It has reinforced our contention that far from being inevitable, much of what we see around us is the result of political choices and priorities. Some of the suggestions that might have seemed utopian when the chapters were initially written in the autumn of 2019 have come to pass: all but one of the parties in the Scottish elections in 2021 raised the possibility of replacing benefits with a Basic Universal Income, a feature of a number of the original imaginings. The rise of Zoom and Teams for online working and conferences has shown what disability rights activists have long argued: that rethinking the 'workplace' to be more inclusive can be done. Again, it has been shown to be a matter of choice, or imagination. Concern for public health was such that the political will was found to take homeless people off the streets and into shelter, highlighting that priorities in spending was why this hadn't been done before. In the long days and weeks of lockdown, we came to value the green parts of our cities, the sound of birdsong and the possibilities for escaping our homes and workplaces into the fresh air. When it was removed from us, we began to long for time with older relatives and the simple pleasure of sharing food with friends. In the early days of the pandemic, it did seem that many of us had begun to reflect on what truly mattered to us and to reconsider our priorities.

But it has often been said that while we are all in the same storm we are not in the same sea-worthy vessel. While a pandemic affects all, it soon became clear how much it exposed and deepened existing fissures in society. The immunising effects of working from home were available to some only by exposing others to the virus. Minority communities and the poor suffered noticeably higher rates of infection. Despite apparent progress in the workplace pre-pandemic, the move to lockdown seemed to reveal the persistent deep gender inequalities that run through domestic arrangements.

It seems no coincidence that during the pandemic we saw the rise of protest movements against the treatment of black lives (most notably sparked by the murder of George Floyd by police officers in the US) and women (sparked in the UK by the murders of Sarah Everard and Sabina Nessa and the subsequent policing of vigils for them). Thus, another key thread running through the original collection – a desire to reconsider whom we value, and how we support them in the national community – is also reinforced.

Until the last couple of years, the concept of public health had begun to seem rather dated in the west. The future of medicine was coalescing around genetic tests and personalised care, not the collective efforts of handwashing, mask wearing and social distancing. We could see how the prevailing cultures of different parts of the world led to different outcomes – from the individualised mask politics of the USA, to the collective support for monitoring and surveillance in South Korea. That some of the simplest interventions – such as mask wearing – are more about protecting others than the self, and that pandemic health is about society and not individuals, has brought into sharp focus the effects of years of concerted attempts to erode the social and collective.

Despite being launched into the pandemic, the first edition of the book sold out. We were gratified to hear from people who had found the book a source of hope during the most difficult times of the last two years, and that this had stimulated them to imagine their future more positively. We couldn't resist using the occasion of the publication of a paperback edition of the book to invite a few more folk to contribute, and so we have nineteen new voices in this second edition. But we are saddened that not all of those who contributed to the first edition are still with us: our country and our personal lives have most definitely lost some of their sparkle and their creative spark with the death of Marilyn Imrie in 2020.

Finally, we have often been asked what we would imagine ourselves. This collection is a shorthand for our vision. As we noted in our introduction to the first edition, we felt compelled to curate this book because of the rise of a toxic culture driven by social media within which it seemed impossible to have real exchange. We still long for a society in which people with different opinions, views and experiences can come together, to discuss, listen, learn and understand. A society where, at the end of discussion, both will have learned and been willing to adjust their views. Or perhaps each will have the same view as they started with, but will have a better understanding of where the other is coming from.

But at the heart of this is a respect for difference. Because, of course, utopia is a problematic concept – it is a singular. One person's utopia is often another's idea of hell. So, our imagined country is multiple – it has the maturity to respect differences, to start from a place of inclusion and to work through the challenges together.

Come along with us and imagine your own country.

Val McDermid is a writer and broadcaster. Jo Sharp is Professor of Geography at the University of St Andrews and Geographer Royal for Scotland.

VAL MCDERMID
AND JO SHARP

Imagine a country . . .

Close your eyes and put your fingers in your ears and shut out the angry chaos for a moment. Now take a deep breath and imagine a country you want to live in, a country you wish existed, a country where you'd feel truly at home . . .

That's what we asked a cross-section of Scottish society to do. (All sorts of people, except for politicians, because they already have plenty of opportunities to tell us what they think.) This extraordinary collection of ideas is what they imagined.

We believe it's time to take those imaginings seriously. Because if we're going to enact change, the first step is to imagine it. If we can't imagine a different way of being, if we can't imagine a different future, how can we reach escape velocity from an unbearable present?

Like so many of you, we have succumbed too often to rage and despair in recent times. We've seen battle-lines drawn where once we negotiated; vitriol and hatred dispensed where once we'd have listened and debated; fake news, deepfakes and barefaced lies where once we could believe. Too much of our political debate has shrunk to a nuance-free 280 characters. It's no surprise that we find ourselves pushed into polarised positions when we try to engage in that way.

This book is a revolt against all of that. This book is about hope.

There are plenty of voices that shout that imagination is the enemy of the real world, that imagination is for the artists, a luxury we can't afford in these times of austerity and cuts. But the fact that one of the first targets of austerity has been libraries reveals how subversive imagination really is. For libraries offer myriad possibilities. Where else can you come into contact with so many alternative visions of the world, both utopian and dystopian? Libraries are dangerous and provocative places.

Our intention in putting this book together is to stimulate debate, not shouting matches. This book is not a manifesto, it is not a singular voice: reading through the contributions should be more akin to walking down the street, sitting on the bus or in the pub, eavesdropping on a number of conversations, rants, daydreams and hopes, rather than reading a neat or coherent agenda. We have tried to draw in voices from across our nation – geographically, socially, politically. The book is not aligned with any party-political position – indeed, we hope we can use some of these ideas to hold our future politicians' feet to the fire.

Just as a library contains books that we disagree with and others we love, there will be some pieces here that you agree with, and some that will make the steam come out of your ears. And this is exactly what we're hoping for. After all, true democracy is about making space to hear the many voices; it is about us encountering different views, debating them and then reflecting on our own position, rather than hearing only the most confident or the loudest or the best-funded. It is perhaps only by hearing some of those voices at odds with our own that we may begin to break down binary thinking and start to open up more connections and alliances.

We set our contributors a tall order: to 'Imagine a Country' in 500–800 words (or an illustrative alternative) in the space of a month. Those 500–800 words aren't much, but we hope (that word again!) that it will stimulate conversations and respectful interactions that will engage with the complexity of modern life. Not everyone we invited felt able to contribute, but we are full of admiration for those who took up the gauntlet. Some have chosen to address the big challenges we face, to think afresh and with huge ambition; others have chosen instead to focus on a very specific change they'd like to see us embrace.

It happened that we did most of the work on this book while temporarily attached to the University of Otago in Dunedin, New Zealand, which provided us with focused thinking time. Viewing Scotland from 'the Edinburgh of the South' gave us a critical distance. When so much of the everyday is similar, the differences are all the more striking and that gave us pause to consider how quite small changes can have a significant impact on people's lives.

Take one example. Free public toilets seem to be everywhere in New Zealand. Towns and cities are well provisioned, but so are small settlements, tourist sites and even roadside viewpoints. They are all clean and well stocked; they are free from vandalism.

Not so in the UK, where many public toilets have been closed. Where they still exist, most charge for entry. This might appear a trivial issue, but it's not. It affects most of us at one time or another, when reliable access to toilets can make all the difference – parents with young children, pregnant women, people with disabilities, older men, drunk people, menstruating women, homeless people . . . The lack of toilet provision impacts our comfortable use of public space and makes our towns and cities less welcoming.

Small thing, big impact.

And, finally, what do *we* want? We want to live in a society where value is not measured by narrow economic criteria but a wider understanding of contribution. We want to live in a society which does not turn its back on the vulnerable, and instead is one that seeks to help everyone to achieve their potential. And if this means those who can afford it pay more in tax, then they should see evidence that this is the price for living in a civilised society. Enacting some of the ideas in this book would certainly provide such evidence.

We also want to sing and dance, to laugh and to enjoy all Scotland has to offer.

The idea for this book emerged from conversations provoked by the Edinburgh International Book Festival's 2019 theme: 'We need new stories.'

This is the first chapter.

Val McDermid is a writer and broadcaster. Jo Sharp is a Professor of Geography at the University of St Andrews.

LEILA ABOULELA

Some countries have double the number of public holidays Scotland has. In Indonesia, where my family and I lived for a few years, there were seventeen holidays, some of which were more than one day. As expected of a country in which almost 90 per cent of the population are Muslims, there were the two Eid holidays – al-Fitr and al-Adha – Islamic New Year, the birthday (Mawlid) of the Prophet Muhammad, and celebration of his Night Journey (the Isra and Miraj). There was also Christmas, Easter and Good Friday; there was New Year's Day and Chinese New Year – that's now adding up to three new year's days per year! Hindu and Buddhist feast-days were also public holidays, as well as Labour Day. I loved all these holidays, especially when they came mid-week; my husband and children at home, the working week disrupted. There is no better way to celebrate diversity than by sharing each other's festivals. I would love Scotland to be the same. Fewer working days would enable us all to live better lives.

If religious holidays are not to everyone's taste, then how about secular ones? Let's make Valentine's Day a public holiday. Burns Night, Guy Fawkes, Midsummer's Day. If Scotland gains independence, will there be an Independence Day holiday? Imagine . . .

Holidays mean more rest and more togetherness; more precious time, more valuable hours. This great spinning world, let's slow it down, let's have a break. A break from the internet would be nice too. A relief from the news. A recess from advertising. We do not need to shop 24/7. We do not need to know the news every hour. We do not need to be able to do every little thing on every single day of the week. For the sake of the climate, we can take time off from electricity, from heating, from travelling. Short pauses here and there. To catch our breath, to hear the birds, to see the stars, to listen to each other. To feel idle. There is nothing wrong with occasional idleness. Staring into space, thinking thoughts or thinking nothing, swinging on a hammock, sitting gazing into the flames. Our fingers need a rest, as do our eyes, our minds. Shopping has become the new oppression, as has acquiring likes on social media, the endless expenses of self-improvement, and keeping up with the latest celebrities. All this comes at the price of more drudgery, more hours spent earning, more days at work.

The four-day work week is not a fantasy. It has already been adopted in Germany and Denmark to some extent. Fewer working hours are better for our physical and mental health. The four-day work week would reduce pressure on the environment. A 2013 paper published in *Global Environmental Change* shows that countries with longer working hours consume more resources and emit more carbon.* Reduced working hours, they suggest, could contribute to sustainability by decreasing the environmental intensity of consumption patterns.

Research by the Trades Union Congress has found that UK full-time staff work almost two hours more than the EU weekly average. Yet staff in Denmark who worked fewer hours were more productive. Resting more and having adequate time for recreation improves the quality of the work we produce. By working fewer hours, we boost our output instead of reducing it.

Sadly, the reality in Britain is that many people are working longer hours or the same hours for less pay. Working harder to become poorer, working more to end up with less. Writing in *The Conversation*, economist David Spencer says: 'The continued force of consumerism has acted as a prop to the work ethic. Advertising and product innovation have created a culture where longer hours have been accepted as

---

* 'Could working less reduce pressures on the environment? A cross-national panel analysis of OECD countries, 1970–2007', K.W. Knight, E.A. Rosa, J.B. Schor, *Global Environmental Change*, 2013

normal, even while they have inhibited the freedom of workers to live well.'*

More public holidays – religious, secular or national – a reduction in the working week, time off from the internet, from the media, from travel and energy consumption, would reduce carbon footprint and give us more of what really matters.

Leila Aboulela's fifth novel, Bird Summons, *was shortlisted for the Saltire Society Scottish Fiction Book of the Year 2019.*

---

* 'Four-day work week is a necessary part of human progress – here's a plan to make it happen', David Spencer, *The Conversation*, 2019

TURAN ALI

I want to imagine a Scotland where the First Minister has a same sex or trans partner. And not just any old same sex or trans partner but the loudest, most obvious queen or dyke or trans person imaginable. The sort of person who screams *queer* from 200 metres just by seeing their outline, their gait or their fabulous outfit or hairdo, or by hearing them speak. It doesn't matter if it's a gay or lesbian couple, or a same sex, mixed sex or non-binary trans couple: any of these options would be a superb boost to the international image of Scotland as a modern, diversity-embracing country.

If at the time of this joyous event, of a queer 'First Couple', Scotland happened to be an independent nation, all the better, because then the First Couple would be trolling off to many more international destinations to commune with and be photographed next to national leaders from countries with very different policies about LGBTQ+ rights. With the First Minister and 'First Partner' together at official diplomatic events, representing the country, it says loud and clear that 'the First Minister and their partner are queer and that is fine by us.' It would be a provocation and shaming of the anti-LGBTQ+ regimes and laws in countries worldwide. If the First Partner is not welcome on the trip, then it does not happen, and Scotland explains why. We would be a global leader in true equality.

The necessity for the First Partner to be a glaringly obvious example of a queer person arises when the First Partner is alone, not standing next to the First Minister, but being photographed, filmed or interviewed separately. The maximum impact of Scotland's proudly LGBTQ+ First Couple would be achieved if every photo, even the tiniest video snippet and just the first few words heard from the First Partner on their own, all instantly said, 'Yes, dear, I'm queer and I represent Scotland – get used to it.' If this were in a Scotland that is still part of the United Kingdom, there'd be fewer international opportunities to parade the deeply symbolic couple, but there would still be massive international media interest, which should be fully embraced, showing Scotland as a world-leading diverse democracy and as the most progressive nation in the UK.

Actually, I don't think this would be a particularly difficult or controversial thing for the vast majority of people in Scotland to champion. For those who would struggle with having a queer First Couple leading the country, it forces a shift in recognising the status of such relationships as valid and equal. But this is only half of the double whammy – and its benefit – that I would like to imagine in a future Scotland.

The other half, which might be more challenging for many in Scotland, is to have a First Couple who were also from different cultures.

When my Scottish partner and I moved to Scotland in 2003 from London and bought a Highland cottage, I asked him, 'What do you think is going to be the bigger problem, that two gays are moving into the village or that one of them is English?' He looked at me with raised eyebrows that said, 'You know the answer to that question!' and he was right. We have not had one homophobic word from any Highland neighbours in the nearly two decades since we moved our home and businesses to Scotland. But being English has caused me to button my lip and feel hugely unwelcome on many occasions, in many parts of Scotland, to this day. I say 'being English', even though I don't have a single English gene in my body. I am of Turkish Cypriot and Austrian parentage. I just happen to have been born and raised in London and speak with a southeast English accent, which gets me damned instantly on opening my mouth by some people throughout Scotland. It is a source of continued sadness and creates a low-level constant feeling of being allowed to live in Scotland on sufferance. When people get past my accent and find out my ancestry, and I mention their initial hostility, they tell me, 'I didn't mean you. You're not really English.'

I want to imagine a Scotland where people are not welcomed or rejected just because of their accent or genetics, but rather for what sort of human being they are. Having a much-loved, flagrantly visibly and audibly queer First Couple, whom the people of Scotland relish having as their national representatives, is only half my imagined Shangri-La; the other half is imagining a grown-up Scotland thinking, 'the First Minister's very queer partner is very English, and both are fine by us.'

Turan Ali has been producing, directing and writing BBC drama, comedy and documentaries for over thirty years, and for the last decade has also been a stage storyteller with regular nights he hosts in Edinburgh (Queer Folks' Tales at the Scottish Storytelling Centre) and Vienna (with his Vienna Storytelling Collective).

LIN ANDERSON

Travelling between my home village of Carrbridge and my work-place in Edinburgh over many years, I know every kilometre of the A9 very well. I also know all the views from the train and more recently the bus.

I first travelled the route north as a teenager when studying at Glasgow University, heading home to Carrbridge for an occasional weekend or holiday. The road itself is vastly improved. The trains sadly have shrunk in size to three coaches, whereas in former times they were much longer and all stopped at Carrbridge, allowing me a short walk to my old home. A bus used to meet the trains back then to transport travellers into the village, a half-mile away.

This dream, however, is not about improved roads and travel round the Highlands, although this is often on my mind. It is about the landscape we travel through as we head north. How over my lifetime it has changed, but not in the direction I had hoped for.

The saddest and most distressing part of the northward journey for me has to be passing through Drumochter Pass. Here we can clearly see bulldozed tracks scarring the hillsides, many of which come to an abrupt end, because they are going nowhere. They are there so that those who wish to kill grouse need not walk too far to do so. These gravelled roads which require no planning permission, along with huge swathes of burned heather exposing the underlying peat, are anything but natural.

These are the Killing Fields for driven-grouse shooting, which has exploded in recent years. Along with its dense plantations of non-native trees, where no human may walk and no bird lives or sings, Scotland no longer resembles its true self. To discover that self, you must visit pockets of the old and protected Caledonian Forest at nearby Rothiemurchus or even, on a smaller scale, the woods surrounding Carrbridge.

Southwest Norway and Highland Scotland are very similar in climate, geology and landforms; but very different in modern land-use patterns and resulting landscapes. In the early twentieth century the region near Stavanger in Norway was almost completely deforested. It is now well wooded, mainly due to natural regeneration – a conscious and rewarding decision by government for the land and its population, both wild and human.

The truth is Scotland is not a natural wilderness but a man-made one. And what was made can be unmade, or remade. The difference can already be seen near Carrbridge. When crossing the Dava Moor to Forres, the landscape is now dotted with numerous naturally regenerating young pine trees.

Rewilding goes hand in hand with repopulation. Just as the natural covering was removed from the Highlands, so too were its people. In the new Scotland I dream that we would have a clear opportunity to change things. To revitalise the whole of Scotland's landscape, for the many, and not just the few. We can and will recreate a living landscape of which Scotland's people are an integral part.

Lin Anderson is a writer and screenwriter, best known for her series of forensic thrillers starring Dr Rhona MacLeod.

ALY BAIN

Welcome to Hamister, my country. Its name means 'Haven' in our ancient language. It is one of the most beautiful countries in the world, from its northerly islands to its rolling hills in the south. Hamister lies in the far north, surrounded by the sea, which can be wild, rough, treacherous and beautiful. The four seasons are reduced to just summer and winter. We are a small country but we believe small is good! People of Hamister are farmers and fishermen. We live in harmony with each other as we do with the abundance of wildlife that surrounds us. Our traditions and culture define who we are and play an important part in our everyday lives. In my country there is a fiddle in every house and not just as an ornament! The arts flourish and are viewed as an investment in our future instead of a throwaway subsidy. We believe our traditions and culture define who we are as a nation.

Every day in Hamister I see in our young people's faces a belief in their imagination and creativity. Young people who feel their ideas and talents are important and valued, who feel safe and healthy in their homes. Young people who feel connected in their families and communities and who feel it's OK to be a bit different, a bit insecure, but who have a belief that they will get to know and like who they truly are. Young people who can see value in the thinkers and artists among them and enjoy the company of all. Young people who feel they can engage in an education that helps them learn about themselves and their worlds with curiosity and tolerance, and who feel they are valued for who they are but also for what they can do. Young people who understand their cultural and historical narratives. The great thinkers, scientists, writers, artists and musicians. Young people who travel and are happy to say, 'I come from Hamister.' Young people who dream in technology and technicolour, and believe they can create great things in the future, and who understand what it feels like to be taken care of by their country and how to take care of each other.

In Hamister all traces of feudalism have been wiped away. The ancient laws of my country are 'udal', not 'few-dal' – for the benefit of the population as a whole. Democratic courts decide any disputes over land or life regardless of wealth or religion. All schoolchildren have the opportunity to visit every part of their country as part of the curriculum. In this way they learn about the country and environment they live in and how precious they both are. We would like to remove all possible means of pollution from our cities as quickly as possible; we're aiming to make a start with car-free city centres. I haven't owned a car for years. I joined the Hamister Car Club and rent only when I need to.

Hamister takes its place on the world stage feeling confident and secure in its culture, history and individuality. It is progressive and confronts the problems facing the world in an honest and constructive way. The great thinkers and philosophers of my country are dedicated to contributing to a future for all. We have a national broadcaster that's fully independent and funded by the government to represent us with authenticity and courage. Up-and-coming directors, producers, writers and performers are allowed to flourish. In Hamister people are optimistic and hardly ever say, 'Och, it'll never work.' The arts provide the thinkers and performers of the future and are our country's ambassadors abroad.

There are two compulsory things in Hamister that can't be avoided. One is that you must have a sense of humour. People who fail to laugh at least three times each day can be sent to one of the humour schools scattered over the country. People are generally much happier after a few sessions with our happy humour teachers. The other is that every man, woman and child must learn to sail a boat. Our greatest Foreseer of ancient times predicted that one day a wealthy unstoppable force would invade our country and make it into a golf course, so we must be ready to evacuate at any moment.

Tradition is being created every day and reflects the society we live in. My country puts the health and welfare of its people first and foremost. Our elderly are taken care of and appreciated instead of being institutionalised and forgotten about. The family lives and works together for the good of all and is at the heart of society.

I would like every generation to produce the Hamister equivalent of Billy Connolly and Jimmy Reid. One to help us laugh and think well of ourselves and the other to keep our feet on the ground and our hands aff the bevvie.

Aly Bain, born 1946, is a Shetland fiddler who lives in Edinburgh.

NICK BARLEY

Dear Mum,

It was lovely to see you at the weekend. The journey back to
Edinburgh was pretty uneventful: the monorail was a few seconds
late leaving York because there was some kind of glitch with the
electronic passport check – but otherwise we got home within the
hour, and in plenty of time for the street party. I feel bad about
being sceptical: it turned out to be quite fun and the neighbourhood
bore (I call him the Pope) was preoccupied with being in charge of
the barbecue, so I managed to avoid most of his pontificating.

Your brownies were devoured in a matter of minutes – although
most of them, in all honesty, were truffled by Haseeb and Callum
and that bunch of numpties from up the street. It was lovely to be
able to have an offering for the organisers, even though I was
straight off the monorail.

Oh, and I needn't have worried about the cat: Vita had been
feeding him even though we'd forgotten it when we'd sketched out
her work plan last week. She's been pretty amazing actually – miles
better than the wet-drip Cadet who 'looked after' the house when
we were away during the summer.

It was great to hear that your Cadet is working with you to sort
out your garden as well as helping with the cooking. I know it's a
bit weird at first, especially when you've been living by yourself for
so many years, but I promise you'll quickly get over that feeling of
being invaded by a stranger. I can imagine you tutting now, thinking
I'm being too damn relentlessly positive about it. But honestly, the

Young Adult Social Service system has been working for over thirty years now up here in Scotland and it's changed things for the better in so many ways.

I'm not denying it had its teething problems – especially during the School Rebellion of 2024 when that whole generation of school leavers rejected the idea of a compulsory year of fully paid community work. The most ambitious people in that first cohort had the impression it would somehow get in the way of their careers, while the less motivated ones just balked at the idea of a year of shovelling other people's shit. But even the lazy ones soon realised that being a Social Cadet offered a lot more than that. And I guess it wasn't until the pensions crisis later that decade – and the genius *We Can Feed You* campaign – that kids started to see that it was either Social Service, or starvation for thousands of elderly people.

I know when you visited us last year you were amazed at the way the scheme has developed into so much more than just social care. When they introduced the Childcare Support and Healthcare divisions in the early 2030s, it meant not only that parents could finally get affordable nursery care, but also that the NHS crisis abated in a matter of months. When you get to that point down in York, you'll really feel the difference.

It's weird that Rose is already planning for her own Social Service year. She's been doing pretty well in her school work since the turn of the year but she's looking forward to getting some non-academic skills training once her exams are done. This term, she's spending Wednesday afternoons visiting the hospital where she'll be based. It's so much more than just running about getting cups of tea and toast for patients; she gets to shadow various health-care workers and it's going to make such a difference to her academic studies – if she manages to get the grades of course . . . But the great thing about Social Service is that she'll get skills credits that will count towards her university entrance assessment. Assuming she scores highly in her People-Facing Skills and her Organisational Skills modules, they'll count for the same as a couple of Advanced Highers. And best of all from my perspective, good grades in her Socials mean she'll qualify for zero tuition fees. It's win-win for everyone.

Still, Rose is viewing the whole year ahead with a degree of adolescent petulance. A whole year of working four days a week for the Living Wage? And a further whole day each week when she's free to 'do culture'? Only someone as thrawn as Rose could be annoyed about that prospect . . . Bloody teenagers.

Anyway. Suffice it to say that you'll get used to your Cadet soon enough. Just please make sure you're not treating her like too much of a lackey. Don't forget it means you're allowed to stay in that lovely house rather than having to move into a care home!

Loads of love to you, Mum. And look forward to seeing you at Christmas.

Nick xx

Nick Barley is Director of the Edinburgh International Book Festival and a trustee of the Booker Prize Foundation.

DAMIAN BARR

S peak to me of my history. Lean in and tell me stories of the place
where I was born and raised and whose name is right there on
top of my birth certificate but of which I know so little.

Scotland was the stylised logo on the front of all my school jotters
– it floated shorn of islands and chopped off the top of England, just
as Mary lost her head. The heart of it was blown up big, as if a magni-
fying glass had been placed over it, and next to it was this text:
Strathclyde Regional Council. Strathclyde seemed to be the biggest
chunk of the country – which I did not yet think of as a country but
simply as the place which contained Glasgow, where we went to see
the Christmas lights, Motherwell, where we went for messages, and
Newarthill, where everybody I knew and everybody I knew everything
about lived. That I lived in Strathclyde and that it was on the front of
the jotters my teachers gave to me – the jotters we were supposed to
cover with wallpaper at the start of every term – made me feel important. That I could see the regional logo because we barely had enough
wallpaper at home to cover the walls, never mind my jotters, made me
feel ashamed.

I wrote almost nothing in those jotters about Newarthill, Motherwell,
Glasgow or Strathclyde. History had happened elsewhere – on the
battlefields of the Somme, on the *Mayflower*, on the moon. I knew
about Henry VIII and could name all of his six wives but knew nothing
of Margaret, brave little Maid of Norway who became queen at the
age of two and was promptly betrothed to the son of Edward I, but
who saw neither kingdom nor husband because she died aged seven
on Orkney in September 1290. Mary Queen of Scots was a mad slag.

Robert the Bruce fought on a biscuit tin. Macbeth was a play. Shakespeare walks with me still. But Burns was just for supper. Castles were for tourists and the Highlands and Islands were for teuchters, whatever they were.

The Romans had been here. They left evidence of their superior heating engineering in Strathclyde Park – troughs dug for clay pipes traced the outline of the walls of a villa. When I first stepped down into them they came up to my shoulders. Now they're at my knees. The Vikings had also stopped by, which I knew when I looked up at my dad – all six foot six. Now we stand eye-to-eye.

When I was writing my own story, *Maggie & Me*, I stayed in a tower in the Borders. All the doors and walls felt weirdly off and after a while the owner, a friend, explained that the family who'd lived there for centuries, looting farms and switching sides, had been left-handed. They were reivers, and behind their foot-thick walls I finally felt safe enough to raid my own past. I knew how a man 200 years before would have held his sword, but I couldn't tell you what language he'd whispered sweet nothings in or what he knew of the contours of the low rolling hills about him.

So, speak to me of my history – start back when I was at school. I want to know it all, not just the stuff about the Tudors and London and the Industrial Revolution and Empire and Churchill. I want to know all that but I need to know all the rest too – there's got to be more. Help me fill my jotters with what was happening in Newarthill, in Motherwell, in Glasgow, in Strathclyde – in Alba, Scotia, the Caledonia the Vikings raided and the Romans built their walls around. Tell me all the stories about how and who we were.

Speak to me of my history so I might take my place in our future.

Damian Barr is the author of Maggie & Me *and* You Will Be Safe Here.

ALAN BISSETT

There are many, many problems with the way in which societies around the world have been organised. Even naming them would elicit a sigh and a roll of the eyes, so accustomed are we to breathing a vague, gaseous cloud of despair. Capitalism has failed, globally, but has also apparently conquered all enemies. We know instinctively that something's wrong but we don't know how to fix it.

As a result, individuals – atomised and battered on the winds of economic fate – have huddled into the only thing which they feel gives them agency and meaning: tribes. Across a spectrum of identities – whether gender, ethnic, national, sectarian, political or religious – people have picked their side, their righteousness and prejudice multiplied many times over by the internet. People have stopped listening to each other, so engaged are they in furious ideological wars in their minds which entail the final defeat of a perceived enemy. It seems that everyone appears to be guilty of this, to one degree or another. Lord knows, I have been.

The question is what to do about it.

In previous lives I imagined a socialist transformation of society, tying people together in a shared economic project, or a cultural revolution whereby we all read our way to enlightenment and defined ourselves in our imaginations.

Now I think, to borrow a phrase from Alastair McIntosh's book *Soil and Soul*, we need to dig where we stand. We need to go back to the source of our humanity: place.

What do I mean by this?

Each of us – or, rather, those of us fortunate enough to have homes

– lives somewhere. We all open our front door on a city, a town, a village, a street, a road, a close or a tenement in a physical location where other humans live. Yet how many of us feel a real sense of connection to our actual neighbours? We often pay lip service to 'community', but the vast majority of our daily dialogue is with those in our workplaces, or our social media feeds, people who live dozens, maybe hundreds of miles away. We consume hours of national news and televised stories dreamt up by committees in media centres far away. The people who live a few doors from us only get a cursory nod in the street. This is why we don't see the homeless person inhabiting the same space as 'one of us'. They are objects to navigate on the way to somewhere else we're being paid to be.

This is how our tribalism is different from that of ancient societies: theirs was local. It was specific to a place, a small place at that. People made their truest connections to those into whose eyes they could actually look and in whom they were obliged to invest trust because the survival of the tribe depended upon it. But globalisation means our tribes are now vast, imaginary networks which stretch across time and space, encompassing people we'll never meet, but who embody 'our' values. Paradoxically, this geographical stretching of our networks has led to constellations of similarity and fewer encounters with difference. These 'echo chambers' are, perhaps, an inevitable effect of the technology available to us.

Regrettably we've come to treat with suspicion those who physically surround us. Even traditional spaces in which conversation would once have been expected – public transport, for example – find us disappearing into our private worlds of headphones and noise. People in pubs turn their eyes away from each other and focus on BT Sport. Couples, families, friends stare into phones at restaurant tables.

Of course there are situations in which we should be careful of strangers. Some people are dangerous. And I'm well aware there is more peril for women than men in a random conversation with a stranger.

Nevertheless, what we have lost outweighs this.

What we need is to think of ourselves as occupying a country of thousands of small locations, full of people who contribute something *to that place*: volunteering for the toddlers' group, organising a local club night, checking in on the old people, helping out in the charity shop, taking part in the gala day, *starting a gala day*, volunteering for an arts festival, going on litter-picking walks, and slowly, slowly learning the faces, names and backgrounds of the people with whom we *actually* share a life.

You don't have to agree with everything they say. You just have to accept them for who they are, and give them the chance to be their best self. Hopefully they will do the same for you. If we must have tribes, let them be porous, welcoming, based on willingness to contribute in a meaningful way to the people with whom we share space.

It's how human beings thrived in the past, and the only way we'll survive the future.

Alan Bissett is an award-winning novelist, playwright and performer who grew up in Falkirk and now lives in Renfrewshire.

CHRIS BROOKMYRE

To build a better future for a country, you need to look to the new generations that will populate it, and I believe one of the most valuable things we could do for them would be to introduce the teaching of philosophy from primary-school age.

One of the most corrosive effects of social media and the self-curation of our news consumption that it has facilitated has been the 'footballisation' of our political discourse. People who might otherwise have expressed little interest in an issue (and who often retain a lack of curiosity over the complex detail) are nonetheless encouraged to take sides, and to regard politics as a zero-sum game in which the other team must be defeated at all costs. Any amount of misbehaviour, dishonesty and hypocrisy is excused as long as it is in the service of your side's success; indeed, getting away with terrible behaviour is in itself viewed as a form of victory, a demonstration of strength.

Through philosophy, children would learn to take the tribalism out of discourse. It teaches them how to think, not what to think: how to evaluate ideas according to their merits, logic and insight, as opposed to the adversarial instinct that causes us to defend ideas because we feel personally invested in them or tribally identified with them. It would be invaluable if our children could learn to confront challenges to their arguments without the fear of losing face, and to understand that it is not a sign of weakness or surrender to change your mind on the basis of new information or changing circumstances.

And if all of this sounds implausibly idealistic, it may surprise you to learn that it has been tried before, on opposite sides of the globe.

In Australia in 1997, Buranda State School in Brisbane introduced a philosophy programme involving structured debates addressing philosophical questions the kids themselves had come up with. The children's academic test results improved considerably and were maintained or improved upon in the years that followed. However, perhaps more significant was the impact on social behaviour.

According to a report on the programme:

> The respect for others and the increase in individual self-esteem generated in the community of inquiry have permeated all aspects of school life. We now have few behaviour problems (and we do have some difficult students). Students are less impatient with each other, they are more willing to accept their own mistakes as a normal part of learning and they discuss problems as they occur . . . A visiting academic commented: 'Your children don't fight, they negotiate.' Visitors to the school are constantly making reference to the 'feel' or 'spirit' of the place. We believe it's the way our children treat each other.

A similar experiment was carried out right here at home, with equal success. In 2001–2002, a number of primary schools in Clackmannanshire, including ones in deprived areas, took part in an experiment whereby eleven- to twelve-year-olds were given one hour a week of philosophy teaching. The study involved a wide range of tests and was observed in comparison with a control group of schools with no such philosophy programme. The study found that, after one year, the incidence of children supporting opinion with evidence doubled, but the control classes remained unchanged. There was evidence that children's self-esteem and confidence rose markedly. Class ethos and discipline improved noticeably. All classes improved significantly in verbal, non-verbal and quantitative reasoning, while no control class changed. Children were assessed as being more intelligent (by an average of 6.5 IQ points) after one year on the programme.

Most significantly, those benefits were retained by the pupils when they moved on to secondary, even though no such philosophy teaching followed them to their new schools.★

We are living in what might be called the Information Age, bombarded with data, with ideas and opinions as never before. I imagine a country whose future generations are equipped to process this information, to evaluate it and to reach valid conclusions. Most importantly, they would learn how to respond when someone else reaches *different* conclusions.

Chris Brookmyre is the author of more than twenty crime and SF novels, as well as writing historical fiction with his wife, Marisa Haetzman, under the pseudonym Ambrose Parry.

★ For more detail on the Buranda and Clackmannanshire experiments, seek out *The War For Children's Minds* by Stephen Law (Routledge 2006).

TRESSA BURKE

E very day I hold fast to a vision of a better country – one that *is* possible and offers hope for over a million disabled Scots. I witness disabled people moving from hopelessness to becoming civic leaders, inspiring and working with others to create positive changes. I see people contributing to families, communities and wider society – with just a little bit of support. And I have the privilege of being a civic leader alongside them in an organisation run by, for and with disabled people, with the biggest groundswell of disabled members in Europe: 'Nothing About Us Without Us' is our mantra and echoes disabled-people-led organisations (DPOs) across Europe and internationally.

It should shock and shame us that the UN has declared the lives of disabled people in the UK 'a human catastrophe'. This is due to the perfect storm of welfare reform and austerity measures at the hands of the UK government, measures that are seen by the UN as being driven by a 'commitment to achieving radical social re-engineering' (Annual Report, UN Special Rapporteur on extreme poverty and human rights, 2018). The erosion of rights and removal of protection has prompted further cuts to local authority services and community supports, including social care which is fundamental for disabled people to live their lives and fulfil their potential.

Disabled people are amongst the worst hit by austerity and make up almost half of those in poverty. They are more likely to be unemployed, in insecure employment, or economically inactive, as well as being less likely to have formal qualifications. Disabled people experience health inequalities and poorer life outcomes all round. The Office of National Statistics reveals that their life expectancy is shorter and suicide rates are higher. Loneliness and isolation can compound this inequality, creating a sense of despair and hopelessness.

None of this is inevitable. It is all a result of political choices. Disabled people need not bear the brunt of austerity. Instead we should use the new tax-raising powers available in Scotland to better support our communities. There is a glimmer of hope in that the Scottish government have already taken steps to mitigate austerity, and we have a First Minister committed to creating a 'Wellbeing Economy' which will focus on what matters to people rather than solely economic growth.

Our collective vision is for disabled people to have the same freedom and choices to participate as other citizens, and the support needed. This vision is not a pipe dream; it is part of a collection of rights already enshrined in the UN Convention on the Rights of Disabled People, and is called Independent Living. It's about not having to do things by yourself, but rather, having the support needed to live an ordinary life.

What matters to disabled people is being included, having a sense of meaning and purpose, knowing our rights and having these met. What matters is playing the lead role in our own lives instead of being a bystander. Disabled people frequently tell me that it also matters that we are treated with humanity and with kindness and compassion – but not as a replacement for fundamental rights: more, as a demonstration of them. It matters that we are able to participate and, just as importantly, to make contributions to our families, communities and wider society.

To ensure the involvement of disabled people in realising the vision of Independent Living we must support disabled people's aspirations and help them grow so that they can realise their potential and dare to dream about what is possible. Not to do this risks losing their amazing contributions to our country. I have witnessed tremendous strength, courage, resilience and a sense of collective and mutual support between disabled people who have dared to dream. This has been supported by accessible peer-learning, capacity-building and consciousness-raising which enables disabled people to have fun, build skills and meet others in the same boat; and for many to continue their education examining and deconstructing their inequality and oppression, understanding their rights, taking control of their situation and planning for change individually and collectively.

Organisations led by disabled people have an essential role in making this vision a reality. But everyone in our country has a part to play. A wider conversation is now needed with Scotland's people so that they better understand the barriers facing disabled people and the reality of our lives, before deciding what kind of society we want to be.

Tressa Burke is a disability activist and equalities campaigner. She was a founder member of the Glasgow Disability Alliance and has been Chief Executive Officer since 2006.

JOHN BURNSIDE

Imagine a country where a handful of individuals 'earn' millions without lifting a finger, simply by 'owning' vast tracts of land, much of it taken by force and passed down by some long-ago ancestor who provided his monarch with a service that Michael Cohen would refuse even to consider. A country where one individual can own land and property in excess of 200,000 acres, with a turnover of £55m, simply by being born lucky, while another sits by a railway station or a cash-point, begging for small change so she can buy a meal and a night's shelter. Could there be anything more absurd?

Now, imagine a country where nobody is homeless. A country where every child has a garden or a park to play in, a room of her own and at least one adult who *listens*. A country with adequate facilities to treat mental illness, along with a sound-enough safety net for those who, having suffered a temporary setback, need a little support to keep going. Imagine a government that laughs at the idea of taxing working people in order to hand over huge sums in subsidies and grants to landowners and corporations. A government that goes out of its way to provide its citizens, no matter where they live, with the educational, health and leisure facilities that their labour, ingenuity and their taxes pay for. A government for all of the people, not just political donors and 'stakeholders'. It goes without saying that this is a country worth making a little effort to live in.

Now, imagine a way of moving from the first of these countries to the second and so finding justice, at last – and consider the possibility that it would only take three steps.

First, we would have to recognise that our current situation is not the fault of any one individual, but of a system. As Australian economist R.F. Dyson pointed out long ago (*Natural Prosperity*, 1931): 'The private collection of land rent is worse than burglary because it is a continuous and increasing theft, and also it keeps opportunities unequal. That is economically wrong because incomes gained in that manner are not limited by the natural productive powers of the recipients, and consequently a few people receive incomes far in excess of their needs. Further, it causes an unnatural subdivision of wages, which means that no producer can receive his full earnings.' In short, large-scale land and property ownership is unjust, not only because it accumulates wealth within a narrow social stratum, but also because it denies everyone, including the members of that *soi-disant* elite, the opportunities to grow and mature that contributing to the greater good allows, summed up in Marx's notion, from 1875, 'From each according to her ability, to each according to her needs.'

Second, through a series of steps involving taxation, education and financial management (including, to begin with, a degree of careful policing) we would have to move to a new system, where the land belongs to nobody, but exists as a national treasure, not just as a source of rent and resources, but as a sacred space, as it once was for our ancestors. Here, we could encourage the revival of holistic farming practices, reverent land-management and a respect for the environment and the creatures that live there – and we could work to bridge the insidious gap between 'town' and 'country' that was maintained for so long by the landed gentry. To those who object to such measures, we should simply say: 'You've had your cake. Now go away and eat it.'

Before we take these steps, however, we need a body of policies that protect the land from further exploitation, as the unscrupulous lawyer-up to take advantage of the new status quo. To that end, we need a universal land ethic, based upon an expanded understanding of Aldo Leopold's proposal: 'The land ethic simply enlarges the boundaries of the community to include soils, waters, plants, and animals, or collectively: the land . . . [A] land ethic changes the role of Homo sapiens from conqueror of the land-community to plain member and citizen of it. It implies respect for his fellow-members, and also respect for the community as such.'

Imagine a country with such a land ethic, and a people for whom justice outweighs individual wealth. A country where a teenage boy with social-anxiety problems is not condemned to sit on a cold street, begging, while a man born into millions slithers by in his Bentley on the way to a banquet.

John Burnside writes poetry, memoir and fiction. He lives in rural Fife, with his wife and two sons.

JOHN BUTT

The problems facing the world are clearly unprecedented. Climate change surely comes at the top of the list, followed by less tangible issues such as automation and the consequent displacement of enormous communities of workers (on top of the growing inequality that we already have), and, to cap it all, the proliferation of arms in increasingly untrustworthy regimes. With all this facing us, I find myself staring into two chasms when thinking about Scotland's future: on the one hand – given such global issues – surely any positive material change in Scotland is going to have very little effect, particularly if some of our bigger neighbours insist on behaving badly. On the other hand, there is the opposite problem: the self-righteous view that if Scotland gets its act together it will be a paradise for right-thinking people, regardless of what goes on in the rest of the world.

If we are going to avoid falling into either chasm, the most obvious imperative is that Scotland engages with both the large and small solutions to global problems, coordinated at both international and local levels. But a world without borders, involving the necessary security (preferably with more intelligence and less weaponry), must surely seem overly idealistic in our current situation, when we are bombarded by divisive nationalisms on every side.

Does my allergy to a world of borders and competing nationalisms mean that I am essentially tone deaf to Scotland's identities, history and unique potential? Absolutely not: Scotland clearly has a deep-rooted historical image, bringing along many customs and quirks; it is one of the most beautiful and bountiful countries we could imagine and, in a world where people are fundamentally the same everywhere, the people of Scotland still stand out in having developed their inheritance with tremendous spirit and generosity. In short, I do not want to live anywhere else and am entirely willing to share in at least some of the mythologies that sustain the rich range of Scottish identities.

Without mythologies, without dreams, we are surely condemned to a pretty drab existence, but the crucial rules should surely be that we are free to pursue our own mythologies and beliefs, share these with cognate groups, but *never* impose them on those who do not desire them or who are forced to share them against their better inclinations. Scotland has already made a good start in this direction, with the ongoing acceptance of many forms of difference and diversity that do not impinge on others' freedoms. The progress from the astonishingly late legalisation of same-sex relationships in 1981 to full marriage in 2014 is nothing short of astounding; and the welcome to Syrian refugees on Bute suggests a very promising advance for a country that has been relatively unused to racial and cultural diversity.

But I would love to see an even greater acknowledgement of the full range of possible Scottish identities. The establishment of the Scottish Parliament has brought immediacy and flexibility to the community, but I would be keen to see government devolved further to regions, cities, traditional or emerging groupings, even to some of the traditions that predate a unitary Scotland. Some areas (e.g. law and most aspects of social services) need unified systems, but there are surely other areas (e.g. education, both for children and adults) where the needs or strengths of a particular region could foster more diversity. Although a multi-cultural country is a must, it would be good to come to a more nuanced understanding of Scottish history and its cultures, including distinctions such as Highland and Lowland society (the latter customarily somewhat ignored, since it has often been assumed to be less distinctively 'Scottish'). Perhaps each area, city, region or linguistic community should search for ways to participate in activities, cultural, historical, physical or even scientific, that are particularly appropriate for them. This might be a reasonable step towards anticipating ways in which populations could be employed if and when there are fewer work hours. All this would provide an excellent balance to Scotland's participation in much larger global groupings.

How can we achieve such a participatory and multi-level democracy? Citizens' assemblies seem an excellent way of involving more informed policy-making and Scotland's existing educational promotion of 'modern studies' should surely be rolled out on a larger and more ambitious scale.

Should there be something called 'Scotland' about which we can be proud and around which we can assemble with our various identities? Absolutely, but it should surely be geared towards the very real advantages that a small country can bring. We have strong traditions, remarkable achievements in the arts and sciences, and diverse emerging talents. We can surely work out which issues we should share with larger blocs and those which should be enthusiastically solved on a local basis. Small may be beautiful but it can also be nimble.

John Butt is Gardiner Professor of Music at the University of Glasgow and Musical Director of Edinburgh's Dunedin Consort.

GEMMA CAIRNEY

A report from 2026: Scotland has rapidly proved itself as a place where progress and radical innovation take top priority at every level over borders, rulers and capital gain.

It is 2026 and the country now boldly focuses on the revival of the soul and humanity which has been lacking in many areas of a fragmented modern western society; what better place for this ambition than beautiful Scotland? A land of plenty, reverberating with beauty and hope. The lust for wealth and corporation pre-pandemic has been dismantled and replaced with that of a country-wide focus on empowerment for all instead. This has been achieved in a number of remarkable ways: we now publicly encourage integrated health for our minds, bodies and the natural world for everyone born here and everyone who comes here, regardless of age, gender or race, and completely free education models have been rejuvenated. One of our proudest examples is a focus on resilience; community and nature have been introduced to schools and other places of education from nursery level to education throughout life.

Lessons in *Resilience* form a sense of self-safety from a young – toddler! – age by combining mindful techniques, discussions on how relationships shape our lives, an embracing of the power of digital detoxing, and therapeutic movement and dance for all pupils.

The *Community* classes are available to anyone who lives within a five-mile radius, which means different generations learn together, whether through multi-media platforms such as simultaneous online streamed sessions or workshopping in the room, where those present benefit from the aliveness of in-person interactivity. These are a favourite of many, as locally themed storytelling is an important part of the course and creates grounded explorations of identity within our evolving culture and times. Also, as part of the regular module, there is a segment called 'Better Together' where those who make up vulnerable groups in an area are invited to have their voices heard safely, whilst solutions are collectively brainstormed.

One advanced group in Kirkcaldy have exceeded expectations since adopting this weekly class approach in their local, otherwise unused church hall. An initiative activated over a number of months in 2022 through one particular 'Better Together' session has seen many buildings take on the technicolour challenge of painting homes all the shades of the rainbow, after discovering that the saturation of grey-hued exteriors and bleak winters were lowering local mood.

'Now I almost giggle whenever I approach my front door, when coming back from work, it's brilliant,' said local resident Maggie, 67, who chose a punk neon pink for her two up, two down, just off the High Street.

We've seen outstanding results from the *Nature* classes too, with parents, carers and children alike reporting being inspired by the rich nature of this country and its elemental magnificence from the 'tooling-up approach' developed and taught on practical sustainability for everyday life. We've all learnt how contagious it is to endlessly love our environment. Plastic-free towns are now popping up all over Scotland, leading the charge in providing earth-friendly community frameworks across the globe. Findhorn in the Northern region had already established working systems of eco-conscious living long before, and now offers free residential and top-quality government-funded courses in *Permaculture*. Attendees from all over the UK and the rest of Europe are encouraged to apply (with quotas for those marginalised because of gender, class or race).

New maps have even been distributed to every household marking out inspiring journeys with many transport links made accessible and easy to understand. This has seen the economy of the Isles thrive, and there are now plans for the V&A to open a permanent home on the shoreline of the Isle of Eigg in 2029.

And, finally, the People Protection Act passed in 2023 saw every planner and architect alike put the healing of a nation at the top of their agenda by completing and submitting a one-pager answering the following question: *'How will this project nurture the human spirit?'* This obligatory process has proved fascinating not only for the future of Scottish design but it is leading the way in a reparative way of thinking around the world.

It's fair to say that nearly five years after the start of the end of the global pandemic in our lifetime our country is in a better place. There's a sort of very modern joy for the multiculturalism that has emerged from symbiotically embracing the ancient wisdom of the lands. By embedding a celebration of both diversity and inclusion Scotland is now associated with a warmth and welcoming it has never before been able to claim.

Gemma Cairney is a writer, broadcaster, adventurer, activist; who considers themselves a citizen of the world with roots in Jamaica and Scotland.

KATE CHARLESWORTH

Kate Charlesworth, Barnsley-born graphic novelist and cartoonist living and working in Scotland since 1991, has never, in 2022, been happier to stay here.

JO CLIFFORD

I magine a country . . .
    What if we could . . .
  What if we could imagine . . .
  And I ask this because mostly right now I find I can't even imagine
a country without so many fucking idiots in it.
  But I try.
  And then I think:
  How I also want to imagine a country where we're not always so
angry with each other
  Where we're not always denouncing each other and insulting each
other and calling each other by vile names.
  And then . . .
  And then I want to imagine a place where because we have always
been respected we know how to give respect
  So we never use the act of making love as an insult or a threat.
  Because we have a respect that goes right down to the very heart
of things, to every act of creation
  A place where we all feel in the very root of our beings that sex
is a beautiful act, and an innocent one, and a pure one too . . .
  And so a place where we can't even conceive the need to use words
for vagina or penis to insult each other
  Because we know how beautiful it is to have a vagina
  And we know how beautiful it is to have a penis
  And we know how much they can give us pleasure.
  And that respect goes to every intelligent and creative act of making
or thought

So we don't use words for clever or studious to insult each other

And we deeply understand that everyone has a right to be different

So we don't use words that mean stupid to insult each other with

And maybe even also generally understand where the word 'idiot' comes from

And so we know that once upon a time 'idiot' didn't mean someone stupid or foolish

But meant something like 'private citizen'

or

'one who minds their own business'.

And if there was criticism implied, it was because

Such a person looked after their own affairs and neglected their duties as a citizen and member of the collective

As we all do, because we've been trained to see ourselves as individuals all our lives

Individuals living in sad angry solitude and in bitter competition with each other

And yet maybe somewhere we know, deep inside, that we cannot go on thinking like this

Because the world demands something new of us.

And if we're not able, most of us, in this cruel world to enjoy the sexual contact we need or the tender touch we need

We must try not to be ashamed

We must try to reach out to one another

And it's because we mostly can't that so often in our fury and our frustration and our rage we use these beautiful words as weapons against each other.

So this country that is slowly and painfully taking shape inside me

Is a place where we all understand together

Understand that we are all connected

And that what I do in one place has an effect in an infinite number of other places

Because we all live in the one beautiful world

And that it is no use my trying to enrich myself at the expense of another human's poverty

Because I am also impoverishing myself

And it is no use my trying to enrich myself by poisoning the planet's air or the planet's soil

Because I am also poisoning myself.

And also if I lash out at you and hurt you in my anger and my frustration and my rage

I am also hurting myself.

And what would happen if this was a place

We all knew as intimately and as comfortably

As a second beautiful skin.

I know by myself I cannot make this country happen

And yet I still think:

Yes

I will imagine this country

And try to live in it as if it was already there.

Jo Clifford is a proud father and grandmother, playwright, poet and performer. She is the author of 100 plays.

JENNY COLGAN

'Why on earth?' you always think, looking at other countries that do things better or worse. Why on earth do they do it like that? Why on earth does America have a health care system that will cheerfully leave you bleeding in the gutter, or take your house if you need a caesarean section? Why does England have a house-buying system that allows you to turn up in front of your new home with a removal van only for the owners to demand money with menaces at the last minute?

Change is always incredibly difficult, so I'm going to write a bit about how another country I have lived in deals with a problem I think looms very large in Scotland: how we feed our children.

I'm not making any judgements, I'm just going to explain how the French system (we lived there for seven years) raised our own children to love good food.

French education starts with *École Maternelle* the year you turn three. I assumed most parents would leave their tiny children for half a day but no, everyone dumps them 8.30 and returns to pick them up at 4.30, except for Wednesday when there is no school. This is a bliss for mothers who don't want to go back full time – employers are very accepting of people not working Wednesdays – and children, who run in light and fleet on Tuesday evenings rather than trudging balefully to the weekend.

Lunch is 12–2 every day. There is no generally accepted term for a 'packed lunch'. You eat at the school, or your parents collect you and you eat at home (most French workers also get from 12–2 for lunch).

There is a chef in school and four courses to each lunch: a salad, a main, a '*laiterie*' which will be yoghurt or cheese, and pudding which will be a fruit compote or a square of cake. Drink will always be water (although we used to joke, looking at the menus, that they should probably pair wines).

In *Petite Section*, their first year, children are allowed to refuse a food three times. In *Moyenne Section*, twice, and in *Grande Section*, once. If they continue to refuse the food, you, the parent, must take them home every day to eat with you. Peer pressure pretty much sorts that out. Only when you have sat and eaten nicely with utensils, overseen by teachers and catering staff, may you go out and play with your friends: etiquette is taken extremely seriously. I have fond memories of my younger son, Michael-Francis, aged about four, desperately trying to explain about the big tree he'd had for lunch (they'd had endive).

On a child's birthday, the parent may send in a cake – home-made or shop bought, either way. There is no restriction on peanuts, and gluten and dairy intolerance are rare.

Moving back home I noticed a huge culture of fear around food in Scottish children. When I would cook in France (often things from home I missed, like potato scones), the children's French friends would come in, ask what I was doing, ask to try it. I well remember a tiny friend of my son's, when presented with his first piece of tablet, handing it back to me, announcing in an appalled tone, '*Madame! C'est TROP SUCRÉE*!!!'. I've known Scottish kids who couldn't eat a plate of plain pasta.

Is it expensive, this way of doing things? Sure is. Parents pay a contribution, but the state backs most of it.

It's not about paying for the food: vegetables aren't expensive. It's about taking the time and building the system to make it work.

The cost of diabetes care in Scotland, for a population of 5,500,000, is £1,000,000,000 per year. Around £800,000,000 of that is from preventable causes, mostly weight-related.

So. If I were to imagine a better future for Scotland, well, that's where I'd begin. (Well, that, and, probably, a city bike network that isn't actively trying to kill me.)

Jenny Colgan has written over forty bestselling novels, for adults, children and Doctor Who.

CARINA CONTINI

Home: there was always delicious food, happiness and a feeling of safety.

Growing up I never remember worrying about anything.

Happiness was having my family around me, being loved, a house above a sweetie shop, and more than enough food. Delicious food. Breakfast was a treat from the local bakery. A glass of milk and a scotch pancake with jam and butter. Or rusks with hot milk. An apple in my school bag for break and either a Penguin biscuit or a packet of Salt 'n' Shake crisps. That carton of chilled milk at 10 a.m. break was so refreshing. If you finished first there was always extra if you were quick. I begged to be allowed to stay at school for lunch even though the food was great at home.

Cockenzie Primary School dinner ladies were my heroines. Two courses every day. Either soup or a dessert but always a hearty, filling and tasty meal. There were never any leftovers, never any waste and never a choice. The approach was take it or leave it.

Home time and another two-course meal. Favourites were spicy white-pepper kidney soup and steamed sultana pudding with custard. The steamed pudding would have a 50p wrapped in tin foil for birthdays. The fridge was filled with milk and red cheese. The soft thick end of the pan loaf, toasted with butter, was one for me and one for my father with a mug of tea at 9.45 p.m. just before the news. A bowl of apples or pears was always on the kitchen table. There was never a shortage of treats but they were monitored. Lemonade was for Sundays only, with a little Chianti to turn it pink. Yes, really!

There was no central heating, no exotic holidays, trips to Edinburgh were counted on one hand. The toilet paper was that hard stuff called Izal and the TV was off at 11 p.m.

But time to eat together was a gift. This gift should be there for everyone.

Yes, the food has to be good. Tasty, clean, fair food to match the best Slow Food values. But eating in community is essential for our community's wellbeing.

Eating together works for all demographics. How many children don't eat, or don't have food to eat, with their families? How many homeless people have to go for days without a hot meal? Lonely people eating without company. Eating at our desks in a rush. Our elderly, sitting alone, eating alone. Ready meals are sad meals; made for one, they are no fun. Hospital food lacks the key ingredient of pleasure.

Imagine if we had communities that lived together and ate together.

I imagine a country where good food is valued, shared and not wasted. Where food is grown where our people live. Where food production considers the environment and the welfare of all humans, animals and plants. Where good food is affordable and accessible. Where good food is shared at tables built for more than one. Not eaten on sofas in front of the telly.

There is a saying that a family that prays together stays together. But a family that eats together meets together and has the time they need to *be* human. Being together may be enough to make that happen. Being together must be better than today.

We all have something in common. We all have to eat. Imagine a country where we make that a joy shared with the people we love. The good and the bad, the ups and the downs will never go away but a table of good food shared with people you love is the recipe to help.

Not everyone is fortunate enough to be close to family or loved ones, so we need to build a society where communities form different kinds of bonds. Eating together is the perfect place to start.

I'm lucky that my childhood met this vision. Let's share this with everyone else so we don't need to imagine, we can just be happy, be fed, be safe and be together.

Carina Contini runs three award-winning restaurants in Edinburgh with her husband Victor, and is passionate about serving delicious food to the beautiful people of Edinburgh as part of their third-generation Italian-Scots family business.

LUCY CONWAY

Mainland friends often ask me what it's like to live on an island, to live on Eigg. Sometimes I glibly answer I don't know, because I've forgotten what it's like to live anywhere else. It's a cop-out answer, because the real answer is so fantastically complicated and verges on the fanatical. The real (short) answer is that living in a beautiful sea-surrounded rock inhabited by 110 or so incredibly strong-willed, capable, compassionate and resilient people is a privilege. It's also a constant process of learning, about yourself and about what 'community' means, what it is and does. I feel constantly challenged, yet safe and cared for.

Eigg was one of the first community buyouts in Scotland. It saw the island move from being owned by a single individual to being owned by the Isle of Eigg Heritage Trust; a community trust with the majority of its directors elected from island residents. Now, instead of one person being responsible for the stewardship of Eigg's past, present and future, all those who live here play their part.

Eigg isn't an asset to develop and monetise to service economic growth. Instead the development of Eigg is about sustaining and growing life, both human and in nature. That development is the responsibility of the many, collectively, rather than the few. Sharing stewardship isn't easy, but it does provide us with a greater sense of empowerment and pride; we believe we can make the future better.

The people who live on Eigg are all very different from one another. One hundred and ten-plus people with different beliefs, politics, habits, income, and more. We disagree all the time, but all agree on one thing. We love Eigg, otherwise we'd live somewhere else. That love of place, of community, means we all strive to make Eigg a place to call home.

Homes are the core of a thriving country. In my ideal country the majority of houses would be owned by the community, by the populace. Houses would return to being homes and not investments. There would be little talk of a property ladder to scramble up, but instead pride in the range of good-quality, warm, community-owned homes, with enough light and space to support joyful and ambitious living.

In my ideal country what we currently call social housing would be the norm, except instead of a general acceptance that it is likely to be of a lesser standard of space, design or efficiency due to restrictions on public investment, it would be the benchmark. Social housing would provide homes of a quality that everyone would want to live in.

A home is somewhere you feel safe, warm and secure. A place you go out into the world from and be your best. A place you come home to, to rest and be well. A home sustains you, and in return you care for and sustain it for those who will come after. A home is somewhere you share through the years, enjoying or adapting what those before you have done, making it better for those who will follow. A home isn't about its value on a balance sheet, it's about how much value there is in feeling secure and able to live life to its fullest and best.

In the same way the future of Eigg feels better and more secure in the hands of a community who love it and take their turn in shaping its future, I believe so too could a community which owns its housing stock. Community homes, owned by the community, lived in and loved by the community.

Lucy Conway has lived and worked from the Isle of Eigg for fifteen years; a perfect place to be amazed by the power of small communities and creativity.

STUART COSGROVE

Once a week I walk though Alexandra Park near my home on the east side of Glasgow. It is one of the sweeping parks that has made the city famous as 'The Dear Green Place' – a place that is generously endowed with green spaces and inner-city recreation.

If you walk to the top of the park's gentle hillside, you can see Ben Lomond in the misty distance and for me part of Alexandra Park's charm is that it connects an area once synonymous with social deprivation to the magical landscapes of rural Scotland. It is a place of social binding and national coherence. Throughout the park you can see many different collisions where the rural and the urban meet and where industrialism gives way to leisure, recreation and to a busy outdoor gymnasium.

At the heart of Alexandra Park is the now treasured but decaying Saracen Fountain, a masterpiece of cast-iron which provides a reminder of the city's great industrial legacy. It could do with a clean but its rusting brilliance unintentionally says something about the loss of industry. Grieving loss is what I'd like to propose in my imagined country.

What always touches me emotionally is a small cluster of trees near the right-hand entrance to the park, as it drops down to a duck pond and the children's play area. At the foot of the trees are dying bouquets of flowers, sodden soft toys and rain-stained letters from grieving mothers to their dead children. Over several years now, women who have experienced still-births and miscarriages have used the trees as a makeshift garden of remembrance, a place to cry and think about the child that might have been. The messages they leave are heartbreaking and are often laced with primitive and deeply distressing poetry. In the cold frosty days around Christmas, the messages reappear again, sometimes with small gifts and whispered words of love from Santa and kind relatives. 'Your Auntie Julie bought this cause we thought you'd like it. Play forever my darling daughter.' The unresolved sorrow lies deeper than any snow.

I have been so taken by these small shards of remembrance that it's made me think I would like to see a society that responds more openly to child bereavement, and supports a network of recognised places where mothers and their families can find room to remember.

Death is never easy, at any age and in any circumstance, but perhaps the most difficult of all is the death that passes without the symbolism of a funeral, a cremation or a remembrance ceremony. It is a sad, lonely and emotionally complicated experience, where conversation is difficult and where the right words freeze even in the mouths of those who love you.

Many women talk of feelings of shame, failure and unspoken anxiety. That they have not been able to 'deliver' a child and so are somehow complicit in a death. An unborn child at Christmas, with all the twisted symmetry of the nativity, deepens grief. As family and friends rush round to buy presents, how are they to know that the festive season brings deeper distress?

In my imagined country, there would be dedicated civic space for bereavement, where people could remember the still-born and those often unnamed victims of infant mortality. Each park would have a trained caretaker capable of all the tasks of that vastly undervalued role. The job would be to take care, to tend the area, tidy the trees and to be available to people who needed help, especially women whose grief is sometimes beyond the ken of their own family. These caretakers would have skills in grief counselling, be human advice centres and have learned to listen without judgement.

It would be a place of comfort, where grief could be emotionally managed and where soft toys and sentimental poetry would be more than welcome.

Stuart Cosgrove is a writer and broadcaster. His award-winning trilogy of books on soul music and social change are published by Polygon.

MARK COUSINS

A generation before it happened, few would have predicted that Scotland would change its name. Sri Lanka changed its name, and Myanmar and other countries too, but they did so to decolonise.

Scotland's name-change in 2040 was the result of something else, another story. Where did the story begin? Maybe with a 2019 drone-shot filmed above a canopy of trees? The trees seemed to sway around each other, to move in unison like starlings in the evening sky. The shot was shown on TV and widely shared on social media. It seemed to touch a nerve, or awaken something. Or maybe the seed was planted a year earlier, with scientific reports that trees could communicate with each other through their root systems? The idea that these apparently mute things could, as it were, speak, was astonishing.

Whatever the starting point, things accelerated, or became visible, when Glasgow decided, in 2025, to enter for the International Forest City of the Year (IFCY). Kiev and Kolkata had won in previous years, but they were already afforested. Glasgow's radical mayor's decision to enter the IFCY by planting 800,000 pine trees within six months captured the world's attention, and that of the International Association of Forest Countries. Tourism increased, flights from Finland and Canada doubled. The smell of the city changed.

In tribute to this bold urban rethink, the National Gallery of Edinburgh did a re-hang. Paintings with people, Christianity and history at the centre of their stories were replaced by pictures that featured the beauty and power of trees. In the same year – 2027 – Grangemouth's decommissioned oil-refinery complex was replanted by a community collective. Much to the collective's bemusement, they won the Turner

Prize. But it became clear that a deeper change was happening – that Scotland's roots were in dialogue, that its people were intoxicated by new ideas – when Hearts and Hibs football teams decided to share one Edinburgh stadium – Tynecastle – and glass over the other – Easter Road – so that it could become the biggest Yunnan cypress house in the world (a project financially supported by the Chinese government). This vast Asian experiment (a joint initiative of the Royal Botanic Garden and Edinburgh Zoo) will introduce its first golden snub-nosed monkeys later this year.

It was the conversion of Easter Road that led the right-wing press to start to use the word 'contagion'. As millions of cuttings were taken from the Caledonian Forest in Strathspey to cultivate the Central Belt's 'forest corridor', the tabloids compared Scotland's fascination with trees to the Dutch tulip mania of the early 1600s. However, young people across Scotland, and activists of all ages, were quick to challenge such comparisons. They made the point that tulip mania was a speculative bubble, a forerunner of subsequent financial crashes, whereas Scotland's new 'arbour ardour', as it was dubbed, was far from inflationary. Consumption was slightly down year on year. By 2035, deep changes in Scottish society were taking place as a result of the realignment. Within a year of the school curricula being re-thought to centre on dendrology, tree ecosystems and the literature and aesthetics of trees, and with the consequent shift to outdoor study for children, young people's nationwide wellbeing scores saw a 19 per cent increase. And the greening of cities and new rural trends in leisure activities were responsible, according to mental health experts, for reductions of adult anxiety across all demographics.

The changes in housing were a particular case in point. Wood construction methods proliferated. Finnish and Swedish kit houses were affordable and widely imported, and what architects called 'arbour composition' – building houses around existing trees or with those trees as an aesthetic focus (what some dubbed the house's 'beauty spot') – was all the rage.

What was less predictable were the subtle shifts in medicine. New R&D incentives discovered that tree phenols, flavonoids, sterols, resins, waxes, sugars, gums and carotenoids had hitherto unexplored uses in the treatment of skin diseases, ENT infections and auto-immune diseases. At the time of writing (May 2041), a consortium of eight new Scottish hospitals has invested in an extensive range of tree-derived medication patents.

The last decade – the 2030s – saw Scotland's arboreal realignment widen and deepen to such an extent that even the sceptics conceded. Government select-committee reports demonstrated that the improvements in education, medicine, mental health, housing and – of course – air pollution levels, were substantial and systemic.

The first calls for the change in the country's name came in late 2037. Many traditionalists were against it, of course, but the case was made that Scotland's renaming would be a radical statement of intent, a post-industrial rethink, a sign to the world that Scotland was not afraid of change, an end to the Anthropocene.

And so, what for a thousand years was 'Scotland' became Tìr nan craobhan. Pays des arbres. Land of the Trees.

Mark Cousins is a filmmaker and writer who has lived in Scotland for thirty-six years, and hopes to do so for another thirty-six.

LEE CRAIGIE

In the most densely populated areas of our wonderful country, creativity and community cohesion bubble under concrete surfaces. In our towns and city centres our desire for connection is palpable and yet the way our physical environment is structured makes connecting to others, our natural environment, and to ourselves, a challenge. To counteract this desolation, we are scrabbling about online to drown out our aching loneliness. We've forgotten how to feel the richness of human interaction, the value to our soul from communing in green space with something bigger than just us.

Now imagine if the streets and communal spaces in our built-up areas were designed to prioritise our connection to each other and to nature instead of focusing on shifting the largest possible number of cars about. Imagine if every school, home and business premises had to be constructed with our physical and emotional health at the core of its design and that moving between these places was a treat and not a smelly chore. Imagine opening your door to birdsong and fresh air, and having permission to take longer to walk or cycle to school or work, everyone safe in the knowledge that happiness and productivity stroll hand-in-hand. If we all began our day by walking, running, riding or wheeling our way through areas where flowers and insects thrive this might go some way towards reconnecting us to the essence of what it means to be a living, breathing, caring human on this planet.

And it is possible. The Scottish government has announced a Climate Emergency. We all know we have to change the way we move around for our health and for the environment, but it needn't feel like a weighty, insurmountable challenge. In 2006, Transport Scotland adopted the Sustainable Travel Hierarchy and placed it at the heart of their National Transport Strategy, where it remains today. It states that consideration for pedestrians and cyclists must be at the very top of the priority triangle in our transport system. Below them comes public transport in the form of trains and buses. Below that comes the private car and other forms of carbon-heavy transport. This is what our country has signed up to and yet, currently, many of us are still choosing to drive our cars into towns and cities because it remains cheaper, more convenient and more reliable.

The emissions from our convenient private vehicles are killing us and our planet but are disproportionately affecting those who can't afford their own cars. Our collective carbon emissions in the west are causing environmental disasters that are affecting people with less choice. This is an environmental issue but it's also a health and social justice one.

This can change. Luckily the solutions are right there to be adopted by our town planners and our transport providers. We can create fairer, safer, quieter, healthier and greener spaces to reconnect with our neighbours, nature and ourselves.

We need a radical rethink of our priorities to make it both harder to drive and easier to travel actively. We must start diverting our roads budgets to the creation of safe and attractive cycling and walking infrastructure. At the same time, we must make driving a less convenient option. Finally, we must celebrate when we get it right. We need carrots to travel actively and to use public transport (segregated, attractive infrastructure and reliable, affordable trains and buses). We need sticks to encourage people to leave the car at home (convoluted driving routes and parking levies). And importantly, we need tambourines to celebrate the benefits our communities and our planet will reap from being bold enough to do all these things at the same time.

Take a moment longer to get to work. Invest in your future self. Walk or cycle instead and show our decision-makers what you value over and above all else. People and place first over convenience and power for the few. Come on, Scotland. The world is watching. This is our time to make a difference.

Lee Craigie was British Mountain Bike Champion in 2013, member of Team GB at the World and European Championships, represented Scotland at the 2014 Commonwealth Games, and now rides long distances through wild places all over the world. She is the Active Nation Commissioner for Scotland.

LYNDSEY CROAL, CAMERON MACKAY AND EILIDH WATSON

No one is too small to make a difference.

This is the key message from the burgeoning youth-climate movement that first began in 2018 and has since swept across the world. Nobody would have guessed that a teenager from Sweden would be the catalyst for a global political movement that intends to hold the polluting neoliberal system accountable for the damage it has caused for generations. A system left unchecked and unanswered for decades. Whilst Greta Thunberg is just one voice amongst many climate activists from across the world, together these voices are united. We would like to imagine that this is just the beginning. The beginning for Scotland and for the world.

As part of a contingent of young geographers with the Royal Scottish Geographical Society, we had the pleasure and privilege to travel to Sweden to present Greta with the Geddes Environmental Medal in the summer of 2019. We travelled across land and sea, brought together with other environmental activists by our shared goal of addressing the climate emergency and our passion for telling stories. Over the course of the journey, we discovered the diversity of our ideologies, faiths, identities, but that together, this diversity made our approach stronger. Similarly, the process of writing this piece collaboratively is exactly the sort of collaboration we imagine and hope a future Scotland would adopt: we want to be part of a country that takes into account every voice and is therefore able to make a greater impact than the sum of its parts.

When we met Greta, Scotland had been hailed as a world leader in climate-change action, even before passing the responsible and ambitious climate legislation it adopted later in 2019. However, the measure of leadership is changing and so Greta's message to Scotland was clear: *every* country must act, and *every* government must do more. Many argue that as a small country, Scotland's emissions are insignificant in comparison to other nations. But we believe that climate change is everyone's responsibility and it is irresponsible to accept no blame for a problem to which we, as a nation, have contributed. Currently the impacts of climate change are disproportionately borne by poorer countries and communities. Often the people most vulnerable are those who have contributed least to the human causes of climate change. This injustice is just one of many reasons to make a change.

Today there are glimmers of what a positive future could look like in Scotland. From community energy and a flourishing renewables sector, from shared allotment space for local food production to circular resource- and tool-sharing networks, we have the knowledge we need to move forward. Scotland has the potential to continue on this path, to invest in a better future and to become an example of what sustainability that works for everyone looks like. It is not too much to imagine a future where inclusive, welcoming and sustainable communities lie at the heart of our culture.

So, we imagine a country that has embraced the shared message from Greta Thunberg, global activists and our own home-grown Scottish climate campaigners.

We imagine a future Scotland that prioritises climate justice; a Scotland that is not afraid to stand up for those that are voiceless.

We imagine Scotland leading the world by example: empowered by an inclusive, innovative and sustainable society whilst at the forefront of challenging some of the biggest problems facing the world today.

We imagine Scotland's land delivering benefits for nature, biodiversity, climate and society. A Scotland with a clean and affordable energy and infrastructure system that is just and provides benefits for all.

In that future, we will have listened for solutions not only from politicians or businesses, but from the younger generations, minority groups and others who have traditionally been separated from decision-making.

The way we structure our economy will be tied to a global green agenda, and Scotland will continue to be at the forefront of forging that path internationally.

Just as no one person is too small to make a difference, no single country is too small to make an impact and bring forward change.

Lyndsey Croal, Cameron Mackay and Eilidh Watson were Editors for the Royal Scottish Geographical Society's Young Geographer Magazine: Arctic Perspectives *in 2019. Eilidh is a PhD researcher focusing on climate, energy and gender justice issues, based at the Centre for Climate Justice, Glasgow Caledonian University, Cameron is a documentary filmmaker with a focus on environmental stories and also works in the Scottish sustainability sector, Lyndsey works on environmental and climate-change policy in Edinburgh, as well as being a writer and recipient of a Scottish Book Trust New Writers Award.*

ALAN CUMMING

When I was a little boy I heard two grownups arguing about politics. The man had voted SNP and the woman was telling him it was a waste of a vote. I've never forgotten that.

The idea that voting for something could be a waste, that just because you weren't going to win you shouldn't vote at all, hit me hard. Not all of us have a voice, but most of us have a vote. Both then, with my childish idealism, and now, with my middle-aged benefit of hindsight, I think voting was and is the most important thing you can do to make a change, to be heard.

I remember leaping for joy in a hotel room in Prague on the night in 1997 when the Scottish people voted for devolution. It felt so exciting that my country wanted to take some control, to forge a modern identity for itself that wasn't totally dictated by or dependent on a system that had failed it so many times.

The National Theatre of Scotland, newly formed and financed by the equally new Scottish government, brought me back to my home-land to work for the first time in many years: first to play Dionysos, the wandering rock-star god who returns to his place of birth looking for approval (much as I was doing some 2,500 years later!) and then to play the most Scottish of all roles, in Shakespeare's canon at least, Macbeth. (In fact, I played *everyone* in Macbeth!)

I began to see the manifestations of that historic devolution vote on those trips home: a new confidence was palpable. We couldn't just blame Westminster for all our woes now. It felt like we were growing up, realising our potential.

I sometimes feel that it's only by moving away from a place that you can look back and truly see it. The phrase I most remember from my childhood in Scotland is 'That's not fair!' The lack of fairness, or an injustice, or not looking out for someone less fortunate than ourselves, is anathema to the spirit of the Scottish people. It's important to us that no matter who you are, you have a chance to succeed in life.

Had I been born in my adopted homeland of America my parents could never have afforded to pay for me to go to drama school. But, as we lived in Scotland, they didn't have to. I had a full grant to live on too. And after I graduated, I cut my teeth as a young actor on the stages of Scottish repertory theatres, funded by the then Scottish Arts Council. I always say I am an actor only thanks to the generosity and values of the Scottish taxpayers.

It's not just our belief in the value of the education system that is under threat these days though. Our precious health service, once so sacrosanct and such a certainty in our lives, is seen now by its supposed guardians as an asset to sell rather than an essential service for our people. For so long many vital decisions have been made for us – often against our will – and eventually those decisions will erode our core values.

The independence referendum of 2014 was a true stramash of misinformation and lies. Fear was the weapon used to keep us all in our place. It saddened me that so many were too afraid to see through the lies, and to step back from the edge of a new, fairer Scotland.

Now we seem to be on the threshold of another referendum – hopefully this time without the economic lies and the subsidy-junkie smears and the endless condescension and undermining of our potential. Hopefully a referendum where we won't need to use fear and lies to win.

But maybe we need to change how we think about voting. Maybe the only way to change the convictions of people like that woman I overheard all those years ago is to stop voting being something we choose to do. Too often, we've made that choice based on what we perceived the likely outcome to be. A perception based on lies and manipulation, more often than not these days.

Imagine a country, our country, where voting was compulsory. Where we have a day off work to make sure we can do it. Where the political process is hallowed and our participation in it is a civic duty. We're all affected by the outcome of an election or a referendum, so why shouldn't it be compulsory for us all to take part in it?

Imagine a country where not voting would never be an option, where no vote would ever be wasted.

Alan Cumming is a Scottish-American artist and activist.

BARBARA DICKSON

I hail from Dunfermline in Fife. I was born there in 1947 to a Scots father and Liverpudlian mother. So much that has happened to Dunfermline since I was a girl disturbs me. However, the invitation to imagine a country has given me permission to restore Dunfermline to its rightful place in Scotland: at the top!

In my mind, there are two important sites in Fife. One is St Andrews and the other is Dunfermline. St Andrews gets quite enough attention in my opinion but that's not the case with Dunfermline. Dunfermline has a terrific City Chambers built in 1879 but since the main decision-making processes in Fife were moved to the 'new town' of Glenrothes, many years ago, Dunfermline has never recovered its confidence. Or at least, that's how it seems to me when I visit from Edinburgh, where I live now. That notion consumes me while I'm there.

Our once dignified town centre, full of proud banks and proper shops, has now faded into the façade of a town on a Hollywood film set: all front and nothing behind. It pains me when I walk down my beloved High Street to notice the buddleia sprouting from all the ledges, a sure sign of terminal decline and nature reclaiming her own.

What has happened? A large part has been the death of the coalfields and Rosyth Dockyard. They'd employed thousands of local people and generated prosperity for the whole community. But it is not just that.

I observed about twenty years ago that Dunfermline looks outwards, away from its ancient, medieval core, with all its glory, and now bows towards Edinburgh, only a spit across the Forth by car. Not the case when I was little. Before the road bridge was built the capital was distant. We had to go to the Lower Station (yes, there was an Upper!)

to catch the train. If you had a car, you could take a ferry across at Queensferry, but if that crossing was closed, you faced a long journey via the Kincardine Bridge.

The massive ancillary accommodation which has sprung up around Dunfermline to the east has meant that the town feels cockeyed, and out of kilter with its history. Scotland's capital a millennium ago is now a suburb of Edinburgh and the cheaper housing it supplies hasn't received a quid pro quo in exchange.

Despite Fire Station Creative, the new Richard Murphy library extension that has given the Abbey Church a new aspect after two hundred years, and a few remaining Carnegie institutions, the Royal Burgh is depressed.

You'll need to go to 'The Glen' – Pittencrieff Park, to give it its Sunday name – to feel the love once again. You can still explore the Pavilion and the sublime wilderness of the pathways beside the burn, where children have hidden and fantasised since Andrew Carnegie gave us that estate all those years ago.

But when you emerge, you can't miss what's happened to Dunfermline. The difference is palpable.

The folks are the same warm-hearted, kind people who still have to deal with their own trials and tribulations.

This isn't a problem unique to Dunfermline. As I tour around the country, I see many other towns suffering the same blight, the same apparent lack of love, and I would extend this same imaginative blessing to them too.

This project allows me to give back to Dunfermline what we all want – her dignity and her confidence. We can raze to the ground the 'new bus station' and the shopping mall which has bombed the heart out of the town!

I'll have to live with the 'new' early-nineteenth-century Abbey Kirk, built without any backward glance towards St Margaret and the Scottish Royal Family. Unlike Haddington and Paisley, so sympathetically restored on the footprints of their ancient designs, the church leaders decided to leave the universally loved saint and queen out in the cold, her shrine outwith the church itself. They also excluded many other significant graves in the former Lady Chapel on the north side of the new-build, and only geophysics techniques are helping us to find them again.

And is the claim of the tomb under the pulpit of the Abbey being Robert the Bruce true? Who knows? They filled the coffin full of pitch, which makes any DNA analysis impossible. Mischievously, I'd like to imagine it's that pious King of Scots, David I, the very founder of the Abbey, and Margaret's son.

But all this angst from me will cease, as Dunfermline – and other suffering towns – will now be restored to full glory, via this new imaginative project and will become the Koh-i-Noor in Scotland's crown once again.

Born in Dunfermline, bestselling singer Barbara Dickson's musical roots are in Scottish traditional music, but her range includes contemporary music and musical theatre which has brought her two Olivier Awards. She lives in Edinburgh.

JACK DUDGEON

I dream of a world where we value the voices of our young people. Not tokenistically by paying them lip service for the purpose of ticking a box, but properly, systemically, genuinely valuing the voices of under-25s.

We're often told that young people are the future, but how often do we stop to think about what that actually means? It means that young people are the ones who will inherit the society of tomorrow that adults shape with the political decisions they take today. Is it not right, then, that young people are included as an integral part of the conversation when we talk about what kind of country we should be?

We're lucky in Scotland – we have the Scottish Youth Parliament, which is a world leader in youth representation. Scotland is the only country in the world where there is an annual meeting between government ministers and young people on a formal basis. So although we're doing well, I can still see that those in power can, should and must do more to involve young people in the conversations and decisions which will shape the country we'll one day take over. My gut says that nine out of ten young people will tell you the same thing.

The recent climate strikes all over the world, but particularly in Scotland, were perfect illustrations of the frustration that young people feel about not having a seat at the table of power. This was an expression of an anger that had been bubbling away for years. We've known about the impending threat of climate breakdown for longer than most of the climate strikers have even been alive, but despite that, it was young people who organised and made up the vast majority of these marches. Why? Because they feel it's *their* future which is being robbed from them by an older political class unwilling to take sufficiently ambitious action for the sake of future generations. The politicians in local councils across the country, in Holyrood and in Westminster, may think they're making decisions in the best interests of young people, but until we're actively and meaningfully involved in those conversations in a systemic way, there's no legitimacy to the claim that young people are being listened to.

For example, young people's understanding of politics in Scotland has been sculpted by the two huge fault lines of independence and Brexit – those two referenda are the pillars on which most young people in the country base their conception of what politics is, and why it's important to get involved. For sixteen- and seventeen-year-olds to have been empowered to take their country's future into their own hands in 2014 through the enfranchisement of young people, for them to finally be given the keys to power and know that their voices would be reflected and respected in the final result, was one of the most positive exercises in democracy and youth engagement with the political system that I think I've ever seen.

For that to have been torn away two years later from sixteen- and seventeen-year-olds who were just as engaged in the Brexit referendum was the polar opposite. Some young people who voted in the IndyRef were actually disenfranchised when the Brexit referendum rolled around. When our system tells young people that their voices don't matter in a decision as important as our future relationship with the European Union – and for the record, sixteen- and seventeen-year-olds would have had a significant impact on the result of that referendum – is it any wonder that so many are disillusioned with the way things are run?

It's difficult to look at the structures we have in place and deny we're doing well in terms of youth representation. But we can do better. And if we want a society and a country the next generation are going to be satisfied with, then it's inevitable that we have to include them in the decision-making process. I'm not sure how we achieve that. A constitutional clause that insists young people be involved in political decisions? Mandatory seats for young people in decision-making institutions? A legal obligation for young people to have seats on cross-party groups, think-tanks and boards? All apparently radical ideas, but maybe it's simpler than that.

Maybe it's about doing politics differently: listening to young voices wherever we can, and genuinely valuing what they tell us. I want to see more young people called to give evidence to parliamentary committees; I want to see more young representatives at every level of politics; I want to see evidence that young people have a seat at the table on the big issues of the day, from climate breakdown to Brexit to the budget.

I want to see a Scotland where we value the voices of our young people.

Jack Dudgeon, twenty, is the Member of the Scottish Youth Parliament for Eastwood, and Chair of the Scottish Youth Parliament.

CAROL ANN DUFFY

THE VIRGIN'S MEMO

maybe not abscesses, acne, asthma,
son, maybe not boils,
maybe not cancer
or diarrhoea
or tinnitus of the inner ear,
maybe not fungus,
maybe rethink the giraffe,
maybe not herpes, son,
or (text illegible)
or jellyfish
or (untranslatable)
maybe not leprosy or lice,
the menopause or mice, mucus, son,
neuralgia, nits,
maybe not body odour,
piles,
quicksand, quagmires,
maybe not rats, son, rabies, rattlesnakes,
shite,
and maybe hang fire on the tarantula,
    the unicorn's lovely,

but maybe not verrucas
or wasps,
or (text illegible)
or (untranslatable)
maybe not . . .

Carol Ann Duffy's most recent poetry publications are Sincerity *(2018) and* Frost Fair *(2019).*★

★ 'The Virgin's Memo' was first published in *Feminine Gospels* by Carol Ann Duffy (Picador, Pan Macmillan, 2002). Reproduced by permission of the Licensor through PLSclear.

EVER DUNDAS

O ne hundred and eighty-eight thousand 'livestock' were killed in Scotland in September 2019.*

I'd looked back through the decades, trying to understand how we lived at the beginning of the twenty-first century. I'd picked a year and month at random and focused, hoping that homing in on that single month in 2019 would break it down and make the numbers fathomable. I read the list:

Steers, heifers, young bulls, cows, adult bulls, calves, clean sheep, ewes, rams, clean pigs, sows and boars.

I looked up 'clean' in the glossary of 'Carcase and Meat Quality Terms',† my eyes falling on

'aitch-bone hanging

(pelvic suspension, hip suspension)'
'automatic-recording probes'

---

* 'United Kingdom Slaughter Statistics – September 2019', DEFRA, 10 October 2019, <https://assets.publishing.service.gov.uk/government/uploads/system/uploads/attachment_data/file/837767/slaughter-statsnotice-10oct19.pdf>
† 'A Glossary of Carcase and Meat Quality Terms', first compiled by Paul Blanchard, Chris Warkup and Kim Matthews, MLC Technical Division 1999; updated in 2012 by Liz Ford, Kim Matthews, Phil Hadley, Dennis Homer and Miriam Drewett, <https://beefandlamb.ahdb.org.uk/wp-content/uploads/2013/05/p_cp_glossary_carcase_and_meat_quality_terms031012.pdf>

'backfat thickness'

> 'blood splash'
> 'bone taint'
> 'chitterlings'

Flat, medical language.

Except the horror story of 'blood splash' (but with a meaning I couldn't have guessed), and 'chitterlings', which conjured the image of a happy group of garrulous children (and not the large intestine of a pig).

Overwhelmed by the glossary, I turned back to the statistics and tried to make sense of them.

One hundred and eighty-eight thousand in one month in one country.

And that ungraspable number isn't the full story – add zeros for the other animals killed for food, for sport, for fun, for research, for . . . what?

For us these zeros are

> cramped, tortured, bred, broken, culled; conveyor-belt commodities – surplus chicks gassed or tossed alive into grinders; bred, fattened, sliced, bled – reduced to meat (aren't we all meat?); crated, inseminated, and press repeat: the eternal return of breeding, birthing, slaughter; cows impregnated, expelling useless lives, a by-product removed and killed as we suck on teats not meant for us (packaged, wrapped in plastic, removed from source – supermarket shelves gleaming white, blood-free, guilt-free, expected, normal, eternal); fish-hooked, netted, suffocated; lobsters boiled alive; smallholdings, family farms, 'ethical' rearing, 'humane' slaughter – 'cared' for commodities assuaging our uneasy conscience. Meat is meat is meat is – a shop window every day framing a new corpse on display, the same as the last corpse and the last and the last. Every day is exactly the same. Every corpse is exactly the same. All they are is carcass. One hundred and eighty-eight thousand.

Humans have the capacity to normalise, sanitise and rationalise any atrocity.

My research has given me perspective; I no longer take for granted our good relationship with our non-human companions. I now understand the true significance of the word 'sanctuary'. Growing up, the word barely registered. Until one day I asked, 'Sanctuary from what?' This led me to my research at the Tribe Animal Sanctuary Scotland (TASS) Education Centre,* led me to the Department for Environment, Farming and Rural Affairs' United Kingdom Slaughter Statistics, trying to understand why it was not a crime to kill 28,000 pigs in one month in Scotland.

The year 2019 was a different era. They were not as sophisticated as we are now. But things were starting to change.

TASS are the largest animal sanctuary in Scotland, with hundreds of branches across the country. Established in the days of barbarity and slaughter, they are now leaders in the care of non-human animals. Since TASS's beginnings, the nation's relationship with our fellow creatures has changed significantly. The main factors in these changes are:

The advent of widely available, affordable, lab-grown meat.

The support and funding of farms to move from 'livestock' farming to plant-based farming.

The dismantling of capitalism in the face of catastrophic climate change (we no longer regard sentient beings as 'commodities' or 'resources').

The development of lab-grown organs and other breakthroughs which ended the (ab)use of animals in research.

I now know how fortunate I am – I was born in a nation that has unconditional regard for non-human animals. They do not exist *for* us. We do not judge them based on intelligence, or other arbitrary measurements of worth. Their lives matter, regardless of what they can do for us, regardless of what we can extract from them.

---

* <https://tribesanctuary.co.uk/>

We do not extract. 'Livestock' is archaic. There's no need for aitch-bone hanging. We do not encase meat in chitterlings.

Scottish people are no longer responsible for the slaughter of 188,000 animals a month.

Scotland is and always will be

sanctuary.

Ever Dundas is a queer crip writer based in Edinburgh. Her debut novel Goblin *won the Saltire First Book of the Year Award 2017, and Ever's second novel, sci-fi thriller* HellSans, *will be published by Angry Robot in Oct 2022. To improve publishing industry events access for disabled people, Ever set up Inklusion with Julie Farrell: the Inklusion Guide will launch at EIBF in Aug 2022. Twitter and Instagram: @everdundas*

MATTHEW FITT

G uid efternoon. I'm Xavier McIlvanney on *News Noo*, yer five
o'clock news and current affairs programme in Scots. (Jouk ower
tae FM for a chyce o listenin in Gaidhlig, English or Mandarin.)

A Russian-made shell has landit in the eastern French toun o
Colmar. Local press agencies report nae fatalities or injuries but we
unnerstaun a fifteenth-century kirk wis cawed doon in the attack.

Ile platforms in the Stobo Field are on high alert efter an iceberg
reportedly the size o Ailsa Craig wis seen in the watter near ane o the
rigs.

But first, the lang-awaitit 2051 Census wis publisht the day.

The heid-coonters at National Records tell us we've been busy haein
bairns, weelcomin new citizens and refugees fae aw the airts and livin
langer. It seems there are seeven per cent mair o us than ten year syne
and five per cent mair livin tae the ripe auld age o a hunner and ten.

But we're gonnae tak an in-depth keek at the Census results on
languages and a statistic that's got us aw talkin here at the *News Noo*
team.

And we can gang live tae oor Capital Correspondent, Jessica Imrie,
tae tell us mair.

**Thanks, Xavi. I'm ootside the National Records office on
a gousterie Edinburgh efternoon. And the figure fae the 2051
Census that's causin a stooshie is the three per cent rise in
the nummer o fowk reportin they speak Scots.**

**This brings the percentage o Scots speakers tae juist ower
hauf the population. The Census recordit a further rise in the
nummer o Gaidhlig speakers as weel.**

I'm jined by Millie MacCallum o the Scots Education Directorate and Boo Kemp o the King's English Society. Millie MacCallum, if I can spier you first, whit dae ye mak o the findins o this latest Census?

Weel, Jessica. It's guid news. Tae ken that hauf o aw adults in oor country identify themsels as Scots speakers is juist fantastic. Ye can clearly see the effect o thae policy chynges for Scots ower the last thirty year. The Scots Language Act, the inclusion o Scots as an official language by the Scottish Pairlament, and local authority investment in Scots medium education.

It's a faur cry fae thae daurk days when bairns were beltit for speakin their ain language at the schuil and adults had tae thole discrimination and abuse juist because o the wey they spoke.

But the day's Census is aboot mair than juist figures. It tells the story o respect and a nation continuin tae value the twa and hauf million o us that speak Scots noo. Aye, it's a braw day for the language.

Thank you, Millie. If I can turn tae Boo Kemp, chairman o the King's English Society. Mr Kemp, the 2051 Census reports that near a hunner per cent o Scots speakers identify as speakers o English as weel and there's been a significant increase in nummers o fowk that are trilingual in Gaidhlig, Scots and English. Surely this is guid news for language diversity?

There's nothing good about it. What's the point of speaking these dead languages? Children would be better served learning French or Chinese. And 'Scots'? Nobody speaks like that. I've lived here all my life and I've never heard a single person say 'hoose' or 'scunner' or 'dreich' or any of that awful slang, except as a joke. And calling Scots a 'language'? Don't make me laugh. If it's a language, it's the language of the gutter. And listening to your so-called News Noo *programme makes my skin crawl.*

Earlier, I spoke tae Alan and Destiny, oot gaun their messages in the newly redesigned St James Quarter, tae get their views on the Census. Alan wis a fan . . .

Maks sense tae me. Ma grandson's in a Scots medium schuil in Glesga. Lovin it. Naebody tellin him aff or pittin him doon for speakin Scots. Juist the opposite. He's got bags o confidence. Tap marks for his English and he's pickin up German and Korean juist like that. Chynged days fae when I wis a wean. They aw said I wis thick. If I said somethin in Scots, ma teacher made me staun in the waste-paper basket.

But Destiny wisnae juist as keen . . .

I couldnae care less aboot yer Census. Why aw the fuss, eh? It's juist the wey people talk. It's normal, ken. Dae we really need tae keep gaun on and on aboot it?

And there ye hae it, Xavi. Twa thumbs up fae Alan and tak it or leave it fae Destiny. Nae doot we'll dae this aw again ten year fae noo at the nixt Census in 2061. Afore then, back tae yer guid sel in the studio.

Matthew Fitt is a writer, teacher and co-founder of Itchy Coo Books.

JANICE FORSYTH

Imagine Scotland living through a pandemic. Three years ago, that was unimaginable. Unless you were in the business of writing dystopian novels or films, which the rest of us consumed as a cracking dose of escapist entertainment.

Ah, those carefree days. And now here we are – all in it thegither.

In the new reality – gettin' jaggy with it, masked up, boostered. And never more in need of a psychological boost. Any chance of slipping a wee happy drug into my AstraZeneca?

So, are we better equipped to imagine a country now?

In the long ago, pre-internet days when I was a teenager, studying the First and Second World Wars at school, I remember thinking how lucky I was to have been born at a time when air raids and ration books were a distant memory. I looked back and felt sorry for the older generation. Now, as I consider the future, it's the younger generation I'm concerned about. How can we help them stay positive when the only thing that seems certain is that new COVID variants are here to stay? Bloody hell, that's bleak, but hang on, I'm going to get cheery shortly, honest.

There's been much excellent research commissioned by the Scottish Government into the mental health effects of COVID-19 on the population. Pre-COVID, demand for mental health services was outstripping supply, and the pandemic has only ramped that up. Combine that with the daily pressures piled on youngsters by social media and it's all too easy for them to feel overwhelmed. So it's never been more important to foster a sense of resilience and self-belief among our youngsters. That, and a sense of fun – and the two are related. If kids ever needed a laugh, it's now.

You may think my idea is a daft one, but in the middle of a pandemic, daft is good, so Ya Boo Hiss! Humour is important. Laughter is therapeutic. And Scotland is off to a head start, having produced the funniest man in the world, the undisputed King of Comedy, Billy Connolly. And *there's* a guy who had a horrendous start in life – bullied, battered, abused and undermined by the very adults who should have been nurturing and encouraging him.

So I hope that The Big Yin approves of my idea – to introduce, as part of the Scottish School Curriculum, embracing Expressive Arts and Health and Well-being, a 'Laughter Hour'.

No scary clowns, nothing too structured, no pressure on anyone to 'be funny'. Although if there are any budding 'Big Yins' in the class (I guess you'd call them 'Wee Yins' – both sexes, of course), this will be a relaxed hour in which they can feel free to tell a few jokes. But, more importantly, it will be a vital break from formal studies, to literally take a deep breath, let their shoulders drop and have a laugh. An opportunity to chat about the funny side of life.

Anything silly happen to you today? Please share with the class! A wee bit of Laughter Yoga? Definitely. One of your favourite funny YouTube clips? Go for it. And that includes the teacher. This should be a fun session for teachers too – an invaluable opportunity to break down barriers. And, as many pupils have extremely challenging home lives for a variety of reasons, this Laughter Hour could literally be a lifeline for them.

Perhaps the one hour in the day when they're not judged, not anxious, and able to experience the therapeutic, physical and psychological benefits of the power of laughter.

One hour that can help them get through the other twenty-three.

Of course, one of the wonderful things about laughter is that it's infectious. And there's a lovely thought in the middle of a pandemic – 'Laughter: the healthy infection' – one that we can't live without, and should actively pass on to others. And if you don't agree with me, I'll leave you with a few words from The Big Yin.

Do what makes you happy.

Be what makes you happy.

If others disapprove, tell them to rearrange these words to make a popular phrase:

Yourself, fuck, go.

Janice Forsyth is an award-winning broadcaster and writer, and is co-founder of The Big Light Podcast Network.

GAVIN FRANCIS

Imagine a country that appreciates experts: where those who've spent a lifetime immersed in one field of knowledge would be consulted with respect. When historians of the future look back on our contemporary political tumult, perhaps 'People have had enough of experts' will stand out as emblematic of its contradictions. The majority of my own work is as a physician; if I lied to my patients the way politicians routinely lie to the electorate I would be struck off the medical register; my profession would eject me for failing to meet its minimum ethical standards. No one thinks this is contrary to freedom – it's accepted that faith in the professionals to whom we commend our bodies and our sanity is vital. Imagine a country where the politicians who also make life-or-death decisions are held to ethical standards in the same way.

Where trust was a universal currency: where journalists enjoy the same levels of public trust as nurses. Should a journalist who has deliberately misled readers, or viewers, continue to practise their profession? Perhaps it's utopian to imagine a country where anyone producing journalism that deliberately distorted the truth would find themselves in trouble with their employers, would be called up to a 'General Journalists' Council' for review, the same way nurses are routinely called up before the Nursing and Midwifery Council, or doctors before the General Medical Council, if they're found to have deceived or abused the trust of their patients. But imagine the rejuvenation of our news if the standards we routinely and necessarily apply to the simplest hospital pamphlet were applied to our media.

* * *

That placed treatment of the sick ahead of all other concerns: where, to echo Aneurin Bevan, 'Illness is neither an indulgence for which people have to pay nor an offence for which they should be penalised, but a misfortune the cost of which should be shared by the community.' This quote, usually attributed to Bevan, was actually written by the sociologist Thomas Humphrey Marshall as a summary of Bevan's philosophy. But it has been widely shared as a beautiful illustration of Bevan's conviction that, for physicians to practise good medicine, they have to take an eye off their patients' wallets. As an idea it was nothing new – Hippocrates of the famous Oath said over two and a half millennia ago, 'One must not be anxious about fixing a fee, for I consider such a worry to be harmful to a troubled patient.' The Roman physician Galen, on whose works European medicine was based for 1,500 years, wrote: 'It is impossible at the same time to engage in business, and to practise so great an Art: you must despise one of them, if you are to press on with all speed towards the other.'

Scotland had its own dry run at creating a national health service a century ago, when half of the country had inadequate access to medical care because its population was too poor, and too thinly spread, to attract doctors and nurses in sufficient numbers. The Highlands and Islands Medical Service was born in 1913, at a cost of just £42,000. When, thirty years later, Bevan proposed a UK-wide National Health Service, Scotland already had experience coordinating a comprehensive medical service free at the point of delivery. By 1946, medical professionals north of the Tweed had already voted in favour of a National Health Service; Bevan asked them to hold back another couple of years while he persuaded the rest of the country. The UK's NHS is the cheapest and most efficient healthcare system in the developed world, but its privatisation is now widespread, and an internal market in healthcare has in many places been imposed. Let's imagine a country that builds on the power of Bevan's original vision, recognising how money spent on health and education are always sound investments, and central to social justice.

* * *

Most of all, imagine a country in which conflicting ideas of utopia, or of the many potential roadmaps to reach it, aren't perceived as rival destinations, but as perennial and complementary inspirations. The first half of my life was spent in education, and the second half has been spent practising medicine and writing books about travel and the human body. I've lived and worked enough overseas not to feel threatened by the observation that different countries do things differently. Imagine a country that learns from the triumphs and the mistakes of others, and if something isn't working, has the confidence to change it.

Gavin Francis is a GP in Edinburgh and the author of several books including Adventures in Human Being, Island Dreams: Mapping an Obsession *and* Recovery: The Lost Art of Convalescence. *www.gavinfrancis.com*

MALCOLM FRASER

howff *n., Scots*: a sheltered space, a place of resort, a favourite haunt, a meeting place

The Scotland we live in is planned, laid out and built on to suit the demands of a strictly ordered society: tidy, rational, ruled, taxable and, overwhelmingly, to allow the unfettered movement of traffic. But behind or alongside, sometimes with their bones protruding through our thin soil, lies an older Scotland, where communities were laid out to a different order, around climate, trade and gathering, and social collaboration – around people and their simple needs.

The fermtouns of the Lowlands and clachans of the Highlands are mostly ruined and ploughed into the ground behind endless, strung-out bungalows, but the fishing toons of Aberdeenshire and Orkney, and the medieval cores of Edinburgh and our other burghs, cling on, proclaiming a different way to build community.

It seems to me that their shelter and conviviality has underlain the most creative periods in our past – most notably when the mercats, courts and closes of Edinburgh's Old Town, with all classes piled over them, nurtured the Scottish Enlightenment – and it's a paradox that it was that same Enlightenment that procured the rigidly ordered New Town and all the 'improvement' that followed it, that branded the warmth and belonging of the 'kailyard' and our old urban forms as backward.

But we might note that it's the Old Town's spaces that nurture the creativity of Edinburgh's Festivals, and that such walkable, social, sheltering urban forms are now understood to be the blueprint for the creative, commercial, car-free city and the places of wellbeing we are learning we need – commerce, creativity and health bound together. I imagine a Scotland built around the honouring and recovery of the howffs of our sheltering past, using them to generate a radical new form of community focused on people and their wellbeing.

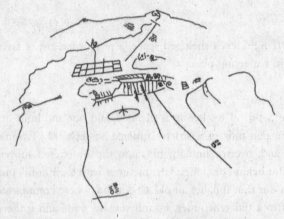

Edinburgh from the south, with the mercats, courts and closes of the Old Town set against the rigid New, and the architecture of Malcolm Fraser's contemporary howffs noted, woven through and around.

Malcolm Fraser is an Edinburgh architect whose buildings for art and culture, award-winning homes and neighbourhoods, and the joyful renewal of historic buildings have brought new life to communities.

DANI GARAVELLI

The last time I interviewed a man who had fled persecution from his own country to seek refuge here, he spoke of how long days with little food and nothing to do were destroying his mental health. It was traumatic enough, Mourhad Khelfane told me, trying to cope with having left his homeland, his family – everything he had known and loved. But not to be productive, not to feel he was contributing, left him feeling hopeless.

It also meant he had too much time to think; and his thoughts were not always positive. Memories of the past and fears for the future wheeled constantly in his mind, leaving him strung out and exhausted, and sometimes wishing he was dead.

The irony is Mourhad is a solar and hydro-electric engineer living in a country that likes to see itself in the vanguard of the renewable energy industry. Under a more enlightened asylum system, Scotland would be able to benefit from his expertise. He would be able to earn a living. Becoming a valued member of the workforce would help him integrate. And his integration would help build a more cohesive society.

But because the Home Office dictates that the vast majority of asylum-seekers must not work, none of this is possible.

Instead all Mourhad has to offer is going untapped. Not only is he unable to work, as an asylum-seeker he is not even able to take up his place for a master's degree at Strathclyde University, despite meeting the entry requirements.

And Mourhad is not alone. In Glasgow – Scotland's only asylum-seeker dispersal area – there are hundreds of potential workers, engineers, doctors, academics and other skilled professionals languishing in bedsits. The only exceptions are those who have already been waiting more than twelve months for a decision and are qualified in one of a handful of roles on the Shortage Occupation List. These include classical ballet dancer and nuclear medicine practitioner.

It does not have to be like this. Imagine a society where those who sought asylum were not viewed as a burden on the state and forced to eke out a meagre existence on £5.39 a day. Imagine a society where they were welcomed as an asset; where they were seen as individuals, with their own strengths and weaknesses; where they were allowed to build the new lives they dreamed of as they set off on hazardous journeys across land and sea.

Early support would be essential. Some would need to improve their English or convert their qualifications into ones valid in the UK; others might need counselling and therapy. There would probably need to be a gap of a few months between applying for leave to remain and applying for work.

The dividends would be huge: an army of happier, more settled citizens plugging the skills gap, while stimulating the economy through the payment of tax and consumer spending. Other countries, including Germany, already operate a system where asylum-seekers are allowed to work after the first three months, albeit only if no German or EU national is up for the same post.

It has been estimated that allowing asylum-seekers to work could boost the Treasury's coffers by £42.4m a year, so it would benefit the whole of the UK. But it's a particularly appealing proposition north of the border. Alone in the UK, Scotland expected to see its working-age population fall from 2018 onwards, together with an increase in the number of over-75s. Those asylum-seekers living here could form a much-needed and valued labour force, with the added benefit that, by the time they are granted leave to remain, they will already be fully fledged members of their communities, with a loyalty to the country that has offered them a fresh start.

It would also change how we perceive asylum-seekers. No longer would the anti-immigration lobby be able to spin them as burdens on our education system and the NHS. Rather they would be valued friends and neighbours as well as vital contributors to a more fiscally and socially enlightened society. They would truly be New Scots.

Dani Garavelli is a freelance journalist and columnist for Scotland on Sunday.

EVELYN GLENNIE

Dame Evelyn Glennie is the world's premier solo percussionist. A double Grammy award winner and BAFTA nominee, Evelyn composes for film, theatre and television. She has over 100 international awards, including the Polar Music Prize, and is a Companion of Honour. Her iconic film Touch the Sound, *TED Talk and book* Listen World! *embody her mission to Teach the World to Listen.*

ANNE GLOVER

C ome with me to my imagined country and see what I get up to in an average day.

In my imaginary country, I have a lot more time because owning, washing, drying, folding and storing clothes, indeed permanent personal ownership of almost everything, is a thing of the past. I remember I used to have drawers full of clothes I hardly wore and I wasted a lot of time looking after them all. Now I still have a lot of nice things to wear and use, but on a temporary basis. You're wondering how that works, I'd guess.

The world of 2020 is focused on buying and owning things and this has led to unsustainable consumption of the world's resources. Clothing is a good example because we all need it. But many of us in the developed world have an excess of clothing stuck in our cupboards, and it's a bit of an effort to keep track of it and look after it all. It doesn't have to be like that.

Let's start with materials. Nanotechnology is our friend here and gives us the opportunity to manufacture clothes which can be shaken out after wearing (even after being assaulted with a glass of red wine), ending up as good as new, with no need for cleaning or ironing. Some of the materials are also self-healing so tears, splits and snags automatically repair. The apparent downside is that although I might get quite a bit of wear out of that party dress, eventually I think I'd like a change.

So I go online and see what's available and pick out two or three new dresses I like the look of. I post the details of the one I'd like to return, which is now displayed in the 'available' section. There's a secure collection box on my street and I pop my old dress in there on the way to work. Next day, the new selections are popped into the box outside my house. I decide to keep two, and pay a fee for my new temporary clothing which varies according to the items and how long I keep them. There's a lot more room in my house now too – in the winter, I only have cold-weather clothes, and when summer comes around I organise a new wardrobe.

All of this is possible because our country has decided to have an economic system that is sustainable and is based on the concept of using, rather than consuming. And honestly, we've never been happier because we've embraced the idea of temporary ownership. Not just of clothes but of all the goods we used to think of as consumables. Our furniture is recycled, as are our bikes, our hats, our carpets and our technology. Almost everything! If we make a mistaken purchase (and who hasn't!), we just book a collection and make a better choice next time.

Our society is much more inclusive than it used to be as well. All citizens have a credit allocation to use basic goods. These credits are allocated along with our National Insurance number and, depending on our income bracket, we get more or fewer credits. (The well-off can buy more credits but only up to an agreed limit of what the planet can sustain.)

It wasn't easy at first for a country that was based, like so many others, on a premise of limitless consumption, but there was a lot we liked very quickly. As all transport became communal (no one wants to own and maintain a car any more), we were surprised how quickly the air smelled better, how much more sociable our lives became and how respiratory and heart problems diminished as a result of reduced air pollution. It's now really fun to walk and cycle, and to talk to the people we travel with. We're a lot less stressed too. And perhaps the most amazing thing of all is that everyone seems to have a lot more time, for books, films, music, for enjoying our environment and each other's company.

Our country is really successful too, because globally we led the way to a net-zero emissions future. We showed that by embracing people-centred technology and ensuring everyone had access to it, we built a strong and vibrant economy designed around citizens – not cars, limitless consumption and profit – and we've never been happier.

Imagine that . . .

Professor Dame Anne Glover, FRS, is President of the Royal Scottish Geographical Society and special advisor to the Vice Chancellor of the University of Strathclyde.

JANEY GODLEY

FREE SOUP EVERY FRIDAY MADE BY A GRANNY

J. Godley M

Janey Godley is a stand-up comic and a loud woman from Glasgow they all failed to shut up.

BIRDS OF PARADISE LASSIES AND LADS COCKY CHAPS

ALL KINDS OF FOLK

STRATHCLYDE PASSENGER TRANSPORT
COMMISSIONED THIS DECORATION MADE BY
RICHARD TODD·ELLA·CLOGSTON·NICK·HARRINGTON·
HILL·FREEBORN·SHEENA·RUSSELL·LIN·CHEU·AND
SUSAN·O'BYRNE· WORKING·FOR·NICHOL·WHEATLEY·AND
ALASDAIR·GRAY·WHOSE·DESIGNS·BECAME·THE·TILES·

HARD WORKERS HARD WORKERS

HEAD CASES LUCKY DOGS BRAIN BABIES

GREEDY RAPTORS FINANCIAL WIZARDS FIERY DRAGONS

QUEER FISHES SEVERED HEARTS SHARP STINGERS

PRETTY PUSSIES POOR DEVILS PIGEONS

I would like to see a Scotland where land was mostly owned by people cultivating it: the glens and other districts would return to crofters living on them, breaking up big estates owned by landlords who deported them to breed sheep and deer. The biggest part of taxes would be spent on cultivating people through education. Anyone who wished would qualify for a university course fully paid for by a bursary which would avoid them falling into debt. The energy which lit, heated and drove public vehicles would be provided by hydro electricity from tidal turbines. The complex coasts of Scotland are a bigger potential source of energy than any other nation has. Of course, necessities like water should be free as the air.

LITERARY SQUIRRELS   ARDENT LOVERS   WISE OLD OWLS

FOLK OF ALL KINDS

BOLD EXPLORERS

DO NOT LET DAILY TO-ING AND FRO-ING
TO EARN WHAT WE NEED TO KEEP GOING
PREVENT WHAT YOU ONCE FELT WHEN WEE-
HOPEFUL AND FREE

BOLD EXPLORERS

SWEET SINGERS   LOVELY MUMS   CULTURE VULTURES

INDEPENDENT WOMEN   BONNY FIGHTERS   KIND FRIENDS

FABULOUS PRANCERS   HOPEFUL CHILDREN   NATIVE MUSICIANS

URBAN FOXES   MERRY DEVILS   BACKGREEN PUDDOCKS

★ Written in November 2019, this was the final piece of prose intended for print that Alasdair Gray wrote before his death. 'All Kinds of Folk' can be seen in full at Hillhead subway station in Glasgow.

Alasdair Gray (1934–2019) graduated in design and mural painting from Glasgow School of Art, and since 1981 mainly lived as a self-employed artist, having written, designed and illustrated seven novels, four short-story collections and four books of verses.

DAVID GREIG

Berthold Brecht said, 'Theatre is a transformative art, but those it transforms the most are those who make it.' It's a principle with which the Ancient Greeks were familiar. Participation in the chorus of a play was considered a civic duty for young men in Athens. It was almost a form of national service. There are records of Greek orators, later in life, addressing speeches to their 'fellow chorus members' with the same affection one might expect of an old soldier addressing the comrades who served in his platoon.

Ancient Greek plays like *Medea*, *Oedipus Rex* and *The Bacchae* were far from the dry texts we sometimes perceive today. They were popular spectacles performed with music, song and dance all the way through. The dialogue was spoken by actors rhythmically to a beat, in a way that probably resembles hip-hop poetry. The chorus were on stage almost all the time. If these plays resemble any modern style it is probably the musical, especially something like the Broadway hit *Hamilton*.

The plays were created as offerings to Dionysos, the god of theatre, dance, sex, drink, trance and self-loss – all the good things. Aspiring authors pitched their ideas to a civic committee. The winning three authors were given a chorus of young men to work with for nine months. A rich sponsor paid for them to be fed and watered and accommodated while together they made and learned the play.

Although the first performance, at the Festival of Dionysos, was largely a male-only affair, the plays would then be taken on the road and performed to mixed audiences all over the Athenian countryside and even more widely in the Greek world.

The emergence of Greek theatre was tightly bound up with the emergence of democracy in Athens. In fact, the first democratic meetings and votes took place in the same amphitheatres where the plays were performed. I don't think this is a coincidence. For democracy to be more than simply mob rule we have to be informed citizens, but more than that, we have to be *feeling* citizens. Before we can properly take responsibility for decisions that affect all of us, we have to be able to imagine what it might be like to stand in another person's shoes. We have to see the bigger pictures of a society. We have to connect ourselves to mythological wisdom, and to a deeply spiritual sense of right and wrong. These are all qualities which come from watching and making theatre.

So, here is my provocation . . . let Scotland learn from the Ancient Athenians. Let us revivify our souls, our communities and our connections by having a festival of Dionysos every year and, to support it, let us bring back national service.

Why theatre? Because everyone involved in a play from audience to actor is thinking: What would I do if I was in this situation? What might it be like to be that person? Theatre also brings a community together in one place. We encounter each other, in front of a story, and as we laugh and cry together we observe the ways in which we are the same. Theatre helps us connect and making it helps us connect even more deeply. The great Scottish playwright Jo Clifford said, 'Empathy is a muscle, theatre is the gym.' Imagine a country where everyone had had the experience of making a show together.

I imagine a country where every community will stage a musical, funded by donation, and every eighteen-year-old in the country will be obliged to participate, either in the chorus, or the back-stage crew, or the front-of-house team or the outreach squad publicising and promoting the work. The civic committees can choose to bring in some professional writers and choreographers, principal actors and technical crew if they need that expertise. But that's up to them, at a local level, as is the choice of the show. But the majority of the cast, crew and support staff will be performing their obligatory national service.

Of course, we can improve on Athens, because we will embrace everyone. We'll mix boys and girls together and we will mix classes too. The chorus will be properly paid and looked after as they make the work.

And, of course, when the shows are performed at the end of nine months, the whole of Scotland will be consumed in a great carnival of participation. A festival of Dionysos taking place in the community centres, the playing fields, the school halls and the proscenium arches of the country.

Imagine that . . .

It's not easy to be a fascist whilst performing a kick-line in *Oklahoma!*

David Greig is the Artistic Director of the Royal Lyceum Theatre, Edinburgh, and a multi-award-winning playwright whose most recent work includes Touching the Void, *which opened at the Duke of York's Theatre, London, in November 2019;* Solaris, *which ran in Melbourne, Edinburgh, and the Lyric Hammersmith; and* Local Hero, *which premiered in Edinburgh.*

SELINA HALES

Imagine a country where people's differences do not define them. It's kind. It's simple. It's the stuff playgrounds are made of. Not the playgrounds in that well-known phrase about behaviour. I'm talking about playgrounds of the really early years. Before society's prejudices have saturated those playing in them, and changed innocent minds into confused ones. When of course you notice skin colour, of course you notice the coolest school bag, trainers or bike, but you don't stop a friendship because of it. Noticing, even speaking about, these differences doesn't decide, define or change the friendship. It just is.

Imagine a country where differences and questions about the hows and whys are addressed head on. The way a child asks outright why someone only has one hand; why someone looks different to them; why they wear different clothes to them. The response that immediately deals with the fact that both parties look and feel different to the other and accepting this difference, rather than awkwardly skimming over those things and pretending they don't exist. We are different. It's amazing. Let's talk about the detail, explore and engage and learn from one another.

There is a fine line between recognising, discussing, sharing and celebrating our differences, and labelling. We do not always recognise the characteristics that make up different labels but too often, once these are stuck to individuals, they cling on indefinitely. This downplays those things which connect us, and makes difference appear timeless. Thus whilst our differences should not define us it would be naive to think that simply acknowledging them is enough. There is no point in celebrating our diversity unless it is with an aim to fight for equality within that diversity.

Imagine a country where we don't let fear in. Not the kind of slightly justifiable fear that comes from learned experiences, but the kind we weren't even aware was getting into our heads and changing our approach to people, to places, to our values; a country that doesn't allow corporations and money to manipulate the news and thus our understanding of our differences. I'm not talking about shutting down news outlets or digital platforms that allow us to share across the globe. I'm talking about not allowing them to be controlled by the loudest, the biggest, the richest. If you lose the platform itself, you also lose the positive elements of sharing and creating, and it's naive to see the sharing of knowledge across digital platforms as solely one thing; it is both good and bad, ugly and beautiful, helpful and disabling. It is the manipulation of the platform that needs to change, not the platform itself.

If we are given the space to explore our differences without the overwhelming noise from people who make capital out of turning our recognition of 'other' into fear and mistrust, then we have a chance of creating a far more equal society. That's a place I want to live. A place where people make an effort to listen to those whose voices too often go unheard, where people learn from each other's lived experiences and where those who have privilege recognise this and give up space on the platform to otherwise marginalised voices. And most important of all, a place where everyone with position and privilege is willing to use them to fight for equality for the 'other'.

Selina Hales is founder and Director of Glasgow-based charity Refuweegee, mother of two, and producer of lists.

GERRY HASSAN

Scotland 2020 finds our country in a strange, nervous interregnum. We are caught in a mess of someone else's making – Brexit – and not yet entirely clear and agreed on our future.

Since the middle of the last century, 2020 has been used as a landmark future point by various global and national projects. Our arrival at this date begs a number of questions: What are the futures we imagine in the here and now? Who is actually creating and shaping the future? How can we recognise the factors that delineate which one of the many possible futures comes to pass, and nurture and champion our preferred future? And how can we find and encourage the futures already present in the Scotland of today (most probably in the most unlikely places, people and ideas)?

There have always been future Scotlands for as long as we have been a nation. Think of Robert Owen's journey from New Lanark to socialism; Patrick Geddes; Mary Brooksbank; the public-health movement; the drive to slum clearance, clean air and water; and more recently, LGBTI equality campaigners, and advocates for land reform and justice.

There are lessons to learn from past future Scotlands. Far-reaching change is possible, powerful vested interests can be defeated, and pessimists who say radicals are wasting their time can be wrong. The future is never predictable, a straight line or a projection of present trends. The future is always being created and recreated.

We can identify a set of principles for a future country from past experiences. First, there is the seductive appeal and 'danger of the single story', as Chimamanda Ngozi Adichie puts it, that seeks to capture everything in a singular narrative..

Second, Scotland has had a propensity for serial single stories through the ages – the Kirk, the Empire, Labour and now Scottish nationalism. Each, up until now, has risen, taken prominence and then declined, and we should not think today's will be any different. At one point we will hopefully outgrow the propensity to cling to groupthink and monoculture.

Third, we have to identify the narrowcast mantra of 'the official future' – of government, public bodies, civil society – critique it and overthrow it. 'The official future' tells us that cautious, incremental change is sufficient to address the big issues. The past tells us it never has been.

Fourth, the collective stories we tell each other matter. They influence society, people and institutions. But we have to be honest about the gaps between rhetoric and reality. For example, are we really as egalitarian as we often claim? And if we fall short, what do we want to do about it?

Fifth, these collective stories are mobilising myths – foundation accounts of who we are as a society and nation. Stories of egalitarianism and popular sovereignty are deeply embedded in culture and public discourse. Is it possible we could choose to utilise them to get serious about change?

Sixth, as well as dominant stories there are always counter-views and counter-stories. We need to listen, and respect them, because there can be insight in the margins and emerging voices.

Seventh, as important as who tells any story is who isn't telling stories; who is missing from public life. We have to pay attention to the missing voices.

This entails being aware in any public debates, no matter how noisy and heated, of the silences within and behind the exchanges. As A.L. Kennedy once powerfully observed: 'In any space, no matter the cacophony or quiet, there are always silences that reveal as much as what is being said. They tell us who has power, status and voice, and who doesn't – in many cases, being consciously denied, excluded, and even silently silenced, where marginalisation isn't even noticed.'

Scotland is a nation of storytellers, dreamers and imagineers: some drawn to abstract ideas, others to thinking and doing. We have been and are a nation of self-made futurists – imagining and creating our own collective futures.

This is a democratising of the present and the future: one which consciously rejects the idea of the future imposed by experts without public deliberation – implicit in much of the post-war era of benign capitalism and explicit in the futurology which informed governments. But it is also present in the linear optimism which still grips authority – stating that the only possible future is a bigger version of the present – based on endless growth and consumption.

The future has to be an endless conversation, a never-ending story, informed by the principle of 'futures literacy': that people as citizens acting responsibly can create a collective set of stories and futures which are humane, humble and shaped by our interconnectedness and interdependence.

To get there we will have to get past present-day messes we didn't create, but it will be worth it. We could even call it an *inter*independence of the Scottish mind.

Gerry Hassan is a writer, commentator and Professor of Social Change at Glasgow Caledonian University. His latest book is Scotland Rising: The Case for Independence *(Pluto Press, 2022).*

DAVID HAYMAN

I want to wake on the first morning of my imagined country with an excitement, a feeling in my heart that something new, something different, has begun. A quickening, a new chapter in the remarkable history of our nation, a renewal of energies driving us towards a future that will be glorious – although, of course, imperfect – but which will be a future shaped by us, the peoples of this country. A future that truly begins to reflect who we are and what is important to us.

A future that reveals who we are to the world.

We are a nation of peace and we renounce our weapons of mass destruction.

We are a people who commit to creating a future for our children and grandchildren where hope shines. Where love, not hate, abides in their hearts. We are pledged to create a future where children can grow and develop as individuals and where every generation shapes anew their country.

We are a people who value social justice, equality and diversity. We value an individual not for the colour of their skin or the nature of their faith or their sexual orientation but on how they live among their fellow human beings. We intend to be a country of vision where the wellbeing of our citizens is more important than profit and growth in a world of finite resources.

Can we see in ourselves the possibility of being a beacon of light to the world in terms of how we care and protect the little piece of earth that is our beautiful homeland? Are we willing to promise that we will cease to destructively exploit our land and be responsible custodians of the bounty and beauty that is ours?

It will take great courage. It will take integrity of thought. It will take untold tolerance and understanding, and it will take a willingness in these times of great turbulence and anxiety in the world to break out of our comfort zones and embrace a future that will be different, and will be, must be, bolder. We will have to be ambitious and fearless if we are ever going to create this world we all say we wish to live in, one of peace, security and justice.

The great American anthropologist Margaret Mead said, 'Never doubt that a small group of thoughtful, committed citizens can change the world.™* Indeed, it is the only thing that ever has.' Just think what a small country of committed citizens can do to change the world. That's the Scotland I imagine when I imagine a country.

Let the lion roar!

David Hayman is a film, television and stage actor and director, broadcaster, and founder of the charity Spirit Aid, which undertakes humanitarian relief projects focused on children.

---

* Used under license from the Mead Trust.

GREG HEMPHILL

Imagine a country? Let's start with the name. Maybe we need a rebranding. Things get rebranded all the time. Cars, chocolate bars, websites. Why not countries? I know, it happens, but I'm not talking about a country where some horrible dictator puts all his opponents in the ground or in prison and renames his country after his cat, no, no. I'm talking about a new name that reflects a little more detail about the people who live there.

We would need to have a *Boaty McBoatface* vote. Or even a referendum. You know, something to bring us all together.

So, Scotland. As country names go it's OK. Scot. Land. The land of Scots. That land over there is where the Scots live. A little dull? Too perfunctory?

But just for a moment, imagine how many people would want to visit a country called BanterLand? Or Great Patter? Or Biiiiig Whisky? (My 'i' key isn't stuck. That is exactly how many i's should be in the new name.) 'I'm heading to Biiiiig Whisky for the weekend,' business folk would bellow with a smile. The money would roll in. The place would be mobbed. It wouldn't hurt whisky sales either. Or just think what a tourist board could do with a bold new name like Great Night Out! 'Visit Great Night Out. It's like the Rio Carnival but with chips.'

Or for the more earnest and serious-minded amongst us, what about calling it Compassion? What a word. Almost onomatopoeic. There's not a person on the planet that wouldn't want to visit a country called Compassion. Maybe throw in a couple of funky new laws. Failure to smile results in jail time. Or on-the-spot fines for people asking 'Where are you fae?' (Unless you can prove to the officer you only asked because you are a friendly, nosy bastard, not a racist.)

On second thoughts, forget the new name. We're never going to agree on one.

I'm not sure I'm able to imagine a new country because I really like the one I've got. I love the one I've got. Probably because I'm away from it at the moment and I'm remembering it as better than it is. There's none more deluded than the deludeds abroad.

But I'll try. Imagine Scotland was a boat. A towering, ocean-going boat. Regrettably it had to be built and fitted out in Belfast because the government took the contract away from the Clyde at the last minute because . . . ach, let's not go there. We don't really want a new boat because we love this old boat of ours. It's beautiful. Sturdy. It's served us well and we are attached to it. We just need a new destination. A little tweak at the helm by a couple of degrees and look at that! The passengers are refreshed, renewed, restored. People on the quay are waving us off and we are on our way.

We'll ignore the fact that half the crew aren't talking to the other half because they were perfectly happy with the port they were in and the rest were determined to set sail. We may have a potential mutiny before we've even passed Dunoon. But we have vast quantities of rum and goodwill and that quells every rebellion.

So where are we headed? Where is that tweak of the tiller taking us? No idea. The captain's pished and mumbling that he's spotted a mermaid. The first mate claims it was an optimistic sunbather at the open-air swimming pool in Gourock. But we do appear to be going somewhere and we're all in the same boat. We might not like it but we're in the good ship Scotland together.

I say we kick back, relax, pull the lid off the Pusser's rum, look out for icebergs and enjoy the journey.

Anchors aweigh!

Greg Hemphill is a comedian, actor, writer and director, best known for co-writing and performing in Still Game *and* Chewin' the Fat.

LESLIE HILLS

The first step was of course the constitution. By universal agreement, it could only be written and passed into law following extensive participation which took into account the specific geographic and demographic singularities of the country. Also central was that much of the discussion was carried out under the wings of our National Theatre, our Youth Parliament and the Local Things. A natural outcome of this was that the whole-life educational curriculum, devised under the aegis of experienced educators, celebrated and acknowledged the primacy of creativity.

The steady progression towards the establishment of universal, secular, state-educational institutions went a long way to enabling creativity to flourish and excellence to thrive. A level playing field works wonders. The place of the arts and their influence on inclusivity, entrepreneurship, effective thinking, research, happiness and a host of other benefits to the polity had long been clear. The big change was the emphasis on creativity in mathematics, science and allied areas which resulted in a release of energy, the flowering of the economy and indeed a palpable increase in wellbeing. An excellent starting point from which to consider the future of our country.

Charged with our unique remit we, the Ganglia Committee, now have a proposal to put to the nation. You may have noticed over the last few years that our members have, in their daily lives, in their discussions both local and national, and in the case of our musician members in their performance, been putting forward, indeed promoting, the notion that: Monolingualism is Curable.

I will come to the results of our investigations below. But first I wish to relate some of my personal experience, though I believe my tale is far from unique. I was taught – I hesitate to say I learned – a European language for five years at school and one at university, in the heady days when a language for an arts degree was compulsory. Little attention was given to speaking the language or using it for anything other than exams. I struggled and privately believed I 'wasn't good at languages'. Years later I went to live and work in another European country and, though I studied the basics, I learned most of what is now a very effective second foreign language through everyday interaction, friendship and, joyfully, love. And I was amazed to find that my first foreign language improved.

I have watched a grandchild, resident in one of our sister countries, effortlessly handling two languages, and, proud of their expertise, plunging into two more with relish. Across Europe I have watched the child negotiating naturally and organically with other small children, until they find some common words to facilitate their play.

Some years ago I revisited a small southern country and was amazed at the level and extent of English spoken, the optimism and activity in evidence. When last I visited some decades before it lay under a form of tyranny; poor, inward-looking and monolingual. Everything has either changed or is changing fast. I asked and was told that English is compulsory in all schools and that all English media is broadcast and shown without subtitles or the dreaded dubbing.

I took two things away from these and other encounters across the globe. That becoming acquainted with several languages as a child and by immersion is beneficial; and that we English-speakers may well find ourselves seriously disadvantaged because our mother tongue has become the international *lingua franca*. In short we are deprived of the benefits of speaking multiple languages, which include but are not confined to: improvement in memory, sharpening of mental processes (ditto retaining of), increased employment prospects and widening of cultural experiences. And I must add here, sheer delight.

So I asked the Ganglia to research advantages of breaking the shocking grip of monolingualism both for individuals and for the country, and to propose how this could be done. Our results are appended.

In summary, our conclusions, which we recommend for discussion in Parliament, are that all subjects at all stages of our education system be taught in part in their own languages by native speakers from European countries on a Europe-wide teacher exchange network (Appendix 9). Second, that all pupils, including those adults who use their sabbatical each decade for learning, should spend several terms of senior years in an educational establishment in a European country whose language they have enjoyed.

We are keenly aware of the inward-looking nature of this proposal, which is for the moment confined to Europe. (For a discussion of world languages, particularly Mandarin Chinese and Arabic, see Appendix 4.)

Leslie Hills is a film producer and writer working internationally and based in Edinburgh and the Isle of Bute.

RICHARD HOLLOWAY

In imagining a new Scotland, a good place to start would be to reflect on the fact that most societies in history have been organised by the powerful and wealthy to suit themselves, though they usually disguise the fact – even from themselves – by theories of government that make their ascendency not only inevitable, but just and morally appropriate. But say we could start over? Say we were honestly determined to fix the inequities, injustices and miseries that have been an inevitable concomitant of all existing systems, how would we go about it?

A good way to start would be to read the philosopher John Rawls' book, *Theory of Justice*. Rawls was interested in what he called 'distributive justice' in society, and the fact that most societies demonstrate the opposite. Distributive *injustice* has been the norm in most societies in history, and is still the norm today. The astonishing fact is that the gap is widening everywhere. Fewer and fewer people own more and more of the world's wealth. But it's not just about *wealth*. It's about social goods such as fairness, health, play, creativity, joy, laughter and the sheer joy of the dance of life. If we wanted to redistribute all those fundamental goods in a new and fairer Scotland, where would we start?

Rawls suggests that we should imagine ourselves setting out to establish the blueprint for this new community by placing ourselves in what he called 'an original position' behind a 'veil of ignorance'. 'Original', because the good society we are creating hasn't been imagined yet. And 'behind a veil of ignorance' because none of us would know anything about ourselves, our natural abilities or what our place will be in the good place we are creating. We would know nothing about our own gender, sexuality, intelligence, natural abilities, physical capacities, colour, income, place in society – nothing!

If we were in that position, we would almost certainly choose a system that granted the most extensive liberties to its citizens, while ensuring them the maximum of justice. And we would almost certainly find ways of ameliorating the condition of those who pulled a weak hand in life. For example, in planning a transport system from the original position, you'd imagine yourself as a wheelchair user, and design accordingly. In imagining the weaknesses that all flesh is heir to, you would place yourself in the position of someone addicted to any of the euphoric substances available on the planet, and you would design not only the best way of helping the addict, you would almost certainly wonder about the wisdom of imprisoning people for ingesting stuff that harms no one but themselves. Come to think of it, you'd imagine yourself into the position of someone sent to one of these already overcrowded prisons, and you would certainly rethink their place, purpose and very existence.

More positively, behind the veil of ignorance you would imagine a society that helped its citizens pass their time on earth creatively and playfully. You would fill its schools with orchestras and dance classes and mad artists desperate to get children drawing and painting and splashing colour everywhere. In a world in which robots will soon be doing most of the heavy lifting, you would help people fill all that empty time creatively. You'd get them walking our hills and swimming in our rivers. You'd get them cherishing and sustaining our frail and beautiful planet. You'd get them singing and dancing. And you'd invite the dispossessed of the earth to come and join us and become part of our caring yet carefree society. Scotland would become not only a more equal place, but a more creative place, an experimental laboratory in human fulfilment – a free and happy nation.

JUST IMAGINE!

Richard Holloway is a writer, broadcaster, former Bishop of Edinburgh and Chair of the Scottish Arts Council (2005–2010), and founder of the Big Noise children's orchestra movement. He lives in Edinburgh with his wife, Jean.

PHILIP HOWARD

I'm lucky. I walk to work. This morning it's sunny, warm for October. A pair of dragonflies the colour of oxblood helicopter around my head. I smile because I remember the talk in the town that the dragonflies must have come with the Eritrean families – it wasn't said unkindly – but no, I'm fairly sure they date from one of the biodiversity projects in the twenties.

On the outskirts of the town I pass the old US Air Force base, famously decommissioned in the first 100 days of the M. Obama presidency, and home to the Eritreans since the new UN Migration Compact. What used to be RAF Roxburgh is now called 'Tamirat', which means, I think, miracle or wonder. It's more of a village really and, earlier this year, after a campaign by the Unbeeching Project, it acquired its own railway station on the new branch line to Berwick-upon-Tweed. Some joker suggested calling it Tamirat Parkway. At least I hope they were joking.

I'm slower to anger these days.

One of the old American aircraft hangars now houses a weaving factory and the collaborations between the Eritrean businesses and the textile mills in Hawick and Gala are breathtaking.

I pick up a coffee from the Yemeni café on the High Street.

Sleep was evasive last night, inevitable before a big day, I know that. But I did hear the wolves, I'm sure of it. At first they were reintroduced into Kielder Forest and on the Cheviots, over the border. But they've been gravitating further north – knowing no borders. I like to think this will only cement our country's reputation for welcoming all-comers. (And to think that, as a child, I would ever have found the sound of a wolf comforting, as I do now!)

From today, it's my term of office as Speaker of the School Parliament, on top of my regular teaching; though a lot of the Parliament workload is carried by volunteer parent-teachers. And as well as Head of Drama, teaching civic society, ethics and human rights on the national curriculum, I convene the curriculum for the Border Region, embracing subjects from Borders Scots to reiver history and – since the Eritreans came – Tigrinya after-school classes. One of my students suggested we're going to have to add lupine language and literature next . . .

Five years ago, drama acquired special status both as a core subject and a cross-subject teaching medium – it can sit on top of and underneath other core subjects to aid transmission and learning through theatre techniques. The results have been astonishing, and there is no doubt in my mind that, wider afield, drama has been key in the assimilation of our migrant communities.

I drain my coffee and turn into the school gates, passing the riverside walk and woodland. A small group of the girls are spilling out of the woodland hide, half giggling, half shushing each other. Just for a second I feel a flicker of irritation that they're larking around – why are they here so early? – but Zewditu and Alana wave me over.

'Sir, sir, sir!'

'What?'

'You've got to see this.'

They push me into the hide and lift the batten.

'What's *that*?'

'That, Zewditu, is a pine marten.'

Philip Howard is a theatre director, script editor and adaptor, and a director of new Scottish theatre company, Pearlfisher.

KERRY HUDSON

I magine a country where every child wakes up in a house that is fit for purpose. Not just fit for purpose but safe and comfortable and, well, homely. Where low income doesn't mean precarity of housing or that the housing is shabby, cold, damp and at the edge of town. The child walks safely to school or takes a free bus. The school day is designed to be modular so that children's parents can have the best chance of not only making an income but also continuing the pursuit of their own ambitions. If the parent can't do this, perhaps because they're ill in body or mind, they are funded, supported, nurtured back to themselves and society. That support is family-wide. The child understands what is happening but doesn't fear it because the adults are taking care of it, just as they should.

At school there is breakfast. It's not a 'breakfast club', a token gesture or a big deal. There's just food there, there always has been, breakfast, lunch, dinner and snacks, since the children attend at different times throughout the day. Since, if it's needed or wanted, a child should be able to eat when they are hungry.

The teachers are well paid and there's enough of them to go around (as in Bhutan, teachers are some of the highest paid government employees in the country). The lessons are spread equally among creative and STEM subjects and the curriculum is self-led, play-focused for younger kids. There are no exams because there's enough teaching staff to monitor and support. There's enough budget for specialist equipment and individual support where needed.

At this school no child ever feels poor or ashamed of that poverty. There is a school library and a school librarian. There is a musical instrument library and a music librarian. There is a school therapist for children and one for parents and staff too. There are trips outside regularly, cultural exchanges, engagement with the local community because, again, there are enough funds for this, because there are enough teachers.

When this child goes to this school it feels safe. It is there only to grow, learn and discover. Nothing is asked of it but that it be there and if even being present is too much, either physically or mentally, that child will be seen, be listened to, be cared for.

In the evenings the school serves as a community hub, with work-shops, meet-ups. There's a communal kitchen where a communal meal is made. There's space to gather as a community and relax, to watch TV or read or play sports together (in fact, most people divide their time between the well-stocked, welcoming library, the subsidised leisure centre and the school – older folks especially).

But the child is home on this night. In their home filled with furniture, having eaten from a cupboard stocked full of food that is good and tasty. The parent who reads them a story may have worries but money, housing and support are not among them.

The child doesn't stay awake, scared of phantom shapes, or the ordeals of the next day. If the child stays awake at all it's because they're excited about what the next day might bring and the day after that. They're dreaming of all the things they might do with their precious life in this country.

Kerry Hudson was born in Aberdeen and is the author of two novels and one memoir.

CLARE HUNTER

History is seen as a guiding light to illuminate the present and inspire the future. What is told, however, of Scotland's past is narrated largely through a male prism. The experiences and exploits of our nation's women are delegated to the shadows. Its women are footnotes, portrayed as also-rans: remembered – if at all – for their part in rescuing Scottish heroes, for their fragility as rulers or as supposed witches and the victims of male disquiet.

I once dreamt up a mischievous antidote to the absence of creative, adventurous and entrepreneurial women from the annals of Scottish history. In the stealth of night, statues in Glasgow's city squares and public spaces were to be enhanced with female attire. On waking, Glaswegians were to be treated to an overnight transformation, an environmental sex change. Those hallowed industrialists, poets, military men and male muses who stood proudly on their plinths were to appear resplendent in skirts. I named the project 'Skirting the City' although, in hindsight, 'Skirting the Issue' might have been more apt. I imagined the discovery of an urban landscape where women claimed a material presence, where they dominated the skyline. The idea remained a defiant notion. But it was born out of a frustration at Scotland's lack of interest in the biographies of its women. My future Scotland has women's defeats and belittlements, their intellect and advancements acknowledged, promoted and celebrated.

Some years ago, in a Reply to the Lassies at a local Burns Supper, I cited the women poets who were contemporaneous with Robert Burns – a surprising number of them. While their names and some of their poems and lyrics are known, the extent of their personal and literary writings are – as, with those of women who came before and after – not accorded the same preciousness as the texts of their male counterparts.

Women of Scotland's past remain largely silent. Not because they did not speak, express opinions and record their experiences, but because what they said of themselves was discarded. I still chill at the fate of the letters of Margaret Macdonald, the wife of Charles Rennie Mackintosh, an extraordinary innovative and visionary artist in her own right. After her death in 1933, her cousin, Joseph Tilly Hardeman, visited her flat to inventory its sparse contents. When he came across a cache of letters he took it upon himself to destroy those that were 'of little use'. He rescued those written by Mackintosh to Margaret but we are robbed of the knowledge of what existed from her to him. Their lack has impinged on the ability to tell Margaret's story. What can be told of her is limited, truncated by a masculine valuation of female worth.

In the knowledge that what they wrote might be disregarded and thrown away after their deaths, women – throughout history and across cultures – have resorted to other media to safeguard some residue of their existence. Mary, Queen of Scots embroidered, in emblematic code, her truth, a material defiance in the face of defeat as a captive of the English court; Scottish women POWs in the Changi gaol in Singapore during WW2 asserted their identity in images and signatures sewn on scraps of cloth to register their share in the wartime nightmare of brutality and erosion of self.

To excavate the history of Scottish women demands alternative research strategies. What remains of them lurks in inventories, is referenced in wills, listed in merchants' order books or is documented in divorce proceedings and reports of theft. Within these lie fragments of women's realities lying unnoticed and under-researched. There are women's belongings remaining uncherished in attics, folded forgotten in sideboard drawers. Their material possessions – procured, displayed, gifted and created – also offer at least a glimpse of what mattered to them in the past, what they hoped might be conserved: clues as to what they needed to say. In Scotland's future I imagine a country excavating, treasuring and displaying the small telling legacies of its women, their meaningful keepsakes: cherishing them as signposts to female concerns, celebrations and complaints, as important insights to Scotland's past.

Clare Hunter is the author of Threads of Life, *a book that explores the social, emotional and political significance of sewing. It was chosen as Radio 4's Book of the Week, reached the* Sunday Times *bestseller list and was awarded a Saltire Award for First Book. Her next book,* Embroidering her Truth: Mary, Queen of Scots and the Language of Power, *is an alternative biography of the Scottish queen, charting her experiences and emotions through the textiles she inherited, displayed, gifted and created.*

MARILYN IMRIE

W alk through Edinburgh's Waverley shopping centre any mid-week afternoon and you'll glimpse a scene being played out all over Scotland's towns and cities. Old people do a bit of shopping and sit over a coffee watching other people's grandchildren run around. They'll be keeping a respectful, non-interfering distance from those kids. These days we all live in fear that our instincts to connect with children, to return a lost toy, or comfort a wee one who has lost sight of a parent, will be misinterpreted.

Imagine a country where easy connections between old and young are restored, and both older and younger generations actively look for ways in which they can connect with those who have fallen through the safety net of family life, those who lack the love of someone with time to spend with them and who understands how they feel without asking.

We have lost so much of this in the last fifty years; my mid-twentieth-century childhood had at its centre a beloved grandad who taught us to sing 'Ye cannae shove yer granny aff the bus', and was always waiting for us after school to see us across the road safely.

It's time to rebuild a Scottish society where *all* children and older people can connect more easily.

We have two wonderful friends who are the kind of grandparents everyone wants, dedicated to family life. When their own beloved grandchildren went to school, what did our friends with hearts the size of football pitches do? They signed up for respite-care fostering and now their house is full once a week with children learning that older people do have time for them. They show the children how to have fun and laugh, how to cook and help tidy up, how to play at pirates – the simple joys of family life which these kids aren't getting anywhere else. It doesn't cost money; only time and a desire to help all our children thrive.

We also need a new model for elder-living which doesn't trap old people in ghettos but gives them a stimulating environment where children and young people share their company, an environment that produces a sense of wellbeing stemming from being needed and being part of a community where they have a role.

Kohab, an intergenerational co-living company in the UK, already builds homes for the old and young to live together in the same space, recreating natural communities. We should plan for more of them all over Scotland. For the sake of all our kids, and our older generations too, I want my future Scotland to put an end to late-life ghettos. No more sleepy retirement homes and entire villages in remote countryside where the median age rarely dips below seventy. Instead, we'd establish a society where children and older people would be positively connected in simple, daily ways – a recreation of natural communities.

There's a successful scheme running in the Netherlands that we could also adopt. There, students occupy vacant rooms in long-term elder-care facilities for free, in exchange for simply spending time with elderly residents. We could put an end to the loneliness, depression and suicidal feelings some young people experience when they leave their familiar home environments, and to the silent despair of old people who have little or no connection with the young and how they think.

I'm emphatically not proposing a patronising, rigorously enforced care system for the elderly and the young; older people are working longer now, and very effectively too. They're sharing their wisdom and much-needed, hard-won skills in the workplace. But they need to be assured that time spent with grandchildren and children from their wider community is also vital, skilled work that they can do better than anyone else.

I hope in my future Scotland we will still be singing 'Ye cannae shove yer granny aff the bus'. And that Granny will likely be up there driving it.

Marilyn Imrie was a grandmother, theatre-maker and award-winning director of audio drama. She was born and raised in Fife and had returned there to live in St Monans.

PETE IRVINE

I can't imagine what it's like to be homeless, sleeping rough or in a shelter night after night here in this country where I live so comfortably, in a comfortable house on a good street in a rich city. Nor can I imagine what it's like to be stateless, to walk thousands of miles to get away from my country in search of another life and somewhere to belong.

When I watch the news, I get angry, perhaps tearful, because it's overwhelming. But perhaps on the other side of their nightmare, there can be an awakening – for us. That something consequential can be done to respond to a rolling crisis that with global warming might engulf us long before the sea does.

In a way I've been in the imaginary blue sky before. Years ago, in another century, I spent a weekend at a golfy hotel in Fife to consider JFK's moonshot dream, when America actually did 'put a man on the moon'. The proposition before us was: 'what could Scotland do with an unbridled leap of ambition?'

In the hotel I felt as often before, an outsider among the suits. Nobody will recall what the proposals were for Scotland's bold future. I had lamely suggested that we should aim to have a bullet train connecting Edinburgh and Glasgow in twenty-two minutes. But like most of the fanciful ideas that day, the train was never going to leave the platform. I decided that if I was going to be engaged in Scotland's cultural affairs it would be best to stick to projects that were at least realistic. Dreams can be sunlit blue and green, then you wake up in the morning to the haar.

The tide of refugees and migrants on Europe's borders will not ebb and it's clear that this Tory government will never address its pragmatic, never mind moral, responsibilities. In Scotland, a small and discrete country, we may have a unique and heroic opportunity. As pointed out for years, we harbour a very different set of circumstances. We are entrepreneurial, compassionate and boast an ingrained sense of fair play. We live on the outside edge of Europe. Most importantly, we have a long experience of migration. Historically our people have had to leave (enforced or otherwise, as migrants do) to find a better life and improve the economic and cultural health of the countries who took us in. And so, we should have the right to create a new system, lower the drawbridge and also to raise the bar on how migrants are received and, crucially, valued.

It's been clear since the Brexodus and in COVID Times that there's a pressing need for workers in many sectors. And the challenge of our ageing population is well documented. We need more people; other people who will enrich us, driving not draining the economy.

So let's ignore the impedimenta of partisan politics and bureaucracy and funding and, in the spirit of this book, head into the yonder. Let's say we could: form a powerful committee; determine realistic objectives to make Scotland a hospitable and viable sanctuary for migrants and refugees; launch a campaign to fire up the public; set the nation on a collective mission to consider all the creative and practicable ways that Scotland could respond. Working with the Scottish Refugee Council, we set new quotas, create dispersal centres in each region and fast-track procedures so that individuals and families are registered, assessed and placed in appropriate accommodation, their needs managed. We would call to the cause squads of local volunteers and the many Scots who habitually show kindness to strangers.

But we could also enlist commercial, cultural and financial organisations, hotel groups, individual hospitality providers, whole islands, farms. Companies from Amazon to Artisan Roast would be directly involved in the recruitment and servicing of a diverse and dynamic outsider work force. Accommodation could be part of the employment package (as many hotels and farms already do). We could facilitate the teaching of English, encouraging empathetically congregated ethnic groups to organise and manage themselves and start their own businesses and social activities the way the Polish did so impressively pre-COVID. How much we could learn from our new friends.

Obviously we can't start a 'flood' of new people into Scotland, but we must significantly turn up the volume on the trickle we're allowed to provide for at the moment. Numbers and where they go would be 'proportionate, manageable, monitored' – politician's words, but our team would have to play in their game. This proposition is simplistic, but sometimes we have to break out, not just think out, of the box, and surmount the red tape and the barbed wire and the hopelessness. And let them in to help us.

Pete Irvine has been the creator and director of many of Scotland's major events and festivals, including Edinburgh's Hogmanay. He is the author of Scotland the Best, *and* The Islands, *his guide and photographic appreciation of Scotland's islands, was published in spring 2022.*

CARLA JENKINS

It is hard to imagine a country where complete equality between men and women would not come with massive implications for our perceptions of its past, present and future. However, if I imagine an ideal country – where anything is possible and nothing has to have financial or practical implications – it would be one with complete gender equality.

That sounds straightforward but the reality would be far more complicated. Is equality even possible? Biologically, women have to endure monthly pain and the agony of childbirth without any balancing compensation in terms of the fruits of their labour. Any attempt to take account of this would likely be met by accusations that women were now oppressing men. We have already seen responses to positive discrimination where some men now consider themselves disadvantaged, just as women have been historically. And yet we are constantly presented with statistics and reports that prove that our structures still fail to achieve even the most basic parity such as equal pay.

It's a big ask, to solve all these issues. So, like those who believe God built the earth, I shall start again and work on one thing after another.

In my imagined country, we will start anew: there is complete equality between men and women. And there always has been. The patriarchy and matriarchy does not, has not and will not exist.

Rather than opting for men to suffer the monthly inbuilt pain that nature inflicts on women, periods are painless and spoken about openly. Sanitary products are free for all, and the cost of making them is shouldered by general taxation. They do not damage the earth or our environment or our bodies and they do not cause us pain. Bleeding is clean and devoid of shame.

Next comes childbirth. Women have comprehensive choice over what they want to feel during this process, but it is not and never has to be agonising pain. Being a mother – or a father – is viewed as a valuable occupation, and parents receive a decent wage for it, as well as the natural wage of love parents receive from children.

Children born into this imagined country are given access to free and wide-ranging education that meets their abilities and talents until they decide they have reached the limits of learning through institutions. Their mothers and fathers are supported in caring for their children in as many ways as they need or want. Access to subjects and training will be free from considerations of gender. Whether a girl wants to be an astronaut or an engineer or a ballerina, their ambition will be encouraged and the same opportunities shall exist for boys, too. Classes are mixed; every child will pursue courses in maths and English as well as life skills such as cooking, how to pay a mortgage and how to make a bed.

Gender is not assigned at birth. Children are brought up in the same way and can identify with the gender they choose as and when they wish. Every public bathroom is an individual cubicle, and no one is forced to share intimate spaces that make them feel uncomfortable. We love who we want to love without fear. We retain who we are even when we decide to join our life to someone else.

Clothes cost the same for women and men and are all made to the same quality. Fashion magazines cover every gender and a comprehensive range of styles. Wearing make-up is a common practice regardless of gender, and people determine for themselves how they will style their hair. Fashions in facial hair and tattooing will be up to personal preference and nobody will be judged for their choices. Equal pay is a fact of life; anything else is inconceivable. Sexuality is never weaponised. Being disrespectful of people's gender, sexuality, race or religion is a criminal offence that will be dealt with by re-education, not by mindless punitive actions. Ritualistic atrocities such as female genital mutilation do not exist.

Our landscape is studded with statues of women and men in equal numbers, for all have achieved amazing things. We celebrate people for what they do and achieve, not because they achieved things by accident of birth and access to privilege.

Whilst all this is just a given, and for many gender is not at all remarkable, others are proud and aware of their gender, and it is not something that is taken for granted. Many women are proud to be women, if that is what they choose to identify as, as are men. Our Scotland is one that is built on mutual respect and love for being alive and for the choices about identity that each individual makes. We are not perfect but we are equal and we celebrate our vibrant, warm, funny character every day by being ourselves, whoever it is we want that to be.

Carla Jenkins is a journalist and writer from Glasgow who won Scottish Young Journalist of the Year in 2019 and who (somewhat controversially) opts for the Diet Irn-Bru option.

DOUG JOHNSTONE

As a writer I'm painfully aware my day job involves sitting on my lazy bum in a dark room staring at a screen. So many of us these days have sedentary lives and it's very easy to get stuck in that rut, turn into a basic blob. Recently I've been trying to snap out of it with regular long walks around the various hills of Edinburgh, where I live. The resulting improvement in my mental and physical health has been startling. But I'm pretty lucky – I'm self-employed and flexible, I have my own means of transport, I'm not in poverty. What about others less fortunate?

This has to start as young as possible. My idea for a future Scotland is to vastly increase funding for access to the outdoors for everyone across the country, and that starts with a massive increase in outdoor learning.

Outdoor learning is nothing new, of course. It's a very broad term taking in any kind of interaction with the natural world, including adventure activities and sports but also, you know, a wee walk in the woods. As is the case with many things, the Scandinavians are well ahead of the curve. For decades countries like Denmark and Finland have had a pervasive culture of so-called 'forest schools', in which virtually all learning occurs outdoors. This in part stems from a more nature-based society, and startling benefits in both health and education were spotted many years ago when regular exposure to nature was delivered to kids as young as pre-school.

In Scotland there is already some outdoor learning but it is restricted, patchy in coverage and, most worryingly, expensive. My two kids both benefited immensely in Primary 7 from attending a week at an outdoor centre in Argyll. It was their first time away from home and while they were both a little nervous, they came back after five days completely transformed. Filling their days with abseiling, gorge-walking, kayaking and more had increased their confidence and made them grow as young people. The benefits are not just obvious for physical and mental health, either. Outdoor learning improves teamwork and social skills, resilience and leadership, all the buzzword guff that the education system requires. It improves society generally and individual people feel better for it.

But it costs. Those trips cost hundreds of pounds, something we were lucky we could afford. And that will be the only time in thirteen years of education they will do something like that.

I would like to see outdoor learning at all levels given a massive increase in funding, and a shift in focus to make it free to all and central to the education experience of every child in a future Scotland. I want regular paid-for trips to outdoor learning centres; outings into nature in schools' local environments as standard; and improvements to infrastructure to make outdoor learning an everyday experience.

Because it works. Back to those Scandinavians again, currently topping all the happiness, contentedness and wellbeing polls you see in the media, something I believe is at least partly down to a culture of outdoor learning.

Nicola Sturgeon recently gave a TED Talk about her desire to shift towards a 'wellbeing economy' as opposed to the rather outdated GDP as a measure of a country's success. I believe increased outdoor learning would be a key building block for Scotland's future wellbeing.

Doug Johnstone is the author of thirteen novels, drummer with the Fun Lovin' Crime Writers, and co-founder of the Scotland Writers Football Club.

PHILL JUPITUS

Homework. Terrible word, isn't it? The bane of every child's evening and holiday, which then of course gets bounced on to the terrified parent: 'Mum, can you please help me with my maths?'

Let's look at the word, though: *Homework*. An unholy collision of a noun and a verb. The place where one lives: *Home*; combined with an activity that one usually does under duress: *Work*. We work because we have to, either to earn a wage or get through the day-to-day tasks which we all have to do as a matter of course.

The work children are assigned is a continuation of what is being taught in class. Part of the aim of homework is to teach the child how to work on their own. Also it's supposed to encourage self-motivation and responsibility. To me this has always felt akin to the actions of those people who throw newborn babies into swimming pools because they believe they will instinctively swim. I remember vividly how I didn't really understand what was being asked of me at big school. Nobody ever just *explained* what homework was. Nobody had ever mentioned it at junior school, and the battle-hardened teachers at secondary school just threw you in. It was sink or swim. I sank.

I have always been of the opinion that school should run on for another hour, till 4.30 (or start earlier, as they do in France), so 'homework' could be done in an environment where one had the help of trained professionals, rather than the hazy memories of somebody who never did better than scraping a C-minus in most subjects and who is also trying to cook your tea.

I realise this is naive in the extreme. The world of education today is a minefield of form-filling and target-based achievement, tests and inspections. Most teachers I know have ten times more 'homework' than their unruly charges. And that's far from ideal. But I'm blue-sky thinking here! A well-educated society thrives.

For students in England, going into higher education carries with it the prospect of a whopping five-figure debt at the end of their studies. How many great minds are we missing out on because of this system and its associated fear of debt? Why aren't more people asking that question?

I would like to live in a world where education was valued more. Where everybody understood that to get the best, we need to give everybody a shot. The net of education needs to be cast wider. Learning should be something to be looked forward to rather than dreaded. Where the sterile metric of test results is not the only means of judging potential.

The problems that the world faces are many. Society is in dire need of people equipped to solve them. I think the way that we get there is by investing hard cash in education and teachers.

I realise that this is but the fever dream of my poor Brexit/Trump-battered mind: four years of confusion, doubt, fear, lies and shrill hyperbole will do that to you. When I'm not thinking about how we might start to fix things, I drift off into dreams of Eton College having an Ofsted inspection: 'Well, headmaster, we can't help but notice that *two* of your pupils have plunged the United Kingdom into the most hideous constitutional shit-storm in living memory, so I'm afraid Special Measures it is!'

Phill Jupitus has been (sic) a poet, stand-up comedian and actor, and is currently studying art in Dundee because he's still not quite sure.

PAT KANE

One of the great challenges of the twenty-first century is not just how we make the transition towards a zero-carbon society but how we make that shift joyous, satisfying and pleasurable. If we don't, then I predict there will be a lot of resistance and revolt.

Over a century of capitalism, our very subjectivity and identity has been shaped by consumerism, advertising and the right to shop. What Angela Carter once called 'the infernal desire machines' of marketing and retail have tapped into our primal and social emotions. Unplugging rudely from those satisfactions will feel like major surgery.

So we need behavioural bridges that people can walk across, and cultural destinations they're glad to arrive at. (By culture I mean all the creative and making activities of a community, not just opera stars and auteurs.) To that end, I want to suggest a new kind of institute for communities. It will focus on giving people options beyond consumerism, engaging their primary instincts for play, care and curiosity in creative and tangible ways.

Indeed, let's not call it an institute – redolent of warders and barred windows – and call it a *constitute*:* a place where we make things, and remake ourselves at the same time. (The German Romantics – and nineteenth-century Scandinavian social reformers – would have called this process 'Bildung'.) And because we're in a Scottish context, let's give it a specific name: the Makar House.

---

* See Pat Kane, 'What Is a "Constitute"?', The Play Ethic, <https://www.theplay-ethic.com/2011/11/whatisaconstitute.html>. Also, for constitutes as a basis for a new politics, visit the Alternative UK, <http://www.thealternative.org.uk>.

Why 'Makar'? It's one of my favourite Scots words, as it links 'poetry' and 'work' (being a literal translation of the Greek term *poietes*, poet or maker). And the offer of poetic/poietic work is, I would suggest, one of the ways we unwire ourselves from consumerism, and rewire ourselves for a more practically joyful life. More about that in a minute.

And why a 'House' (and a particularly well-built, open, comfortable and enduring house, at that)? Because, in the way that Carnegie put his stamp on Scotland by supporting libraries and public rooms that still stand today, we need to make this kind of facility an irreversible gift to a community.

What happens in the Makar House? I envisage a mixture of science and engineering labs, repair and design shops, kitchens, media studios and performance space, a 'library of things' or tool library, and well-equipped meeting rooms of various sizes available very cheaply or free, to make it possible for every act of consumption to be replaced by an act of creation: making, remaking, repairing, inventing, customising, cherishing and restoring.

Communities will be urged to bring all their skills to the Makar House – the electricians and the joiners, the linguists, the coders and the hackers, the facilitators and the managers, the child-carers and the sports trainers, the gardeners and maybe even some poets . . .

'What,' you say, 'and just come up with something? Collaborate and co-create freely and easily, when jobs have to be done, chores have to be completed? What time or energy would we have for that?'

My secret is out. There are two much bigger ideas that sit behind the Makar House – a reduction in the working week (without reduced pay), and a universal basic income.

The first would 'steal' a day (or two) from your working duties, letting you try out this new post-consumerist (maybe even post-capitalist) lifestyle free from guilt; and the second would give you time to be as creatively active as you would like to be within the Makar House.

It's very different from the old 'sports', 'leisure' or 'community' centre, which were 're-creation' places, something to repair and heal you so you could be thrown back into the grind. Between planetary limits, which will force a reduction in human consumption, and radical automation, which will replace most repetitive work, our old models for purpose and dignity are falling apart.

Since this new era needs us to be more active and conscious about the 'stuff' in our lives, our politicians and administrations (and who knows, maybe even a few clever capitalists) have to help us become more self-providing, more materially conscious, more ingenious. Or at least they should, unless they want to face an awful lot of social melt-down when people turn to desperate and extreme solutions to the chaos of their lives.

I imagine that Scots, with their rich appreciation for culture, commu-nity, education, science and technology – what the naturalist John Muir once called 'salt of the earth, and of machines' – would be able to support these 'constitutes' and their enabling policies. And as the Carnegie buildings reflected their era (not unproblematically), maybe the Makar Houses could be the symbols of an independent, lively, sustainable Scotland.

Pat Kane is a musician, writer and indy activist (www.patkane.global).

BILLY KAY

'Thaim wi a guid Scots tongue in their heid are fit tae gang ower the warld'.

That old Scots saw which I got from my parents is a clue to the kind of Scotland I want – one that is proud of its own languages and culture, but that also sees Scotland as part of an expansive European and global nation at hame wi freedom, human rights and rampant egalitarianism.

It begins with linguistic confidence. The union eventually brought economic benefits to Scotland – benefits often built on slave economies within the British Empire – but it also left a legacy of cultural colonialism. My first language, Scots, was the vehicle for some of the greatest poetry written in Europe between 1450 and 1550, but the vast majority of Scots are unaware of this. They presume what is often implied in their education and media – that Scotland has always been a provincial backwater compared to England. Removing that cultural cringe might take decades, but educating our people as Scots and normalising their mither tongues as cherished speech forms rather than dismissed as aberrant patois will surely speed up the process.

When David I founded Royal Burghs all over his kingdom in the twelfth century, he addressed the inhabitants as 'Francis et Anglis, Scotis et Flemmingis' – the French, English, Scots and Flemish people, who lived in a multilingual, multicultural society which gave birth to an identity which was proudly mongrel from its beginnings. My imagined Scotland will retain that diversity but will have knowledge of Scottish cultural history at its core.

Most countries today which have enviable linguistic abilities are ones where there is pride in their native languages alongside the realisation that they need to communicate easily with the world beyond their borders. They chose English as a lingua franca for that purpose – the Netherlands and the Scandinavian countries are perfect examples of this.

Up until the seventeenth century, Scots stravaiging Europe had Latin as a lingua franca, giving us strong roots in that Humanist tradition.

George Buchanan, for example, was regarded as one of the greatest Latin writers in Europe in the sixteenth century – a time when the educated elites all spoke and wrote Latin and it was as much part of their culture as the native one.

Scotland was distinctive because the Scottish Reformation's revolutionary desire to have a schuil in ilka pairish created an educated class with a much wider social base. When James VI toured his kingdom, it was not unusual for the burgh clerks to compose original Latin verse which they declaimed in public to welcome him to their town!

The historical accident of two English-speaking countries, Great Britain and the United States, becoming the world's superpowers for two centuries promoted a monoglot English mentality and *Weltanschauung* among our people. Before that, we regularly produced brilliant linguists who drew on our past traditions. In the seventeenth century, central Europe was hoatchin with Scots pedlars, merchants and soldiers of fortune who spoke German, Polish, Swedish, Scots and Latin interchangeably.

There are countless examples of Scots using these linguistic skills to benefit societies across the globe. Here's one. Henry Brunton of the Edinburgh Missionary Society created one of the very first grammars of an African language, Susu in Sierra Leone, at the end of the 1790s. A few years later the Czar gave his Mission land in the Caucasus and wished them well in converting the Muslim tribes to Presbyterianism. They didn't convert many, but a lasting legacy of their presence is Brunton's translation of the New Testament into the Tatar Turkish language!

I write this as a linguist myself. I am convinced that the reason I have a facility with languages is because I grew up in a Broad Scots environment where we had to learn to adapt to English quickly at school. One of the ironies of an Ayrshire childhood in the 1950s was that bairns got a prize from the Burns Federation one day a year for reciting Rabbie Burns's poetry, then got the tawse every other day for speaking his language! Ye learnit tae be gey gleg an skeigh in switchin fae ae leid tae the ither!

That flexible bilingual background meant I picked up French, German, Russian and Portuguese comparatively painlessly as a young man. I've witnessed the same phenomenon within my own family where my wee Brussels-based grandchildren speak fluent French, English, Italian and Portuguese because they are exposed to those languages every day.

Their grandfaither is now adding Scots to their repertoire and they just love haein heids, shoothers, shanks an taes alang wi nebs, lugs, een an bahookies! I want them to know and feel that they too belong to a proud, ancient and energetically contemporary European nation where linguistic diversity and confidence is just totally normal and lovingly cherished. Imagine that!

Billy Kay is a broadcaster and writer, most recently of The Scottish World *and* Scots: The Mither Tongue.

JACKIE KAY

THE LONG VIEW

When you were born, my daughter, my son
The half-moon grinned and the sun shone

You came after a long song of a labour
Of years and years – and then some!

It was July when you at last appeared, hanselled
With the mace from Her Majesty – Ma'am, Good Day –

Bright-eyed, flushed, newest day!
And the crags at your tiny feet, and Arthur's Seat.

When you were born, bairn,
Red Arrows flew over your city

And everyone you met, pet,
Wanted to join you on your journey –

Between the lochs and the ferns
Between the braes and the bens

Between the crofts and the bothies
Between the rowans and the pines.

Between the high-rise and the tenements
And the Wimpey houses in the big cities

Between the north and the south, the east and the west,
And the land and the seas . . .

★ ★ ★

Now: I know of someone in Kilchoan,
    Ardnamurchan
Who remembers an old Kilchoan man

Saying that he remembers an old Kilchoan woman
Who had once seen all the houses ablaze

And these were the first of your days:
Stories to keep the past alive,

A poem read aloud to knock the future's door.
A song sung by Sheena Wellington, for a' that.

You're twenty now. We couldn't be prouder.
Look how you've grown in stature:

'This is about who we are, how we carry ourselves,'
your godfather's premonition, the day you were born.

We are not a people that takes to the compliment well.
Put it this way – you're twenty! You've carried yourself
    well.

★ ★ ★

Twenty years on, what can I tell you about your birth?
Your birth was a process not an event –

Your wee form emerged between the land and the stone;
A citizen already sitting, seen through the portal.

And the boats carried you out to sea – to see what you could see,
And back to the land, to the bottom of the Royal Mile.

Every way you turned, your smile made others smile;
And, if at first you faced ridicule, and some were hostile,

You held your own and carried on! Ground-breaking land
   reform!
First up with the smoking ban . . . and on, on.

Remember the jubilation when same-sex marriage passed?
When Clause 28 was opposed?

Look how you shone the light on
The darkness of abuse, how you had such a clear vision;

How you let Auld Scotland out
And Modern Scotland in, first footing.

Nane for thee a thochtie sparin'
Earth, thou bonnie broukit bairn!

You knew what was right and what was wrong.
And oh, how your citizens sang their song:

★ ★ ★

Under the Common Weal, weel, weel
Under the Common Weal, we'll thrive

Oh, it was a braw, bricht day when you arrived, alive!
Wee wean, under the common sun, doon,

Doon
Where you'd been coorie-ing doon, coorie-ing doon,

Under democracy's moon
Wee wean, hoping that aw'thin wuid be fine

And you'd get to tell yer story, wee wean
Who kent awready whit was richt an whit was wrang

Wee wean,
Look how you've grown up michty fine

Oh ma darlin', you'll aye be ma trusty fiere
When the dorkness descends,

When the MacPhees roar an the lochans sing, wee wean,
And ye sing tae mak the wurld a better place.

And oh ma Country, ma country,
you will ayeways be loved and respected by me.

Loved and respected by me.
Oh, my country, my country . . .

★ ★ ★

Scotland itself is my country, said Sorley MacLean.
My other country is Ireland

And after it, France, our great Gaelic bard said plainly.
And if he were still alive today, maybe

He'd have been compelled to name
The other twenty-five countries.

★ ★ ★

Scotland itself is my country
And twenty years on, my country has changed!

I remember it once being a country I ran from,
In those days, you felt unwelcome.

You passed. You pretended. You kept your mouth shut
Unless you sang *sing if you're glad to be gay, sing if you're happy
that way . . .*

And now – look – Old Scotland is no more.
Gay men kiss at the Parliament's door.

★ ★ ★

Hope travels all the way round the world.
Hope has people it wants to meet, hands to shake

Hope flies to New Zealand, to the South Island in
solidarity
Hope wears a hijab and speaks out against hate.

Hope comes home – finds a hearth, a country ahead of its
time,
looking out across the lands and the years

Across the cold North Sea, where the waves knit in plain and
purl,
Is a country to sing you a lullaby, a country to rock you
awake.

★ ★ ★

My country has started to speak my language
And I am no longer alone

I used to feel a foreigner in my own land
I used to feel not at home

I used to be a stranger in the mirror
I used to talk to the hand because the mouth wasn't listening

And now you get what I'm saying
How difficult it is for me on some occasions

But these days, you're listening up
And I am not cordoned off

The door's open and I've come ben this bonny chamber
A nod to you two, and you and you and you for taking the
    long view

And the mountains are speechless
If what they say cannot be understood

And the many-voiced ocean is silent
If no one knows its language

★ ★ ★

It must be a bizarre thing being in the same room
As all these people who share the same birthday as you!

Everybody dressed up and looking so fine;
And when you were born, Nicola,

In the middle of the day between Wimbledon
And the opening of Scottish Parliament

You were induced. It was a quick birth.
And your gran jumped over a wall to tell all you were a girl.

And the Hielan cow jumped over the moon,
And the dish ran awa wey the widdin spune!

* * *

And you are the future: Parliament's bairns.
Sworn in that hot July day in '99.

The grass is greener in Scotland, Callum said.
The milk is better and the people friendlier, he said.

It's nice that people can be themselves, Megan said,
And not be afraid.

I'm excited, said Alicja Hertmanowska
In her *Dear Scottish Parliament* letter

To see what the future brings
Here's to the next twenty years!

Under the Common Weal, we're taking the long view.
Under the Common Weal, we're taking the long view.
Under the Common Weal, weel, weel, we're taking the long
    view.

Thank you to Polygon for permission to quote from Sorley MacLean's
poem 'My Country'. Thank you to Carcanet for permission to quote
from Hugh MacDiarmid's poem 'The Bonnie Broukit Bairn'.

Jackie Kay was Scotland's Makar from 2016–2021. Her latest book is Bantam.

STUART KELLY

I live in a village, and do so enthusiastically. Having thrown myself into village life, I have come to see such places as a kind of ethical experiment.

A friend and I were once discussing monasticism. The thrust of his argument was that monasticism is not a retreat from the world, but its opposite; it makes the world closer and more intense. You may have theological differences with other monks or nuns, you may think some are backsliding or hypocritical or proud; they may simply irk you. But you have a moral obligation not to dislike them. To my mind, a village is akin to a monastery.

I am on the Community Council, an Elder on the Kirk Session (and the Worship Committee, and the Mission and Outreach Committee), I attend the monthly village lunch, I go to the pub, I enjoy the screenings of the New York Metropolitan Opera in the hall, and the Historical Society meetings. I use the village shop almost daily.

What eventually struck me was how atomised all these groups are. There are people I chat with in the pub but never see in the kirk, or people who might attend the Community Council meetings but never go to the opera. There are dog-walkers whom I only know to nod to as I go on my daily amble, and allotment owners with whom I chat ineffectually about potato blight and how good the gladioli are this year.

People are perfectly entitled to choose their way of life – I don't go to the bowls, and despite imprecations am yet to join the Scrabble Club. But I do *know* them, in a way that I never knew 90 per cent of the people I passed by when I lived in the city. Of course, there are things that annoy me – complaints about the future of the village shop from people who only shop in the supermarket seven miles away, or the loudly shared opinions of some of the more bumptious individuals. But the point is to disagree agreeably.

The great gift of the village is the gift of being recognised, being known. It is a far more benevolent way of living if everyone recognises the individuality of the other and nobody is a statistic. A village is an antidote to social media, because it is social. Had I my way, I would happily press the delete key on Facebook, Instagram, YouTube, Twitter and every other such platform. It's easy to be derogative anonymously and very hard to be so in a village. If you gossip or bad-mouth, you become identified as a gossip or a boor. Alexa, turn off the future, please.

Although I believe in devolution, I do not think replacing one centre with another centre is adequate. Reality is granular, and policy is a blind and ubiquitous imposition. In Mervyn Peake's divine novel *Mr Pye*, the protagonist elects to go to the island of Sark, as it is a small enough place to make a difference. Indeed, in reading about remote areas, the constant theme is that one cannot fail to be community-minded. Neighbourliness is a prerequisite for survival.

To return to my question – why were the different, engaged and thriving sets of people not overlapping more? It seems to me that either inadvertently or surreptitiously we have been corralled – kettled, even – into binaries of left–right, Yes–No, Leave–Remain – while big business has turned us into a mere aggregate of our choices, and sold that to the highest bidder. A village is an exercise in scrutiny and self-scrutiny, a place where you can actually appreciate differences, where you can change minds, where you can extend invitations to genuine flesh-and-blood humans.

So, if you don't mind, I shan't imagine a country. I'd rather imagine a country which is a constellation of villages.

Stuart Kelly is a literary reviewer and writer, whose latest book is The Minister and the Murderer.

RACHAEL KELSEY

'Q22. What do you feel is your national identity?'
Scotland's Census 2022

Help and Support:
What does 'national identity' mean?
National identity is a feeling of attachment to a nation. This does
not need to be the same as your ethnic group or legal nationality
(citizenship). For example, this could be about the country or
countries where you feel you belong or think of as home.

I f I had been asked in the 1981 census what I felt my 'national
identity' was I would probably have said 'English': at least, that's
what I was told I was by my classmates. There were three of us in our
small Highland school in the 1970s, and there was rarely a day that
we weren't singled out by that definition. The Highlands in the 1970s
was a complicated place – my parents had moved there when I was
two and we were part of the influx of 'oil people'. I would try and
explain that my father wasn't English and that my grandmother was
from the Islands, but I wasn't allowed to be Scottish because I wasn't
born here.

Fast forward forty-odd years and that question felt easy to answer
– I *feel* Scottish. It may be still that what I feel about myself is dependent
on how others see me – I do spend a lot of time outwith* Scotland,
and non-Scots wouldn't think of me as anything other than Scottish:
to them I sound Scottish and my work is advising on Scots law.

But how others see me is not the whole story. Part of why I now feel Scottish is no doubt time – I have lived here for almost fifty years, my children were born here, and my close family all live here. But part of it is also about the fact that I now feel that I want to claim Scottishness. Scotland is not perfect, but it is better than it was. It is a place where a small community in Bute took in twenty-four Syrian families fleeing the war in their country; a place where hundreds of people mobilised in hours in Pollockshields to protect two refugee neighbours; and a place where the leadership response to the Ukrainian refugee crisis has been swift and unambiguous.

As a community we have a huge amount of work still to do in order to give practical effect to the aspiration to welcome others – we are far from perfect when it comes to racism and there continues to be a problem with anti-English sentiment, for example. We have to be vigilant and think of how people in Scotland who were not born here feel. But there are seeds of hope that we have changed in the last fifty years.

As a lawyer, my initial reaction to this question on the census was negative – what kind of useful data could possibly be obtained from a question about how people *feel*? But I've changed my mind on that – we need data on how many people in Scotland feel Scottish when they weren't born here. And I hope there will be many of us. That for me would be the country that I imagine for my grandchildren.

* Seriously, how can I not be Scottish?

Rachael Kelsey is a family lawyer, appointed by the Lord President to sit on the Family Law Sub-Committee of the Scottish Civil Justice Council in 2016 and reappointed in 2019; she is also President-Elect of the International Academy of Family Lawyers.

A. L. KENNEDY

In our country, our good country, we are sisters, we are brothers. Our family makes you a member as soon as you join it, however you join it.

In our country, our good country, we grow trees. When we mourn, when we celebrate, when we start our weeks and months, we plant new trees. We prioritise the diversity of species, the breathability of our air, the purity of our water. We give our people pleasant homes in green places. There are no places which are not green – we cannot afford them. We trap our carbon, we keep it sunk.

In our country, our good country, we learn. We know that ignorance harms us. We know that wilful ignorance harms us more than any other kind and makes us dangerous. We have grown fond of reality and understand it. Whenever it is cruel we seek to mitigate its cruelties. When we make decisions, we make them in deference to reality, in accordance with good understanding and the comfort of our brothers, of our sisters. Our young children study history, anthropology, philosophy. They are taught defences against the sciences of deception. We teach every child in the way that best suits them. We are always happy to help our sisters and brothers if they wish to spend all their lives learning.

In our country, our good country, we attend to our contentment. We acknowledge that without it, without the elements that build and guard it, we would be in pain. We always remember that people in pain make bad decisions and are vulnerable. For this reason we make sure that our people have free access to the law, to healthcare, to peace, to freedom, to social care, to all levels of education, to aids for their disabilities, to hospices for their dying, to midwives and maternity wards for their being born. We seek to ease burdens. To the weak is given assistance. To the strong is given the opportunity of giving assistance.

In our country, our good country, our statues are of whistle-blowers and campaigners, of those who resisted oppression, defended the right, formed good laws. We celebrate the savers of lives. We defend ourselves, but will not place upon our population any requirement to fund hollow military display, overbearing force, or the propagation of conflicts. National service is asked of everyone for three years. Those serving can work with the poor and those in need, can build and mend, can rescue the lost and the drowning, can assist in other countries to ease their harms and hurts, can keep our borders marked with courtesy and all necessary welcomes, can learn the duties of national defence and their proper restraint. In this way, we will meet each other while we work towards a better country. The mind-worker, the hand-worker, the home-worker, all are part of our good country and all may be contained in one person.

In our country, our good country, we will speak to each other in art, cheer each other in art, show each other our humanity in art. We will welcome beauty. The dreams of our hearts will be expressed. We will play games, cook meals, raise children, tend gardens, love our children. We will seek our fulfilment. We will seek to create fulfilment in others. We will cultivate gratitude and all that causes it.

In our country, our good country, we will all pay a little for the common good, according to our prosperity. We will regulate the natural flaws of public and private life with due oversight. Governing our leaders, our law-makers, our police officers, our teachers, our politicians, our farmers, our businesswomen and men, our councillors, our nurses, our doctors, our neighbours, our lovers – governing all of our brothers and sisters in the family which is our nation – will be this principle: *First Do No Harm.*

In our country, our good country, we will seek to do no harm. We will love each other, as best we can. We will fail and then fail better. We will cherish proportionate hope.

A.L. Kennedy is an award-winning writer of novels, short stories, non-fiction, children's books, plays, scripts for TV, theatre and radio, and stand-up comedy routines. She has twice been chosen for the Granta Best of Young British Novelists list and is a Fellow of the Royal Society of Arts and the Royal Society of Literature.

DEBBIE KING

Imagine a country where there is a safe, affordable and well-designed home for everyone.

Imagine a country where individuals have the power to get out of homelessness quickly because they not only have the right to a safe, affordable and decent home, but also the support to assert that right.

Imagine a country where people are not turned away from their council's homelessness office when they desperately need a safe place to stay that night.

Image a country where temporary accommodation makes living better and not worse.

I work for Shelter Scotland, a housing and homeless charity, as a community organiser working with people at a local level to create a movement for change, to take action and to make a positive difference. Unfortunately, the housing reality for many people is so stark that they have given up hope for a better housing future. We live in a wealthy society and it is unacceptable that we still see people being ground down by the struggle to find and keep a decent and affordable home. Surely by 2020 we should be living in a society where everyone has a proper home?

However, there are more than 14,000 homeless children in Scotland and nearly 11,000 households in temporary accommodation. We also have rising numbers of people sleeping rough on our streets across the country, with many more sofa-surfing or living in dangerous or inappropriate accommodation. The housing emergency is forcing many people to make the desperate choice between feeding their family or paying the rent. Others are struggling with life in temporary B&B

accommodation for months, and sometimes years, on end. Insecure housing has a substantial negative and enduring impact on people's mental and physical wellbeing and their life chances. Nationally this also damages Scotland's ability to achieve the aspirations of ending child poverty, of education equity, of reducing health inequalities and of creating a healthy, socially just society.

Research by Shelter Scotland on how many homes in our country meet the 'Living Home Standard',* a measure created by people across the UK, shows that there is still a glaring housing divide. A staggering one in three homes in Scotland did not meet this standard. The people most likely to be living in these substandard homes are young people, families with children, renters and people on low incomes.

We must therefore address not just how many homes there are, but how those homes are placed within reach of those who most need them. Not just better standards, but better systems to deliver those better homes to the people who need them most. Not just better legal protection, but better accessibility and clarity to allow people to exercise their housing rights.

So, I am imagining a country where a decent, safe and affordable home is not a privilege, but is a realised right for everyone. Where the tens of thousands of people who are currently struggling with homelessness, poor housing and the often-crippling housing costs are empowered to insist on their right to a well-designed, high-quality, decent and affordable home in a thriving and supportive community.

Imagine living in a country where everyone has a home that allows them to settle into a safe community where they can access education, work, childcare and healthcare services. Imagine a home which is a safe retreat, where you can bring up your family, and it doesn't cripple your bank balance and create the kind of stress and anxiety that can affect your mental health. A home should be in a friendly, supportive, mixed community and when you step out of your front door, you should feel safe, and have access to well-designed surroundings. Where

---

* Shelter Scotland, Living Home Standard, 2018 <https://scotland.shelter.org.uk/50/living_homes_standard>.

parks, sports facilities, a GP, shops and schools are right on your door-step.

It is outrageous that we still have to imagine something as basic and obvious as a safe, affordable home for everyone in the twenty-first century. Sadly, we are still battling the legacy of decades of under-investment in decent and affordable social housing and a lack of an urgent commitment to make sure that families and individuals do not have to struggle every day without something as essential as a place to truly call home. It's time we acknowledged the housing emergency and made it history.

Debbie King is Senior Community Organiser at the homeless support charity Shelter Scotland, where she works with people in the community to identify key housing issues, supports them to challenge the status quo, and helps bring about positive change.

SANJEEV KOHLI

My vision of an ideal country would centre on the development of a device that would be issued to every single citizen. Let me explain . . .

The perceived physical beauty of humans has always been vastly over-valued. In the sense that it's valued at all. For example, the metric distance between your eyes is seemingly a measure of your trustworthiness and will directly impact on the shrift you receive at the returns desk in Debenhams. And we're supposed to be the most evolved of the animals.

Surely, as a species, we should have transcended this biological imperative. And yet many of us are guilty of perpetuating it. I am certainly as much a slave to this phenomenon as anyone; I care *way* too much about my appearance. Despite approaching fifty, I still use 'sludge', 'mud', 'fudge', 'mudge' and 'ectoplasm' in my hair. And I still attempt to rock jeggings, despite the fact that they make me resemble an amputee spider.

However, I am far from the biggest offender: this phenomenon has been magnified exponentially by the Insta generation, one of whom I witnessed flicking her mermaid hair around whilst taking pictures of herself on her phone for the *full eighty-minute duration* of an Edinburgh to Glasgow train journey.

Maybe she was an influencer; maybe 100,000 people were locked in suspended animation whilst awaiting her verdict on an eyebrow pencil. In my world, though, no such creature would exist. Because physical appearance would no longer be any kind of measure of value. And this would be down to the Humanitometer™.

The Humanitometer is a device, to be issued free to everyone, which measures human decency, empathy and kindness. It will be either hand-held or perhaps strapped onto the forehead – this might seem ridiculous now, but in my future looking ridiculous won't even be a thing.

How does the Humanitometer work? It will be calibrated to detect and measure the positive alpha and beta waves that emanate unseen from the empathy centre of the brain. OK, I made all that up, but I'll make sure that the right boffins get the right funding so that one day we can value people by their humanity and not the curve of their buttock or the gap between their thighs or the price of their Yeezy Boost 700 Inertias (they're trainers, Grandad).

In fact, to formalise the arrangement, your Empathiscore™ will be converted into credits which will then in turn be converted into a tangible equivalent. So if (for example) you give up your seat on a heaving train, you will be able to purchase an M&S dine-in deal. If you nurse a small sparrow back to health in your kitchen, you will be entitled to a high-end squash racquet. And if you help to lift a stranger's fridge to his top-floor flat you will get a second-hand Vauxhall Astra.

This will of course have a massive impact on the economy, as it will effectively result in mass wage restructuring. Basically, the wage you earn will be more directly reflective of the joy, comfort, help and enrichment you bring to others. Nurses, social workers and primary-school teachers will have their salaries tripled; venture capitalists will receive a tenth of what they used to; and Katie Hopkins will actually have to pay people every time she opens her mouth. Who doesn't want to live in a world where that happens?

Sanjeev Kohli is a writer, actor and presenter, probably best known for writing and performing in BBC Radio 4's comedy series Fags, Mags and Bags, *and playing Navid in* Still Game.

MARC LAMBERT

The Queen was dreaming, dreaming all the way back to when giants walked the earth: clearing mountains in a stride, striking left and right, giving blood and mythos to the land.

And now? Nothing, just the memory of them on the wind. If you cared to listen.

So many ghosts. No wonder she had her head in her hands. She had been a giant too, nearly a millennium ago. But now, diminished, she had finally been found, in the sand, on the Lews shore, along with her king and retinue – berserkers still at hand, hopped up on fly agaric, eyes bulging and armed to the teeth. How they had once stormed! But now, once again? They had been sent (oh, for heaven's sake!) *to London.*

The Queen awoke to gawking crowds. Crowds who looked without seeing, ghosts in their own time, though they didn't know it. *These are not my people.*

Being captive in London made the Queen reflective. She had been at many a court, including this one, but none as mighty as her own. It was the perfect image of history and geography inverted, this London sojourn. Because back then, in her time, north had been south.

(She had only come across the true map once in modern times. Improbably, there it was in a book, the frontispiece of Kevin MacNeil's *The Stornoway Way.*)

Time, she determined, was a concertina. It expanded and contracted, and the future was already there in the past.

The Queen thought of Walter Benjamin, and his interpretation of Klee's 'New Angel' , the one which looks to the past as the storm of progress propels it towards the future. An angel turned to the disasters of the past, even as the future flows through it . . . In spite of having been buried in sand for a thousand years, the Queen had clocked all the ideas and all the ghosts, every one, rising out of their time, vanishing into the past, only to flow back again into the future.

Some of these ghosts were benign, still intact.

But thou shalt not worship false images. Others had been traduced and turned, through no fault of their own, into zombie notions, sucking on the blood of her people like vampires. Adam Smith, for instance. How unquiet was his grave? How was it to be co-opted by the oligarchy? To stalk the land, leveraged, godlike, as an instrument of oppression? Poor Adam. She would restore him to himself, laying the dishonourable ghost of his alienation to rest.

As for the King, he was as enraged as ever. When would he be able, along with his warriors, to draw his damned sword? Only those who looked carefully could see his arm shaking with the effort. These days, she pictured the King like the disconsolate knight at Bannockburn in George Mackay Brown's *Beside the Ocean of Time.* But she, the dreamer, channelled his squire, Thorfinn Ragnarson, who was cleverer than anyone had suspected.

Well, she would release her king to do what he did best. She remembered the passage:

A wave in the Sound – one of those seventh waves that comes in higher and colder and more rampant than the six ordered predictable waves on either side of it – crashed against the round ancient ruin on the shore, and carried away another stone that had stood for twelve centuries.

The King would be her seventh wave. He would be her 'invisible hand'. She enjoyed the irony of that description of him. One hand – his – invisibly wielded in the service of her nation, to deal a death-blow to another – Adam Smith's idea of the social benefits of self-interest, a notion monstrously distorted by time and opportunism. There would be no laissez-faire in her new Scotland, because it had only brought suffering. There were false ideas and interpretations to kill, false ghosts and gods to slay, in this reimagined land. She had arrived through time to her true purpose, turned like a compass to true north.

She thrilled to the purpose of it. Touching the King, she sung a spell, summoning the Angel to free him: '*The music goes on and on, unheard for the most part. Through this lifetime of vanity we creep, stumble, march, follow, plough and scythe, linger, hirple on a stick, until at last the feet are folded and lie still: but seen through the angel's eye, it is an immortal spirit that dances from birth to death, all the way, from before the beginning till after the end.*'

'Go!' she commanded.

Marc Lambert is CEO of Scottish Book Trust.

PATRICK LAURIE

The best thing I ever did as a farmer was have folk from the local Alzheimer's group out to see a field of oats I grew. Many of them had worked on farms their entire lives, but more recently most had been cooped up in residential care. It pleased them to walk the field with the sound of skylarks above them, and what a wealth of memories came pouring out of men and women who forgot they weren't at home again.

They told me how the old harvesting machines used to work, and one woman said she could still smell the sweat of her father's heavy horses. One man never spoke a word; he couldn't, but his fingers were busy with something from the moment he arrived. Just before he left, he gave me a corn dolly he'd plucked and folded from the heads of my own crop. God knows how he'd made it; it would have taken me years. I thanked him and he smiled, and later I pinned it above the door in the kitchen. It's so beautiful that people ask where it came from, as if it couldn't have come from here.

That group came to visit the farm because their families hoped it might do them good to get some fresh air. They were right, but that visit bothered me. Because even in a tiny glimmer, I'd seen something of what we used to be in this place: a community of people bound in a shared memory of our own traditions. Now, writing this on a winter's night in Galloway, I look up from my desk to the window and find an entirety of darkness outside: no lights, lamps or traffic. I know there are heather hills in that view, five old farms and a marsh, but in the darkness there is nothing more to see than stars.

Farming was never meant to be a lonely business, but this place has never been so quiet. Modern farm subsidies have created landscapes where the hills belong to a steadily diminishing handful of folk. Owing to a kink in global markets, local farms are now being bought by investment companies and pension providers who turn fields into cash by planting dense plantations of spruce trees. In the last few decades, my neighbours have vanished to be replaced by Dutch or Austrian investors who've never even been to Galloway. There was a financial adviser on the radio at New Year saying that 'Now's the time to put your money into land', but there are better things to put in the land, and surely you should start with your heart?

It's easy to feel like we're reaching an end in this glen, but my urgent hope is that some of these patterns can be reversed and the view from my night-time window might prickle again with a bit of light. I'd love to feel a sense of others here, and I'm not trying to make this place seem like a feeble thing; we don't need to be coddled or wrapped in cotton wool. Bugger that, I'm talking here about sustaining a sense of life and tradition in a landscape that's never asked for anything until it found itself finally choking on the edge of collapse.

What we need is folk to love this place and make it their own. There's often talk of repopulating the countryside with young people, but they don't stand a chance against investment banks. I have no doubt we can change this situation and make it fair, but it also bothers me that each year there are fewer old people in this glen. At a certain age we move them out or pass them into care, but a community needs folk of all ages and abilities. Those visitors to my oat field brought a new perspective: a warmth and a connection to place which felt both crucial and creakily fragile. Their love blew from them like down from a willow, but it's all too easy for the tree to fall, leaving nothing more for the wind to carry. I have so much hope for the future here, but the first step is to bolster the soul and a sense of justice in quiet, starlit places like these.

Patrick Laurie breeds pedigree Galloway cattle on a hill farm near Dalbeattie. His 2020 book Native: Life in a Vanishing Landscape *was a* Times *bestseller and was shortlisted for the Wainwright Prize for UK Nature Writing.*

MARIOT LESLIE

I imagine living in a Scotland full of confidence and curiosity. A country whose people enjoy leaving it to learn, live, work, travel; and who love coming back home again. A country which has a realistic understanding of its place in the world and is wise in its choices of partners and projects. A country which is proud of what it has to offer others, as well as humble about learning from them.

Most of us have taken for granted the security and prosperity of our corner of Europe. That certainty is over. Globalisation, climate change, migration and the digital revolution are all putting national and global institutions under strain. The challenges are plain to see: the rise of China; a United States which has become a disrupter rather than a norm-setter; conflict in the Middle East; an aggressive Russia; a return to strong-man politics in some newer democracies; pressure on standards in public life and the rule of law here in Britain and elsewhere in Europe.

A small, nimble, well-educated country will still be able to thrive if it plays its cards right. That means sorting our domestic problems and choosing our friends well. Unquestionably, we ought to put effort into close friendship with England and our other neighbours in the British Isles. For an independent Scotland, with our geography and our history, this must also mean wholehearted membership of the EU and NATO. As the US and China square up to divide- and-rule world trade, only the EU has the counterweight to protect a way of life which combines high standards of environmental and social welfare with strong support for innovation. Only the EU is big enough to take on the tech giants and regulate the internet and artificial intelligence in a way which reflects these priorities. Only the EU offers a top table in world affairs where a country the size of Scotland can be sure of its own seat and a voice on everything from agriculture to foreign policy. EU membership comes with the right to study and work with 500 million people in 27 countries to extend our own small home base. My future Scotland would be diminished if we did not go for it.

Security has also become harder in a world where cyber, terrorist and covert 'hybrid' attacks are increasing and there is an arms race in new technologies which Scotland could never afford on its own. An independent Scotland would be vulnerable without allies. Membership of NATO would be essential to deter aggression and to build Scotland's own military capacity. Mutual membership of NATO would also be a valuable confidence-building measure with England. Scotland has much to offer its allies, including our strength in maritime and medical sciences, some world-leading AI and space applications, a territory which abuts strategically important Arctic routes, and experienced service personnel with a proud military tradition.

I'd like my future Scotland also to remember its history as a nation of emigrants, including those who, for good or ill, jumped at the opportunities of the Empire. Around the world there are people with Scottish roots. There are many places in Africa, Asia and the Caribbean where there is still a fond memory of Scottish teachers, doctors, nurses, engineers and administrators – as well as places to which we owe a debt of conscience. Let's build on this inheritance, and on newer links through communities which have made their home in Scotland recently.

Above all, I'd like Scots to be proud of being good citizens of the world. Small countries cannot do everything, but they can build a reputation for being great at what they do best. Our research and universities are real assets, as are our civic-society organisations, our professions, and our creative artists. The English language makes them accessible and attractive to many.

I would love to see a Scotland which became recognised as a problem-solver: for the thought-leadership of our government or the high calibre of Scots who choose careers at the UN. It might be because exchanges between Scottish and foreign schools prove transformative for pupils in both countries. It might be for the excellence of the medical teams we send to humanitarian emergencies, or the ingenuity of our solutions for mitigating climate change.

Let's not wait! We can make a start now by demanding better language teaching in our schools, by encouraging the organisations to which we belong to seek out international partners, by egging on our young friends when they are hesitating over an Erasmus place or a job opportunity overseas, or by asking committees and boards if they have considered international evidence. There's a big world out there and Scots are as much a part of it as anyone else on the planet.

Dame Mariot Leslie is a former British diplomat and ambassador.

CAREY LUNAN

Health inequalities mirror poverty across the world and Scotland is shamed by its unenviable status as the 'sick man of Europe'. The poorest people in our society lead not just shorter but also sicker lives. The community that I care for, as a frontline GP, has an average male life-expectancy of just fifty-eight years, whereas in the most affluent parts of Edinburgh life expectancy is over twenty years more. I believe that the biggest unaddressed challenge to the Scottish health service is this enduring difference in health outcomes between our most and least affluent communities.

Of course we need, primarily, to tackle the root causes of poverty, but something more fundamental needs to change about the way we deliver healthcare, particularly to marginalised and vulnerable groups. All aspects of healthcare are, to a greater or lesser degree, underpinned by caring relationships, no more so than in the GP consulting room, yet, for many people, their earliest experience of a caring relationship, often within their own family, may have involved significant adversity and psychological trauma. This means that for many of our most vulnerable patients, their ability to accept healthcare is compromised, and attempts to offer healthcare are met with anxiety, resistance, mistrust, hostility and sabotage. So here lies the rub: the people who need care the most are often the least able to accept it, sometimes to a life-threatening degree, and this harms patients, doctors and our wider society.

Our medical training does not address this paradox. Ours is traditionally a transactional model, where patient narratives are sought, symptoms collected, diagnoses made, treatments offered . . . and usually accepted. The complex factors at play in these consultations, if not understood, can result in complicating responses from both patient and clinician: hopelessness, nihilism, threat, punishment, abandonment. These erode our compassion and lead to burn-out.

Our healthcare systems are not tolerant of this paradox. They are designed by healthy people, for use by healthy people, who are able to negotiate such systems with ease. They necessitate a degree of health literacy and the ability to turn up for, understand and accept the care offered. They do not work for people whose lives are chaotic, whose literacy is poor and, crucially, whose experience of caring relationships is fractured.

Health services must be at their best where they are needed most, or health inequalities will continue to worsen. Adequate resourcing in areas of high need is important, but resource alone will not solve the problem. We need to rethink the way that services are designed and delivered.

I imagine a country where the success of our healthcare system is measured not by targets, but by the quality of the relationships within it.

There is no more important place for this than in general practice, where continuity of care over time, within communities and across generations, has been shown to improve both quantity and quality of life.

This 'low-threshold, high-fidelity' model of general practice describes a system that is defined by the ease of accessibility for those who are most commonly excluded, and its faithfulness to those who are commonly abandoned along the way. The first doctor–patient encounter is considered the most important, and is focused on welcome, acceptance and the building of trust. Our aim is to create the conditions for subsequent encounters in which they can build a committed, kind and consistent relationship over time.

Addressing the problematic relationship with care that many vulnerable and marginalised patients have necessitates an enhanced approach to the care of both patient *and* doctor. This requires a stable and adequate workforce of GPs, working within systems that promote both continuity of care and time to care. This also requires a recognition of the 'emotional labour' of relationship-based care, with doctors receiving time and support to reflect upon and understand the dynamics at play, building resilience, tolerance and empathy into day-to-day practice. Furthermore, to help doctors understand and relate to the complex challenges faced by their patients, we must aspire to a medical workforce that is more representative of the populations we serve by widening access to medical schools.

GPs have the capacity to rediscover their role as social activists and advocates, in partnership with their patients, and develop, in the words of past Chief Medical Officer Harry Burns, a 'compassion that stands in awe of the burdens that others carry, rather than one that stands in judgement'.

In this imagined country the newly established NHS Cross-Party Group declares that a society with less health inequality not only costs less but is also more at ease with its sense of social justice. Surely this epiphany has the power to vaccinate the NHS against both politics and privatisation.

Dr Carey Lunan is a GP in Edinburgh, caring for one of Scotland's most socio-economically disadvantaged communities. She is the Chair of the Scottish Deep End Project.

PÀDRAIG MACAOIDH /
PATRICK MACKAY

I have always felt buoyed by the sight of lights across water. Looking across from Sleat to Mallaig, say, with house-lights studding the dark bulk of the mainland and streaking and smearing across kyles: there's a sense of community at a distance there, a reassurance. Growing up on the west coast of Lewis there was no such permanence, though there would be, looking out onto the ocean, the passing dots of ships taking the main sea-route, the largest lit up and spread out like a floating town-ship. Our own villages, meanwhile, would be austere strings of Christmas lights draping the coastline; not too near the edge, for fear of dropping off. There is vertigo to so much darkness, to the heaving mass of an invisible ocean, to those millions of stars refusing to stand still overhead.

What does it mean to imagine a country? Is it the same as imagining a 'community'? Or imagining what it means to belong – deeply, friv-olously, superficially, sceptically, transitorily, however – in or to a place? What of *this* country? Any country, any Scotland I imagined, would have to incorporate the Western Isles where I grew up, and Edinburgh where I now live. And the emotional, let alone physical, connections between them seem tenuous: those lights twinkle dimly. For Gaelic speakers like myself, Edinburgh has often felt (despite an ongoing attempt to develop a Gaelic centre and a dedicated Gaelic secondary school in the city) like a distant irrelevance. For centuries, if Edinburgh existed in the Gaelic imaginary it was largely through the threat of Calton Prison, the risk of having your wallet tricked from you on the High Street, or of meeting your end at the hands of the common executioner. (Uneasiness still comes from having a military garrison at the centre of this capital city.)

But the problem is not just Edinburgh. For most of my childhood, any town or city – Stornoway, Portree, Inverness, Glasgow – felt like an unreality, a not entirely welcome necessity, a historic mistake. One of the great things about the Highlands as a space is the *lack* of a definite centre, of a clear hierarchy (who, again, is the clan chief?). And though in my childhood there was a castle looming over Stornoway, by then it was no longer the mock-baronial nineteenth-century drug-hazed dream, but a somewhat run-down college, shabby and apologetic for its past (even if its current incarnation as museum and luxury hotel has brought its own problems).

I can't imagine, in other words, the contemporary Highlands – or, by extension, Scotland – through that traditional British image of the oak tree, one continuous organism in which we are all sheltered by the canopy of [fill in the blank of your own centrifugal or hierarchical fantasy: London, Edinburgh, Inverness, an aristocracy, old wealth, etc]. Instead, the Highlands are, for the better, a forest, or some kind of rhizomatic entity, with many different growths appearing dotted around the place, in a way that is erratic or unruly or, indeed, creative. This may be just another fantasy version of a country, one in which the eccentric, the small, the marginalised can find its own place, can be its own centre. But it is the country I would imagine: one which has rejected the open market, the (inevitably wealthy, white, male) visionary who would happily buy the land and bend it to their will, and shape the idea of community as they see fit.

It is a country in which those glinting lights of community exist all year round. Where caps aren't doffed. Where fuel poverty is not endemic in some of the most (renewable) energy rich parts. Where there's a Universal Basic Income so that everyone has the chance to take little – or big – risks, and not live in constant fear of poverty. Where Gaelic speakers – especially in the Highlands and Islands – have affordable housing, jobs, the possibility of making a full life there. Where clean and affordable travel between all parts of the country is possible to imagine. Where every village, each community has a cracking festival celebrating the oddest, weirdest, most localised thing they can imagine and which they hold for themselves first and foremost (and *after* that all tourists are welcome). The Festival of Bogcotton? The Lewis Kabaddi Festival? Aye, sign me up.

Peter Mackay is a poet, broadcaster and lecturer; originally from the Isle of Lewis, he now lives in Edinburgh.

FRED MACAULAY

I magine a country where the citizens can receive free treatment for health issues regardless of their income, postcode or age. That is our country.

Imagine a country where refugees and displaced persons are welcomed and treated with respect and dignity. That is our country.

Imagine a country where our national football and rugby teams perform so well that we have expectations of them that can rarely be achieved. That is our country (sometimes – look up 'Quarter Finals' in the Scots dictionary and you'll see it says 'Things that other countries take part in').

Imagine a country with scenery of lochs and mountains that is envied the world over, that people from other countries flock to see in their droves.* That is our country.

Imagine a country that gave the world golf, whisky, television and the telephone (four of the things that caused Tiger Woods's marriage break-up . . .), and many other inventions and discoveries. That is our country.

Imagine a country where 90 per cent of the border is coastal – so all of its energy could be generated through tidal and wave power. That is our country. (Most of it is the North Sea, but if you go in it above your waist you'll declare: 'It's Baltic!')

Imagine a country that stands on its own and doesn't blame others for its faults. That is what our country should be.

Imagine a country that's not perfect and whose people are not

---

* **droves** *n.* tartan trousers made of inferior-quality cloth.

perfect. That is our country. That is us. That is who we are. Yes, even me.

Imagine a country that punches above its weight in sport, business, science, the arts and technology. That is our country. (Mind you, it's also unfortunate that we measure our successes in terms of violence and obesity.)

Imagine a country where a parliament votes four times on an issue that the public were denied the chance to vote on a second time. That is not our country. And it's arithmetically as well as politically problematic.

Imagine a country where a Home Secretary smirks when she says that she is stopping the free movement of people. That is not our country. (I've been having free movements every day since she said that, so it's not working.)

Imagine a country that was first to publish the *Encyclopaedia Britannica* back in 1768. That was our country. (Ten years later, Samuel Johnson published his first *Dictionary* and people were able to look up the word 'Encyclopaedia'.)

Imagine a country that pretends one of its lochs has a monster in it and we're still getting away with it. That is our country. And the only monstrosity is the deception we perpetuate on our visitors.

Imagine a country whose people – according to a Cambridge University study – are the most emotionally stable of the four countries of the UK. That is our country. (When I read that . . . I filled up with tears.)

Imagine a country where our breakfast of choice is porridge. That is our country. Nothing sums up our national mood better than porridge:

'What are you having for breakfast?'

'Grain.'

'What with?'

'Water.'

'Anything else?'

'Aye . . . salt!'

'You put salt in your porridge?'

'No . . . I pour it straight in my eyes. Because I've been asleep. And when I was asleep I maybe had a dream. And in the dream I was maybe *happy*. So I pour salt into my eyes to reset the pain.'

Imagine a country with a deep and dark and long-lasting national sense of humour . . . That is my country.

Fred MacAulay is one of Scotland's best-loved stand-ups.

STUART MACRAE

PIECES FOR A NEW COUNTRY

we are open...

free...

open-hearted...

open-minded

...and welcoming

STUART MACRAE
Oct. 2019

...a warm place

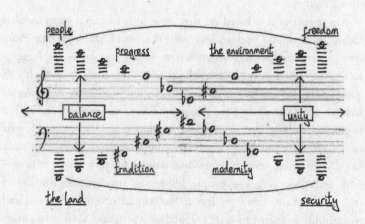

Stuart MacRae is an Edinburgh-based composer working in a variety of genres, including opera, orchestral, choral and chamber music.

ANDREW MARR

I know what my country looks and smells like. It has slant winter light, coming over a stormy, steel-grey eastern sea, and tussocky glens, with thick clusters of silver birch, rowan, oak and pine. The stone-built, modest villages smell of woodsmoke and baking. In summer, the rich dark soil is covered with golden barley, oats and tattie shaws. On the lower ground there are sturdy, shaggy beasts; higher up in the glens, anarchistic and disreputable sheep. Call it, for want of a better name, Pictopia.

My dream of it is based on that drearily fashionable word sustainability. Pictopia is a land, trading with the world, whose people grow enough food and make enough warm clothes and sturdy implements to live good lives without despoiling everything around them. (It's an absurd idea, obviously; but it's also maybe the way we're all going to have to try to live.) In Pictopia, people have taken a step back, and begun to unplug the extraordinarily intelligent and wasteful gear designed in California and built in China to drive everybody mad. Locally designed wind turbines and wind kites provide most homes with enough energy. The people, leaner and sturdier than the rest of us, have learnt to use their legs to get around. Nimble-fingered and thoughtful, compared to their neighbours, they make their own entertainment, some of it between the sheets.

In Pictopia one generation passes down to the next a landscape essentially unaltered. The same grey stone dykes divide the same mixed, grazing and arable farms, where each year the same migratory birds land and are admired, without being shot.

On all sides, true, climate change rudely thrusts against Pictopia.

That must be so because it can be found on this planet. But left to themselves, ancient woodlands turn out to be remarkably resilient, the peat has not dried out, and the rain has not so far relented. When beaches are eroded or coastal roads are grabbed by the rising sea, the Picts shrug and adapt. They don't like it; but they have learned to thole what they cannot change.

There are oddities about this small territory, it has to be confessed. Its democracy is participatory, which means there is endless, and some-times wearisome, talking. Arguments weave and curl in on themselves, and float languid in the air over every settlement. Decisions? Well, they may take a while. The pace of what used to be called modern life decelerated here from motorway-fast to bridleway-patient.

Once there was a famous dominie who knew her Herodotus and was much taken by the story that the Persians discussed every impor-tant decision twice, the first time sober and the second drunk, and only acted when their verdicts matched. So the Parliament of Pictopia is strictly divided into two barns. The lower barn is the house of water and calm deliberation. The other, the 'hot barn', contains a maze of shebeens and saloons and permanently stinks of the water of life . . . hence the popular expression, drunk as a lord.

The Picts are no great believers in the specialisation of labour. Everyone who can does some manual, outdoor work; everyone is their own political newspaper; everyone is taught to mend, craft and build. In one way or another almost everyone has an art – music-making, storytelling, the decoration and painting of surfaces. Pictland, say the tourist-visitors who are made very welcome, sounds lively and looks beautiful. Its food may not have been to everyone's taste – the endless meaty broths, fruitcakes and rhubarb pies – but the whisky is second only to Islay's.

The whole point of Pictopia, however, is that it is fertile, quite heavily populated land which manages to give its people a good living without destroying all the other living things, vegetable and animal, around them. It never goes to war. Possible invaders consider the endless, intricate and weary conversation that would be required to keep order in this place, and quickly decide it would be too tiring to dominate.

Unfortunately, long ago, after a heroic session in Pictish Inn, the UK Ordnance Survey team completely forgot to put Pictopia on the map. But it isn't hard to find. It's a little north of Aberdeen and south of Dundee, over to the east of Laurencekirk and west of Kirriemuir. Down in London I met a pipe-smoking, grey-haired old man calling himself Grassy Gibbon, or some such, who said you really can't miss it.

Andrew Marr is a writer, a journalist and a broadcaster; he edited The Independent *and was the BBC's Political Editor.*

ALEXANDER
MCCALL SMITH

HEALING

We have so much to regret;
The things we once had
That we have no longer, and those things too
That we hoped we might one day have,
But which, when the light shifts,
We see are impossible, dreams perhaps,
Fond imaginings with no grounding
In any world on offer.

Most of us who have lived
More than a handful of decades
Remember a Scotland in which
We knew who we were; that country
Was full of holes, yes, and injustice,
Full of small lives lived
Under the stern gaze of those
Who did not much like
The idea of freedom and people
Being who they wanted to be;
That, thank God, has gone,
But something else has gone with it,
In part, if not in whole:
The idea of community, of being
In it together, or being bound

To one another by a fabric
Of shared references and associations;
Of sharing things that make us laugh or cry
According to the moment; the world
Is frighteningly large, its forces
Are hard and impersonal, give
Little incentive to embrace the other,
To tend to the needs of those
Who are lonely and in need;
For those social goods to flourish
We need to feel that those around us
Are our brothers and our sisters;
Those simple words that still
Sound so powerful, and so true.

So if it were given to me to wish
For one thing, it would be for that,
For the restoration of a sense
Of being joined, as one, with those
With whom we share our country;
So that we are with them in their needs
And in their sorrow and in their joy,
Citizens in the sense in which
Political philosophers have struggled to define,
But that our poets have known in their bones,
As Robert Burns did, and Hugh MacDiarmid too
When he spoke of Scotland's little rose,
Enough for him, still enough for us.

Alexander McCall Smith was a Professor of Law at the University of Edinburgh before he became the author of The No. 1 Ladies' Detective Agency *series and a number of other novels.*

KARYN MCCLUSKEY

By the time we realised that this brave new world we had created through our scientific advances and smart technology was turning us into creatures less connected, less happy, or just less, it was almost too late. Like boiling a frog, we had changed our society, imperceptibly, one degree at a time, until it was too hot and we began to wilt and die.

Almost too late.

Sometimes old ideas are the remedy for the modern condition and so Scotland embarked on a new old journey. It wasn't easy. People argued, 'This is just diagnostic progress. These increases in mental-health issues are not correlated with this world we have created.' 'These increased numbers of suicides cannot be linked to the bullying and unrealistic ideals sold on social media,' they said. But we decided that the faces of the dead and the pain of those caught in the tar pits of technology were reason enough to create a new reality.

We decided to create places of digital detox, calm places in communities around Scotland, invested in and cherished by young and old. Sure, we employ technology – we bought high-quality comprehensive cellphone jammers to ensure protection for those who seek refuge from the online screams of those trapped in the digital world. People who enter our places know that their phones will be useless, and the compulsive hand-flick and thumb-tic that connected them online can be stilled for a time.

They're safe, these places, carpeted to deaden the sound of the other occupants. Seats are comfortable and the temperature is neither too hot nor too cold, for we want you to stay, to take a break, to remember what the world has to offer, and what you have to offer the world. We have a clock of course – but analogue.

These places make no judgement about your background or your motives for being there, you can just 'be'. When the question came about how we would engage and keep you interested, we thought long and hard, and then decided to fill these rooms with books: books about animals and ecosystems that were under threat; books that required you to think of different ways to engage with this fragile world we live in; books about fantasy, people and their adventures; books for young and old.

The smell of these places is comforting. Most of those in their thirties have a Proustian moment, a remembrance of things past, a smell that they can't quite describe. For those Generation Zs born after 2000, the experience is unfamiliar and discombobulating: in the beginning they're like the discoverers of new countries, awkwardly navigating and sampling the wares. After a time, they settle on a chair, skim-read a few pages, then find themselves completely sucked in. Their lives outside are challenging, unpredictable and sometimes dangerous but our spaces have become comforting and a place of safety.

Parents and babies come in their droves to the rooms in our places. We've created friendly areas where the babies can be fed with colours to stimulate them. We give books to parents so they can take the experience of the written word home to their children, to feed the imaginations of those who will soon become the guardians of the environmental and historic treasures of this small, beautiful country they live in.

Some people have said, 'These places that you spend money on, we had them before, and we closed them down, we took their money away and nothing bad happened.' But we looked around, and decided that something bad had happened. The frog was boiling.

We recognise that the world has changed, that artificial intelligence will revolutionise work and leisure. We understand that we face great challenges for which solutions have not yet been invented, so we need inventors, thinkers and artists. But the stories of other great challenges have all been written down and the roots of new ideas lie within.

And so the people realise that, when they enter these spaces we've created, that we've cherished in every community, that we've invested in and maintained to the highest standard, their heart-rates slow, their breathing becomes rhythmic, deep and contented. They learn from fiction and non-fiction alike. The pace of learning may be slower but it's deeper, and it's real, not fake. In the solitude they can find themselves and thus find connection to others.

We call our places libraries. They are our archives of achievement and our cathedrals of hope. They are monuments to what has been and what could be. They are important and they are necessary. They are a cornerstone of our future and not a story that we tell our children about what we had and gave away. They are where our imaginations live.

Karyn McCluskey is a relentlessly positive violence preventer and justice innovator who remains convinced that, despite the hard work required, the view will be worth the climb.

ALAN MCCREDIE

I was deeply asleep at some unmapped hour of the night when my phone pinged with a message from the other side of the world. 'Imagine a country . . .' it began. I read it, liked it, thought about it and then fell back asleep. I dreamed of expansive worlds and fantastical countries.

In the light of morning, the dreams faded (except the one about the great city of Perth being entirely remade with blue cheese). But the text message was a reality and a provocative one at that.

I soon realised my initial thoughts for this newly imagined land were almost entirely illegal and likely to be banned in this and any other as yet undiscovered worlds.

Being given a blank slate is a daunting prospect. Where do you start when it comes to conjuring up a desirable land of the imagination? A bit like trying to choose your songs for *Desert Island Discs*, I suppose – you come up with what feels like the perfect set and ten minutes later, you remember all the tracks you've left out and your wish-list has completely changed. I found myself exploring numerous ideas but most seemed to be tweaks around economic and fiscal policy. How depressing to be given the keys to the kingdom and only being able to come up with subtle changes to accounting practice . . .

I fell back on frivolity, but I soon had to admit that trying to push my long-held dream of a country where the wearing of white jeans was compulsory would only result in (misplaced) derision. Reluctantly, it was back to square one.

What had seemed like a brilliant opportunity was now proving harder than I'd thought. We've all become victims of a world with too many choices. I was feeling as overwhelmed as I do when I sit in front of Google and think, *I can find out about anything in the history of mankind*, before searching for photos of dogs who look like deceased rock stars.

I took a deep breath and went back to first principles. *Imagine, Alan!* Of course, what came to mind was John Lennon – a man in a white suit (not jeans, sadly) singing about having no possessions while driving around in a white Rolls-Royce. No, that wouldn't do either.

There was only one drastic option left.

I went to the pub, where all great ideas originate.

Cocktail in hand, salt and vinegar crisps open on the table before me, fake coal fire twinkling, my protean thoughts began to take shape.

How about a country where education was an end in itself and not the means to an end? Fully funded universal further education just for the hell of it, and not in order to gain access to a career you don't even want. You wanna study Renaissance art? Go for it, Leonardo. Fancy a spot of Penguinology? It's all yours, Joe. A degree in modern dance? Darcy, darling, you simply must.

Oh yes, I'd like that.

Or how about a country where governments implement long-term policies for the greater good, and not just in order to win the next election. That sounds nice.

Anyone care for a country where it's not been left to children to highlight the most pressing issue of the age, while the blinkered adults wring their hands, muttering that most repugnant of all words, 'real-politik'? I think I'd like that too. Even though it would mean being simultaneously humbled and inspired by those children who actually care about something.

Then, crisps finished, I downed the last of my tasty beverage, and as the barman turned off the mock coal fire I finally settled on my answer. There are many, many ways in which this or any other country could be improved, but most of all – and this finally is my simple pitch – just picture what it would be like to imagine a country where the need to imagine a better country was no longer necessary. Imagine me that, please.

And of course, we all wear white jeans.

Alan McCredie is a photographer and lecturer and the author of several books. Originally from Perth, he now lives in the warmer climes of sunny Leith.

COLIN MCCREDIE

I imagine a new Enlightenment.

I imagine a country with a brand new subject on the school syllabus. A subject for five- to eighteen-year-olds. A subject not taught in a classroom. A subject with no final exam nor any homework.

A study out of school and across the length and breadth of Scotland.

An investigation to take place in art galleries, cinemas or even fields.

This is not a replacement of something else already brilliantly taught in our education system. This is something to complement the lives of our young people. And not just for a few periods but for one whole day a week to be released from the shackles of school. A world where our children can march to a different rhythm and where they can beat the drum of youth.

An education where the proscenium arch will replace the smart board.

The things that inspired and shaped me to become the person I am didn't occur in the school I attended or the provincial town I grew up in. It was when I was immersed in a workshop with the Scottish Youth Theatre or stuck to the sprung floorboards of the Barrowlands. My 'wow' moments were more likely to appear in the unassuming church halls of the Edinburgh Fringe. From grand playhouses to dank comedy clubs, it wasn't just what I saw or took part in. It was the places, buildings and people that ignited a fire in me. Barely a handful of kids in Scotland ever get this chance, but I dream of getting every child out of school, around the country and into the arts.

I want to take them on an Arts Trip.

My vision is a subject without form. An experience forged by sound, music, words and the senses presented to them. A pulsating, technicolour, visual journey through art and the landscape of our country. Throw open the doors of our amazing palaces of art and let our young people embrace our finest artists. Let them sample it. Love it or loathe it. No post-mortem or post-show discussion needed. Just breathe it all in, for next week it will be something or somewhere exhilaratingly new. A day when playtimes really will mean Play Times.

Forget the cost, the logistics or an in-demand actor's availability, and imagine a country like this. I know some might find it poncey, pretentious or po-faced. I know they'd rather be on Snapchat, Insta or YouTube. However, it might just be slightly more appealing than double maths in a sweaty classroom! I know some will moan and claim it's not for them, but hopefully somewhere along this journey something might click.

Can you dare to imagine a timetable like this?

Week 1	Irvine Welsh and Denise Mina at Edinburgh International Book Festival
Week 2	*Black Watch* by Gregory Burke at Pitlochry Festival Theatre
Week 3	Emeli Sandé at Aberdeen's P&J Live
Week 4	Oscar Marzaroli Retrospective at Glasgow Gallery of Modern Art
Week 5	Field trip to V&A Dundee
Week 6	Craig Armstrong film scores with the RSNO at the Usher Hall
Week 7	David Mackenzie's *Outlaw King* at the Glasgow Film Theatre
Week 8	James McAvoy in *Macbeth*, presented by National Theatre of Scotland in Birnam Wood
Week 9	Susan Calman's *Standing Up for Laughs* at Ayr Gaiety
Week 10	The Best of Celtic Connections at Perth Concert Hall

The best of Scotland. The best of art. Free to every pupil in Scotland. Released from their desks and let loose to be inspired and entertained.

My goal is to create a generation and a country with art at their very core. Where every pupil leaving school has been immersed in the best our country can offer. And to take this with them out into the world and beyond.

This is my dream. This is my hope. This is Scotland. This is the country I imagine.

Colin McCredie grew up in Perth and is an actor best known for playing DC Stuart Fraser in Taggart.

SHEENA MCDONALD

I went to visit my sole cousin Jim, who has lived in deepest rural France since his retirement from merchant banking, and where he has spent seven years of time, energy and euros on transforming a dilapidated property into his own fiefdom. He has spacious rooms, a small swimming pool and a large barn which houses several fast cars. Leather furniture and a huge TV screen. It is luxurious – but not *my* idea of the ideal place to live.

So imagining 'the kind of country we all want to live in' which 'does not exist yet' is not so much a challenge as something of a utopian impossibility! We all have very different dreams and ambitions.

I might timidly venture that my urban nirvana (I am no country girl, although I love to visit) might have car-free city centres – and then I remember that my mother fondly recalls the days when one could park outside Jenners on Princes Street in Edinburgh. She craves a return to her good old days.

And Edinburgh City Council is already well on the way to reducing car-use in my home city.

I could reel off the familiar liberal ambitions: protected and monitored free speech; realistic civil liberties; an ecologically sustainable environment peopled by inclusive, selfless folk; sufficient funding to support a year-round spectrum of artistic and cultural activities – but there's nothing provocative in those thoughts. I could ignore sport! That's racy! But my pre-teen niece not only plays four instruments but also enjoys scuba-diving and kayaking.

In her country she would own a (self-cleaning) dog . . .

We know that in our future country driver-free electric cars will fill what streets still allow vehicles, and robots will form a great proportion of the workforce, freeing us up to live life at its fullest, supported by a basic individual income. (Such a country actually stretches the imagination . . .)

And then it happened. I found inspiration in a book written in 1927 and reissued last year by Edinburgh publisher Polygon. Its author, John Buchan, was a child of the manse like me. He was no Bible-bashing evangelist – as *Witch Wood* demonstrates. Nor am I. But in David Sempill, the minister of a Lowland rural parish who attempts to serve his parishioners with mercy and empathy, Buchan has created a hero for any age, and as provocative a voice as one could wish for.

These are the words that leapt off the page. Sempill is being upbraided for not conforming to the fire-and-brimstone traditions of the time (the early seventeenth century, although the narrative and characters seem contemporary and completely recognisable). His response is clear: 'I am a minister of Christ first and of the Kirk second.'

You may never have stepped into a church, or have abandoned your childhood practices. No matter at all. Forget ministers, and church buildings. Set God aside for now. Dare to take a look at the New Testament. Read what it records and recommends. I swear there is no better – nor more provocative – code of conduct for our future. The key is that any imagined future must serve others, as well as me and mine.

Church attendances are dwindling. Fewer people refer to Jesus without embarrassment – or the kind of zealotry that is lampooned in *Witch Wood*! But mighty words were spoken and recorded 2,000 years ago. For instance – and this is a hard call! – 'Love your neighbour as yourself.' Think about it . . .

And if you're feeling lively, try this, written by John, author of one of the four gospels: 'This is love: not that we loved God, but that he loved us.'

In other words, you cannot dodge the grace of God; you can ignore it or reject it, but it is there – immutably. John is pithier.

I should not be surprised to find myself writing this: I was provoked by a book.

Perhaps my imagined country is a library-cum-bookshop. You can buy a book in the shop, or tackle your chosen provocation in the library. Who knows? You may even find yourself nestling into a leather sofa.

Sheena McDonald is a journalist and broadcaster.

HORSE MCDONALD

I was brought up in central Scotland in the sixties. I vividly remember my early childhood as full of carefree, sunny, dreamy days. I felt safe and secure in myself. It wasn't always perfect, but that core memory sustained me, especially through my teens, when I was bullied and chased because of what I was. I was different and I knew that I could never, ever, not be myself. It was a precarious existence, walking a tightrope, always in fight or flight mode. But it was the dreaming that kept me alive, dreaming of my possible future. Reality was too hard. I sang for my life and held fast to those dreams.

Every child deserves love – simple, unconditional love. It empowers and shapes perceptions and wider relationships for life. But today's children barely seem to blink before life smacks them hard in their faces.

In his infinite wisdom, and rightly so, my father would often yell at us, 'Pull up the ladder, I'm all right, Jack.' I understand his sarcasm now. What *have* we become? We are selfish and greedy. When we don't get our own way we get 'shouty', we get angry. We blame other people. We are arrogant and believe ourselves superior to others. We are judge and jury, goading people, plying digital hate-speech. Today's peer pressure comes from complete strangers on an *app*. We are our own worst enemies – at best unkind, at worst cruel. Have we totally lost our instincts and moral boundaries?

I am incredibly proud to be Scottish. I think of my fellow Scots as kind and welcoming, but in reality, this has not always been my experience and I know I'm not alone in that. In my imagined country, no one is made to feel ashamed of who they are or put down for their race, creed, religion, disability, gender or sexuality. We've made huge strides but such prejudice persists and it's not acceptable. We really are 'all Jock Tamson's bairns' and we *all* have value. We have to stop shouting and listen more. We have to work together and encourage mutual respect and tolerance. Everyone needs a sense of belonging.

My recipe for change is simple. Kindness costs nothing – a simple act of kindness daily would make us all feel good.

Our sense of 'family' is different from previous generations, but a broad and extended family is still essential for healthy community: children are our future, but our elders are our pearls of wisdom. As we grow older there's a common notion that our time is up and that we no longer have value. This is *not* true. We must honour our ageing population. We could begin by creating shared space for these two groups in society who have little control over what happens to them. They truly demonstrate the simple things that make us happy. I've seen several moving documentaries in which under-fours attend care homes for the elderly. They learn about each other and have shared tasks. They bond quickly and, in their own ways, respect each other.

Researchers determined that in these projects all adults' physical and mental functions improved dramatically. The children did not see age as we do. They adored these elders as if they were trusted family members. I'd love to see this intergenerational connection more widely adopted. By a natural osmosis, we could potentially redefine relation- ships and remove stigma. That's kindness in action.

Also at the heart of my imagined country is play. We all age phys- ically, but we can still be children at heart. I strongly advocate *play*. Play with music, play with paint, play with words. Sing, join together, use our voices. Dare to have fun. Reintroduce these core, natural, creative elements back into our education system and our daily lives and we will change lives for the better. Being creative is such good medicine.

John Muir said: 'Everybody needs beauty as well as bread, places to play in and pray in, where nature may heal and give strength to body and soul.' We are lucky: Scotland is utterly beautiful! We are blessed to live here. Let us go to the sea, to the mountains, forests and rivers, recognise the creatures that we share this country with and do what is necessary to protect and make all of this sustainable. Go back to having sensory or tactile experiences . . . and breathe!

But above all, we should be kind. If we embrace, support and celebrate every person in our rich and diverse country we *will* thrive. So, dare to dream! We shall all tak' a cup o' kindness yet.

Horse is the iconic Fife-born singer-songwriter with an award-winning career spanning over three decades, one of the Saltire Society's 'Outstanding Women', and 'One of the finest singers in Britain' (Q magazine).

BEN MCKENDRICK

The country that I imagine is one that I want both of my children to grow up in. It's one where everyone is treated with kindness, dignity and respect.

It's one where they, and every other child, live free from fear and want.

Until recently, it was difficult to imagine many people would disagree with that sentiment.

But the language some world leaders are using in 2019 seems to focus on division and difference rather than on unity and shared humanity, and I find that terrifying.

Words matter, especially when they are uttered by the powerful. Not being vigilant about that has the potential to take the world to a very dark place indeed.

But for the moment let us imagine that we all share this vision that everyone should be treated with kindness, dignity and respect, and ask ourselves instead:

How can we achieve that?

How can we turn those words into action and make this vision reality?

We can do this, if we so choose, by taking a human-rights-based approach to everything that we do – in our communities, in our regions and in our nation.

The concept of universal human rights was conceived after the horrors of the Second World War. The Universal Declaration of Human Rights, drafted by the United Nations in 1948, states that 'the advent of a world in which human beings shall enjoy freedom of speech and belief and freedom from fear and want has been proclaimed as the highest aspiration of the common people'.

Lately, it has felt like that vision could easily slip away from us, as political debates and the words some leaders use become increasingly toxic, febrile and tribal – apparently deliberately so. Rhetoric that instructs others to 'go back' to where they came from, for example, sounds as if it has been designed to keep other human beings living in 'fear and want' because the colour of their skin or their perceived country of origin means they don't have the same rights as the rest of us.

Another path is possible, if we choose to take it: putting universal human rights at the centre of all that we do.

We can insist that everyone in Parliament and in government, national and local, has the rights of every human being at the heart of every decision that they make. Every law we enact would uphold and protect those rights, especially when it impacted on the rights of people whose voice might otherwise be seldom heard, or who are already in a vulnerable or disadvantaged situation.

We can make sure that everyone knows what their rights are. Everyone would have an equal right to take part in decision-making processes and to hold those in power to account for their actions. And as a last resort, when those rights are breached it would be clear to everyone how to redress that.

We should regard any breach of human rights as an indivisible attack on us all, and one that must be resisted. We are all humans. If rights are breached for anyone, we should all be appalled and stand in solidarity alongside those who are affected.

Our Parliament can do this already, by changing the way that it works. If it chooses to.

Our councils can do this already. If the politicians we elect choose to do so.

And so can our government. If it chooses to.

In our imagined country, we will incorporate all of the key United Nations human rights treaties into domestic law. That will give us a watertight legal framework for protecting our rights and for taking action when they are breached.

When we do all of these things, we truly will generate a paradigm shift. We will create a culture where everyone is genuinely treated with kindness, dignity and respect, and every human being can live free 'from fear and want'.

Ben McKendrick has worked in and around the political world in Scotland since early 2000, and is currently the Chief Executive of the Scottish Youth Parliament.

CAMERON MCNEISH

Some years ago I climbed up the Great Stone Chute above Coire Lagan in the Skye Cuillin. The Chute is a massive fan of loose scree that gives access to the high tops, but it's a tough route to the summits. For every step you take upwards, you feel as though you are slithering back two.

The reward at the end of all this hard physical graft is to stand atop one of the Cuillin's narrower summits, Sgurr Alasdair. In my experience there is nothing more humbling than to stand on the summit of a majestic mountain after you've sweated and toiled to reach it. Adrenaline and endorphins create a natural feel-good drug, and the views of the rest of the majestic Cuillin, rising straight from the western sea, remind you of your place in the natural world.

On this occasion, there was something else flittering through my mind, something related to the circumstances which had brought me to the Cuillin in the first place. I had been trying to gauge local feeling about the potential sale of these Cuillin mountains. John MacLeod of MacLeod needed cash to repair Dunvegan Castle and had put a For Sale notice on this iconic mountain range. What price Scotland's natural heritage?

As I stood, still trembling with the exertion of the climb, I couldn't help but wonder what it would feel like to own these hills. I very quickly reached the conclusion that MacLeod didn't actually own this landscape any more than I did. The emotion I experienced as I stood there on the crest of the peak was deeper than mere legal ownership. I felt I had gone through a rite of passage to become part of the fabric of the mountain, part of that community that is made of rock, light and air. That emotion didn't register as ownership, but kinship.

As a mountaineer I've always enjoyed this relationship, this kinship, with the land. By habitual resort, by unchallenged possession, by right of usage and by moral justification, if land like the Cuillin of Skye belongs to anyone it belongs to the community of Scotland. It belongs to the people – to care for it, to cherish it, to sow and reap its bounty. But the vast majority of Scots rarely get the opportunity to experience this sense of kinship. Land ownership in Scotland is still wrapped in Victorian values, an outdated system of land use that sees some 7 per cent of the people owning 84 per cent of the land.

Politically we still value land in Scotland in economic terms. I don't know of a single politician who values land in an aesthetic or philosophic sense. The all-too-familiar argument is that people and jobs come first. But the root of the word 'dominion' is *dominus*, which literally means a caretaker in the house, or a steward of the land. In that light we should consider the wisdom of the ecologist Aldo Leopold: 'We abuse land because we regard it as a commodity belonging to us. When we see land as a community to which we belong, we may begin to use it with love and respect.'

Under community ownership, land is certainly an asset to those who live there and when managed correctly it is capable of sustaining communities. In contrast, too much land in Scotland is managed on a monoculture basis. For example, environments are created not to benefit the local community but so that red grouse can thrive to be shot on a seasonal basis to make money for a single landowner.

Here in Scotland some curious anomalies exist. We take pride in the constitutional claim that sovereignty lies with the people. So why don't the people of Scotland own the land? Why is neither of our two national parks owned by the state? That's almost unheard of in the international community of national parks. And in the national park where I live about a quarter of the houses are reckoned to be second homes.

Much of Scotland's land is owned and managed as a kind of hobby for the wealthy. Some actually live here in Scotland, but many don't.

There isn't even a register to tell us who owns what! Scotland's thriving green-energy industry – wind, wave, tidal and hydro – doesn't make local communities more prosperous, but turns millionaire landowners into multi-millionaire landowners. The income from green energy could be used strategically to house local families, many of whom can't compete with the retirement and second-home market.

Land reform can change the face of Scotland from a feudal nation of declining communities (particularly in the Highlands and Islands) into a vibrant and populous nation. Land should be taxed according to value and used as a means to redistribute wealth. It's time to limit foreign ownership, restrict holiday-home ownership and increase community ownership of land. Only then will we see a repopulation of the Highlands and Islands, with more than enough glorious wild land for everyone who values a kinship with the high, wild and beautiful places.

Cameron McNeish is a mountaineer and author and is an Honorary Fellow of the Royal Scottish Geographical Society.

MARK MILLAR

We don't need jet-cars or hoverboards or teleporters for a better future. We just need everyone to switch their phones off. Not just because there's nothing worse than standing at a bus stop and hearing half the dialogue from a dozen conversations, or people walking through the street like nutcases, apparently arguing with themselves as they talk into a hands-free. We just need a break from the noise. Some time in our own heads again.

On the two-mile drive to school every morning, my wife and I are always amazed to see almost everyone looking down at a device while they walk, earphones plugged in to completely cut themselves off from their environment. Stand on one side of any train platform and every single face on the benches opposite has a blank, blue-coloured hue from their screens as they scroll to see where their friends are having dinner or to get updates on edited lives. The mental-health aspects of all this have been well documented, but the pernicious effect on social discourse troubles me more, complex issues reduced to binary arguments with the passion and mindlessness of an Old Firm squabble. In reality we agree with almost everyone on almost every issue of the day. People are generally very civilised and sensible and will tend towards correct moral solutions. Reduce an argument to 140 characters and it becomes the Coliseum.

Let's turn our backs on internet mobs. On the perpetually offended. On dehumanising people we disagree with on any particular issue. Let's switch off our phones and just talk to each other again, an ancient and global notion that doesn't rapidly escalate to either blockings or unfriendings. I own a phone, but it's a second-hand Nokia from 2002 and usually sits for days uncharged in a drawer, but I still manage to amble through life. I've given up on hectoring my friends with my political beliefs. I doubt we ever change their minds any more than celebrity endorsements swing us behind a politician or an argument. There's a reason there's a curtain on our polling booths. The people who built this fine nation were actually very smart, realising that threat and intimidation are a detriment to democracy and that privacy has an intrinsic value.

I'm not calling for a future where phone masts are pulled down, or for more, insidious government legislation to correct this odd new habit. Let's just be adults and switch these off ourselves. Let's enjoy the comfort of our own thoughts again and reject the narcissistic compulsion to share our every half-baked idea with several hundred people we met at a party fifteen years ago.

Imagine a country where we remember that everyone else is a human being, that we can love someone with a different opinion, and that those people who disagree with us, the objects of our white-hot online fury, are sometimes actually right.

Mark Millar is the New York Times *best-selling writer of* Kingsman, *and* Kick-Ass, *Marvel's best-selling graphic novel of all time. He is currently President of Netflix's Millarworld Division, where he produces and oversees new comics, TV shows and movies for the streaming giant.*

KATE MOLLESON

I n a remote fishing town on the west coast of Greenland is a music
school where the doors are never locked. Downstairs: coat rack (low),
boot rack (snowy). A tiny living room with hammocks and football
tables. Upstairs: pianos, violins, cellos, traditional Inuit drums. A small
team of teachers gives after-school lessons, free for anyone who wants
to learn. The place is buzzing. Raucous. Some children come to practise,
others just to be in the warmth. One shy eleven-year-old is curled into
a sofa in the corner of a rehearsal room. He hasn't signed up to learn
any particular instrument but in a whisper he tells me that being close
to other people playing music makes him feel calm. His teacher later
explains that for many of the children who use the school, parental
alcoholism is a recurring problem at home. Music is an escape, a spur,
a salve. Music is a safe house. My Greenlandic friend says that in traditional Inuit culture, it's taboo to talk about emotions or social issues. Not
so far from Scotland, I half-joke. My friend clarifies: it's taboo to discuss
such matters – but to sing about them is essential.

Imagine a country where every child has access to music. Where every
child can learn music for free. Where, from the first day of primary
school, making music is not seen as an extra thing or a posh thing –
but fundamental to how we learn, love and express ourselves. Where
the benefits of early musical exposure are available to all, not only to
those whose parents can pay. Because those benefits are seismic.

Take your pick of signifiers of mental, emotional and physical wellbeing. Self-confidence; teamwork; discipline; concentration; motor skills;
listening; sensitivity; ambition; self-identity; collective belonging; capacity

for nuance and creativity. The developmental positives of learning music are proven to the point of incontestable, regardless of whether a child keeps singing or playing in later life – and importantly, this isn't about creating a nation of virtuosos, though wouldn't that be a happy knock-on?

Perhaps I should put it another way. Imagine a country that denies its young people this most basic right to become their best selves.

Our northern neighbours act with good sense in this regard, teaching us clear lessons on why root support for the arts really works. Ever wondered about the inordinate number of Finnish conductors leading orchestras around the world? The explosive creative talent emerging out of Iceland, a country with the same population as Cardiff? In Helsinki, home to the world's most celebrated education system, seven-year-olds at state primaries learn Finnish and maths through singing. Not only can these children raise their voices beautifully, not only do Finland's musicians grow up to punch above their weight internationally, but the pervasive musicality feeds their linguistic and arithmetical prowess.

In the foyers of Reykjavik's waterfront concert hall, percussion sculptures hang in windows overlooking the fjord. These sculptures were handmade by local kids, all of whom learn music at school. The concert hall itself was built using public funds while the country watched its banks fail and its assets freeze. That prioritisation was no whimsy for this small northern nation where tourism is an economic survival tactic. Culture is no optional luxury: it is identity and it is industry.

Free music education is a patently achievable dream. Duty of provision should be shifted away from local councils and ring-fenced at national level – which would prevent any postcode discrepancy. Whether in Lerwick, Lockerbie, Leven or Lochaber, no school should have to choose between buying a few fiddles or retiling the loos. Every child should have the chance to learn music like a second language. Every child should have music as a safe house, doors unlocked. Imagine a country of expressive equals. Imagine a country that sings through its taboos.

Kate Molleson is a music journalist for the Guardian *and a presenter for BBC Radio 3.*

ABIR MUKHERJEE

I was five when my folks moved to Scotland, to a village just outside Hamilton in what is now South Lanarkshire but was then just plain Lanarkshire. I had, if you discount the weather, an idyllic childhood, spent amidst a loving circle of friends, family and schoolmates, close to open countryside yet within sniffing distance of the Tunnock's factory.

As a teenager, my horizons expanded: not too far, but far enough, taking those first tentative trips on the old orange trains of Strathclyde Passenger Transport to Glasgow, the city that would be the centre of my world for the next decade. Glasgow, with its galleries, museums, libraries, pubs . . . mainly its pubs.

It was Glasgow where I had my first pint, saw my first fitba match, had my first snog (the Glasgow Kiss isn't always a bad thing) and got my first job (in the days when the great sandstone buildings of George Square, St Vincent Street, Bath Street and Blythswood Square still housed banks rather than bars). But then I left, forced south like so many other Caledonian migrants before.

They say distance lends perspective, and perspective leads to understanding. In my case, it yielded the realisation that Glasgow, at least *my* Glasgow – the West End, the Merchant City; the Southside and the well-heeled suburbs beyond – was only ever half a city. There was the other half. Blighted by entrenched, unyielding poverty, the half that I knew existed but hardly acknowledged: the estates and housing schemes, cut off from the heart but still there, visible at speed from the M8 or from the sky on the final approach to the airport. Castlemilk was as alien to me as Calcutta. Easterhouse as foreign as Johannesburg.

And I'd accepted it without thinking, that crack in the soul of my city. Took it for granted with that other great shibboleth – the one that split the town between the Billy and the Tim.

What I didn't know when I lived there is the statistic that almost 40 per cent of children in Glasgow are born into relative poverty.

Almost 40 per cent . . .

Almost 40 per cent of the children born in my city will suffer greater health problems and social inequalities than the rest of us. Almost 40 per cent are significantly more likely to be obese, suffer more physical injuries, and have poorer general and mental health than their peers born into relative affluence. They're more likely to die in infancy, be born with low birthweight, and suffer higher levels of everything from tooth decay to teen pregnancy. As they grow older, they're likely to have poorer educational results, poorer job prospects and poorer life prospects, thus affecting the prospects of their children, the next 40 per cent.

And it's not just Glasgow. Persistent poverty blights the lives of one quarter of all Scottish children. *One quarter* – all but written off before they've even had a chance.

I'd like to imagine a country where the spectre of poverty is eradicated. Where each and every child and adult is given the opportunities that Scotland gave my family and me.

And it can be done.

It'll take investment. Cold hard cash invested in quality housing, education and amenities; and more cash for families who need it, to provide a decent, living wage to buy the things required to create a home environment conducive to learning and development.

But it'll also take more than money. It'll need the revitalisation of that spirit of self-improvement that working-class Scots were famous for, but which, since the destruction of our heavy industries and our tenement communities, the closure of our shipyards and the mothballing of our mines, seems to have died or at least to be on life support. It'll take the real rekindling of support networks and true community spirit.

None of it will be easy, but then don't we always like to do things the hard way? There's no reason why any of it should be beyond us.

And there's no escaping the fact that we need to do it. There aren't that many of us to start with, and we're writing off a full quarter almost from birth. What a waste of human potential; of national potential.

Imagine a Scotland without persistent poverty. Where every one of our brothers and sisters has a fair chance of attaining their full potential. Imagine what we could do then as a nation.

Abir Mukherjee is the best-selling author of the Wyndham and Banerjee crime novels, set in Raj-era India. His books have been translated into fifteen languages.

ANTON MUSCATELLI

S cotland is at its best when we look outward – welcoming new ideas, new cultures and new energies to our national landscape. In just the last century, new waves of immigration from Ireland, Italy, India, Pakistan, China, Poland and many other countries have at various points given our national identity a new lease on life.

Yet even the immense social and cultural contribution our many immigrant communities continue to make is possibly overshadowed by their economic contribution. In 2015 there were 181,000 non-UK EU nationals residing here, with higher employment rates than UK nationals for all age groups except 35–49-year-olds. Indeed, around 115,000 non-UK EU nationals aged 16 and over are in employment in Scotland – powering our economy and in many cases performing skilled roles that we simply would not be able to fill without them.

As Principal of the University of Glasgow, I see every day the genuinely world-changing work undertaken by my colleagues who've come here from other EU countries – from the arts and humanities, to the social and physical sciences, and biomedicine. In key areas of innovation for my university, like precision medicine, quantum technology and nanofabrication, and fintech, they are the lifeblood of the emerging industries which could be the basis of the Scottish economy for decades to come. That this is being put at risk by policies driven by populist politicians with scant regard for Scotland's specific needs is unthinkable.

It is fair to say Scotland's national conversation around economic migration hasn't been poisoned to the extent that we have seen across the rest of the UK. This is at least partially thanks to Scotland's political leadership – often across parties – being willing to set out the facts and make the positive argument for immigration.

But while we may be spared some of the worst excesses of the scapegoating and negative rhetoric, we will not be spared their conse-quences. While most of Scotland's recent increases in population have been due to EU migration, figures show that by 2041 Scotland's pensioner population is expected to rise by around 265,000, while our working-age population is to rise by only 38,000. Without freedom of movement and the increased migration from EU countries this would bring, the hit to our economy could be monumental.

This will not simply make itself felt through slight falls in GDP figures, which barely register with ordinary people. If we were to see a significant decline in the number of EU nationals contributing to Scotland's tax base post-Brexit, there would be a direct impact on the resources the Scottish Parliament has at its disposal to fund the NHS, education and other core services we all rely on – almost certainly hitting the poorest people in our society the hardest.

The case for Scotland to have its own immigration system tailored to our specific needs is unanswerable – even those who would deny the moral and social argument cannot deny the bare economic facts staring them in the face.

We in Scotland should not be wasting a second of our time discussing precisely how best to pull up the drawbridge and restrict migration when this is exactly the opposite of what we need. And even more to the point, nobody else should be discussing that on our behalf.

The key questions for Scotland in the coming years will be whether we can build a society and an economy that works for everyone – with truly inclusive growth ensuring no community is left behind – and whether we can marshal our collective skills and energies to join with others across Europe and the world to meet some of the huge global challenges we all face.

From the climate emergency to the migration crisis, Scotland has a valuable contribution to make to what need to be cross-border, collective responses to these important issues – and it would be an act of national negligence if we were to turn our backs and look the other way.

We will simply not be able to play our full part in these endeavours or meet our full potential without the many economic, social and cultural benefits brought by those born outwith our shores but who wish to make Scotland their home – and to refuse to use all of these talents would see us diminished in every way.

Instead, let us build an open, inclusive immigration system designed to fit an open and inclusive country – and let the next generation of people who wish to make their lives here leave their mark on our constantly evolving national identity.

Professor Sir Anton Muscatelli is Principal and Vice-Chancellor of the University of Glasgow. An economist, his research interests include monetary economics, central bank independence, fiscal policy and international finance.

JEMMA NEVILLE

Dear Sula,

Daughter of mine, mini-maker and artist-to-be.

Here is a story. A true story about imagination.

Once upon a time, there was a hut in the woods where good ideas grew tall. This is a time in the future, the not-too-distant future. So really it should be once upon a time, there will be a hut in the woods where good ideas will grow tall. And, baby girl, you will have grown taller by then too. The woods will not be a distant, magical place. They will be a near and real place full of rowan, birch, alder and oak. And rather than a hut, it will be a cabin. A cabin with a log fire, bookshelves lined with poetry, sturdy walking boots at the door, a very comfortable bed and a big table at which to eat, think and make.

What's the difference between a hut and a cabin? Quite a lot, potentially. When a group of mostly elected and sometimes clever people gather around a big table to discuss important matters of state, it is called a Cabinet. There is a Scottish Government Cabinet chaired by the First Minister. The word comes from the name for a small and private space used as a study or retreat.

Your study or retreat in the woods for the nurturing of good ideas could be a cabin-et, if you will. The 'et' being all the ands that make it special and link it to a network of other studies or retreats for creative play in the woods. For example, it will be a private space for you while you stay, but you cannot keep it or sell it. It is not an exclusive holiday home for the few. You do not need deep pockets to stay. You need only normal-sized pockets in which to put any pine cones, shells or scribbled notes of the first good ideas that you find there.

The cabin is a thing of beauty but is not so achingly stylish that you will be shy about getting mud from the sturdy boots onto the floor or folding over pages of the poetry books you pick up from the shelves. Perhaps most importantly, you do not need to complete long application forms in advance to assess whether or not you will be creative enough. You will be enough because you are enough. You do not need to shape your ideas into narrow definitions of what art should or should not be. And, daughter of mine, any children or dependants you care for at home will be provided for while you stay here. Like this, your creative spirit can flourish without guilt, worry or financial hardship, in the same way as that of your twin brother's.

The cabin in the woods is yours for when you need some time to yourself. Quiet time, thinking time, messy time, making time. In the making time, you might sketch the outline of a great painting, compose the lyrics for a song, or write the chapter of a novel. But first of all, you will likely want to take naps in the big bed, skip through the woods as though you were a little girl again, sing loudly and joyously to the birds in the trees, or feast on the delicious food in the well-stocked cupboards. Then, and likely only then, will creative seeds tumble out of your pockets and take root on page, paper or paint.

The cabin, and the others like it, will be built and maintained by a network of cabin custodians, some of whom live nearby and so can be contacted if you need anything. Each will take pride in keeping things warm, safe and comfortable because they once benefited from a stay in the cabin too. And because some of their own ideas that grew tall were so good, they can afford to extend the hospitality. With this trust and love, free from the exhaustion of childcare responsibilities and the monotony of money-making work for just a few days, you will start to believe in the artist that you are. You, and all those who stay in the cabin from time to time, will become residents in art.

Nourished by rest, the fresh air and imagination, your confidence will soar. It is likely that good creative work will be made. You will know it is good because you will simply feel good. The only condition is that on leaving, you must pass the keys to the cabin on to another. It need not be someone who shares similar experiences and background to your own. Better that it simply be someone else in need of creative time and space. Then when you meet this new acquaintance, rather than asking *what do you do?* you might begin a conversation with *how do you do,* or even *how do you make?*

But all of that and more is ahead of you. For now, you have stories to hear and dens to make and play in.

Jemma Neville is mother to twins, feeds the birds every day and writes when she can; her first book, Constitution Street: finding hope in an age of anxiety, *is part memoir, part social history and a call to action.*

ANDREW O'HAGAN

The facts alone make self-love a cosmic joke.

Planet Earth has existed for 4.543 billion years. If you aren't from Glasgow and you don't eat too many Caramel Wafers and you don't fly a light aircraft, you could live to be ninety. And that will mean your vital existence – so beloved, so indispensable, so interesting – will have taken up exactly 0.00000198 per cent of the planet's history.

That's not very much.

You can halve that percentage for Robert Louis Stevenson, Montgomery Clift, and Anne Sexton (all of whom were dead at forty-five). You can reduce it a bit too for Abraham Lincoln, Mahatma Gandhi, Boadicea, and Mary Wollstonecraft. It's a blink from their time to ours, and their lives are infinitesimal in the grand scheme. So who are you to feel so significant?

I dream of a nation in which we are collectively and momentarily something because we are nothing much in ourselves. I dream of the death of narcissism. I dream of a country where we are ambitious for the world because we do not see it for long, and the world is our legacy, which gives us the freedom to plant wonder in place of our ego. It allows us to create radiance and fairness and make a golden helm of our visit.

Free at last from the movements of fear. Free from violence, which always begins in self-love, which always begins in self-hatred. Free from the need to conquer. Free to sow the betterment of those who will live beyond you, knowing that they will come to enjoy that freedom in their own turn, and thank you for the memory. Fellowship is an aid to self-governance in the minds of the free, an enjoyment of collective potential for its own sake. We are bored on our own, and ravaged by short concerns; we are drugged with needs, and soon gone from the scene of our self-importance. What is money, what is power, what are dominions and cars, but a passing tip to the delinquency of our unconnected selves?

We are lost where we love ourselves most. We are failing before the light. In the great denial of our unimportance we are bereft of reality. I imagine a country where brutality and exploitation are obvious acts of self-slaughter. I see a nation where the defilement of others is a mark of the plague, and narcissism the sport of slaves.

You are no longer stronger because others are weaker and no longer bright because they are dim. I dream of a world where the wee streets give direction to the great, where real people love the earth, and where single and ceaseless acts of kindness are the main currency in our exchange, with hearts open. I dream of a land where we enjoy our differences and where no one knows her advantage by hating others.

Nothing is too small for such a small thing as man. Decency is slow, carelessness is quick, and self-love is the denial of our place in time.

I dream of a world where narcissism died. The dream flowed from tenement building to island farm to redeem our better nature, and found us willing, and found us ready, and found us keen to live beyond the old habits of pain. Freedom, we said, eye to eye, let us make it new, year to year, and excel by knowing we are nothing much.

There are 7.7 billion people in the world. That means you represent 0.00000001299 per cent of living humanity.

That's not very much.

A great nation is an assemblage of people who know this.

Andrew O'Hagan writes novels and non-fiction stories and lives in London and Edinburgh.

GEOFF PALMER

I was born in St Elizabeth, Jamaica. My late mother and I are part of the Windrush Generation. She arrived in London in 1951, I joined her in 1955. Because I was one month shy of the school leaving age of fifteen, I had to go to school in London and that led me to many subsequent years of education and work in England and Scotland. My interest in Scotland's history began in about 2007 when I realised that surnames in my family included: Larmond, Mowatt, Gladstone Wood and Gordon. I also noticed that most of the surnames in the Jamaican telephone directory were Scottish.

Scotland's direct involvement with chattel slavery in the Caribbean extended from the seventeenth to the nineteenth century. During this period, slaves produced the likes of cane sugar, coffee, cotton and spices which helped to transform Scotland from a poor to a rich country. Scotland also exported products such as linen to clothe slaves, and ships that serviced this slavery. About 30 per cent of the slave plantations were owned by Scots. Servicing slavery also provided employment in many professions and trades such as business, management, medicine, engineering, building, surveying, the military, government and the law.

Scotland's historical links with slavery are reflected in the names of streets, roads and places in Scotland and the Caribbean. The majority of Scotland's heritage buildings were built with the profits from Caribbean slavery. But, until recently, this has been a hidden history. Taking responsibility for this brutal slavery, where a slave had 'no right to life' and could be 'murdered', has been difficult for some people who, for self-serving reasons, believe Scotland abolished slavery in 1778, well before the 1838 Act abolishing slavery in the British Empire, in which Scotland remained heavily involved. To compare the release from 'servitude' of the young black man Joseph Knight in Edinburgh in 1778 with the release of about 800,000 chattel slaves from a brutal slavery, where slave-owners were compensated for their 'property', is deception. Such national pride, perpetuating the falsehood that Scotland abolished slavery fifty-five years before England, is unacceptable.

In 2018, Glasgow University, after careful research, courageously declared that it had received about £200m in legacies from this slavery. As a result, the university has allocated £20m as part of a reparative justice programme in education, in partnership with the University of the West Indies. Glasgow will also provide scholarships to African and Caribbean students in the United Kingdom. On 23 August 2018, Glasgow University accorded me the great honour of unveiling a marble plaque in the memory of those who suffered chattel slavery. The plaque states that the university received benefits from slave-owners who profited from slavery, and commemorates the lives of those who suffered as slaves.

The reparative action of Glasgow University serves as a first and important light on the fact that we cannot change the past but we can change the consequences. Robert Burns described the slave-owner as having 'hands that took but never gave'. Glasgow University's action is the opposite: giving after taking.

Scotland has become a diverse society with a large non-white diaspora. Diverse societies require diverse attention to make a country a home. A sense of belonging gives people the confidence and contentment they need to contribute optimally to society. Diverse representation is an important feature of a just society because it eliminates the racism that recently led someone to assume I must be the chauffeur when I said I knew the boss.

Sadly, many of the 'equality rights' of our society have to be protected by laws. This reflects badly on our humanity. As human beings, we have the capacity to observe critically, reason fairly and act justly. It was pride in my slavery heritage and a strong sense of belonging that enabled me to take the opportunities which I used to teach students and contribute to my community.

The country I imagine will teach the truth about our national past, and only by doing this can we change attitudes and eliminate the racism that is a consequence of a cruel slavery. Then we can truly recognise that we are different but we have the same humanity; then we can say: 'We are Scotland.'

Professor Sir Geoff Palmer is a community-equality activist. In 2021 he assisted in changing Henry Dundas' plaque in Edinburgh, was awarded the Pride of Scotland Lifetime Achievement Award, became Chancellor of Heriot-Watt University and a Fellow of the Royal Institute of British Architects.

BILL PATERSON

I have a dream that won't save the planet, or force the rich to pay their taxes.

It's just a dream of a small island cutting the automobile down to size.

It began about sixty years ago when the times really started a'changin'.

For the first twenty years of my life, I spent every holiday on the Isle of Cumbrae in the Firth of Clyde.

Specifically, in the little town of Millport which wraps itself round the island's southern bays, turning its wee Victorian face pleadingly towards the sun.

Cumbrae's entire milage of public road, 'round the island' and 'the inner circle' was, and still is, about fifteen miles.

Five minutes cruising with Lewis Hamilton would cover it.

From the late forties to the early sixties, life on Cumbrae ticked along nicely with just a handful of four-wheeled vehicles.

Milk and coal were still delivered by horse-drawn wagons. The pier lorries and the two buses looked like they had recently survived the Normandy landings and the only private cars were a few ancient Humbers and Austins.

This gave Millport something of a reputation as a 'children's paradise'. Especially for children who lived for fifty weeks of the year on the dangerous streets of the biggest city in Scotland.

Thousands of summer residents arrived by paddle steamer from Wemyss Bay and a lot of them, of all ages, swarmed to the bike hire shops. A bike was as essential as footwear. A bike gave you the freedom of the island, and a bike on seaside roads without cars was paradise indeed.

We knew we were blessed, and the late polymath Jonathan Miller described these times as 'the last days of Eden'. He had studied at the Marine Biological Station at Keppel Pier and knew well the joys of Cumbrae.

Then, toward the mid-sixties, around the time that Dylan went electric, the summer hordes from Glasgow and Paisley abandoned the Clyde and fled to sunnier shores. Life would never be the same for the shops and businesses that had thrived since the first steamers had called at the Old Pier.

Little did they know it, but Millport and its couthy town council were facing an existential choice. Preserve the island as a more-or-less car-free haven, or lay down the red carpet for the vehicles that would pour off the proposed new slipway opposite Largs?

I doubt they gave it a second thought.

As on most of the planet, there was no contest. The car simply had to win. It brought a glorious new kind of freedom to the individual even if it imposed itself brutally on society as a whole, and that included Millport.

So, in 1972, they came.

Rolling on and rolling off, loaded with supplies from the mainland that would make them self-sufficient for at least a couple of weeks.

Never mind that the local grocers, bakers, dairy and half of the bike shops pulled down the shutters for good.

Never mind that driving on a small island could only bring you back without fail to the place that you had left twenty minutes earlier.

Never mind that the cars would languish by the town's kerbsides for a couple of weeks and make cycling and walking nearly as little fun as in Paisley.

A few of us, in the spirit of the sixties, shared Joni Mitchell's antipathy towards paving paradise and putting up parking lots, and thought that there might be another way.

We started to imagine an island.

Perfectly proportioned, easily accessible, close to a big city.

A wee bit of the Hebrides thirty miles as the seagull flies from Sauchiehall Street.

We were hearing about lots of islands across the world that had turned their backs on the automobile. Places like Mackinac in Lake Huron, Lopud in Croatia, and Sark.

They seemed to be doing fine.

Paradise could be regained, with a huge market waiting in the wings. We'd lose some but we'd win more.

It seemed such an obvious idea for Cumbrae.

However, you'll be familiar with the phrase 'swimming against the tide', and tides are strong and deep in the Firth of Clyde.

No one in power had any interest in our hippy dippy ideas. Millport became just like any other town.

Now I'm well into my eighth decade and wondering if I've come full circle round the island. Could Cumbrae be freed again from the tyranny of the automobile?

The smart technology of today could make feasible that Sixties dream. Charging and technology can control which vehicles are useful and which are more trouble than they're worth. Low traffic neighbourhoods are all the rage. In both senses of the word, if London is anything to go by.

Me, I'm imagining a country by imagining an island and keeping the dream alive.

Born in Dennistoun, Glasgow, Bill Paterson was a founder member of 7:84 Scotland, and his work includes The Cheviot, The Stag and The Black Black Oil, Comfort and Joy, Aufwiedersehn Pet, The Singing Detective, Smileys People, Outlander *and* Fleabag; *he received a Lifetime Achievement Award from BAFTA Scotland in 2015.*

DON PATERSON

As Scottish independence begins to look less like a dream than an inevitability, my idle thoughts have turned from the vegan Lorne sausage and the elf-staffed high-speed inter-Hebridean rail network to more urgent matters. I would hope that our immediate energies as a new country would be directed towards tackling social inequality. And I think there's a way of doing it which could also harness that energy to drive a cultural renaissance.

A universal basic income would largely replace the benefit system with something wholly more dignified and infinitely less worrisome (and, by some estimates, cheaper). It would supply a wage for traditionally unremunerated but intense forms of labour (predominately, though certainly not exclusively, still carried out by women) such as childcare, care-giving and housework. It would also provide security for the many folk in erratic or low-paid employment: a UBI bump would guarantee not just our nurses and junior teachers a better living wage, but all those forced to take piecemeal or gig-economy work in restaurants, delivery services, factories, call-centres and warehouses to sustain themselves and their families. And finally – my only original contribution to this debate – it would supply a basic wage for young 'cultural contributors'.

A UBI is not a panacea, of course, and would have to be matched with other changes. There is a danger that the school-leaver–graduate divide (the most potentially turbulent social division we'll have to face in the immediate future, and one already starting to pull England apart) could be widened by UBI's too-thoughtless application, and so broadening access to higher education needs to be addressed as UBI is introduced, especially as we head towards a four-day week and a job market shrinking through automation and AI. The very culture of work will need consideration too, because the dignity, community and sense of empowerment lent by work is too often understated by its proponents. We have to do more for folk than cover only the most basic of their needs. However, these needs do have to come first.

Moving on to my second point: if New Scotland wants to guarantee a healthy and flourishing culture, it has to be bold enough to invest directly in its young and early-career artists and cultural contributors. I'd like to see the domain of 'the arts' extended to all those who make a tangible contribution to the culture – and include our comedians, vloggers, political bloggers, DJs, literary journalists, rappers and independent scholars too. UBI can support this.

I believe grant funding to be a pretty flawed paternalistic model: it's far too limited in its scope, and creates too much of the wrong kind of competition at the wrong stage of an artist's development. A lump of cash is no substitute for steady, nurturing support, for mentorship, or for funded scholarship. Young artists mostly need to buy time, and lots of it.

Should anyone think I'm proposing the state should afford these folk a comfortable living, my answer is an emphatic 'no'. There's nothing wrong with artists finding it tough going in the early part of their career. I merely mean the kind of low-level support that a lax and indifferent dole office inadvertently offered me at a young age, when I was signing on as an unemployed shepherd (sheep-related work was pretty thin on the council estate back then), and I needed to spend my days doing nothing but writing or practising, while not distracted by hunger or cold. UBI would supply this minimal support, and likely result in an explosion in the arts. And if I may be blunt: unless Scotland wants an artistic and cultural class populated entirely by the family-subsidised middle classes, it should give *everyone* who is sufficiently driven the opportunity to put in their 10,000 hours of piano practice without wondering where their next Pot Noodle is coming from. It would do so in the knowledge that whatever percentage of good art that then emerges is part of the common weal.

As for our mature and proven talent: 'art is not a democracy', and I have long advocated for a Scottish equivalent of the Irish charmed circle of Aosdána for our 'national treasures', which would come with a modest, means-tested annual stipend. I don't think any of our major artists should be put through the indignity of applying for small arts grants to not starve in their old age. But while *all* arts funding will continue to be the low-hanging fruit for those – sincerely or insincerely – looking for 'economies', everyone knows this is peanuts in the scheme of things. Either way, regardless of how we choose to properly fund the arts – and whatever fag-packet estimate you arrive at – chalk off what you've just saved by not paying for the renewal of Trident, and haud yer wheesht. These are peanuts which will grow us oak forests.

Don Paterson is a poet and musician, and the author of many books of poetry, aphorism and criticism. He is Professor of Poetry at St Andrews University and Poetry Editor for Picador Macmillan.

MARY PAULSON-ELLIS

H er shift began before it was even light. She'd never been good in the mornings. Or perhaps it was just that every day she woke and thought of him. Six months since her father died and still the first thing. She got up, showered, ate breakfast standing at the window. The curtains were drawn on the house opposite. It had been five days now and she'd never seen them open once.

Work was busy. Decent weather for the time of year. Also football season, dips and peaks every weekend to be tracked and reported. Plus the latest internationals, which always tended to fall on the positive side of the graph, win or lose. They still saw sparks when folks talked of the World Cup campaign ten years before, all those women on the pitch carried home like conquering heroes. A demographic quirk, that's what they'd dismissed it as at the time. But there were a lot more collective activities to track now as a result – festivals and grow-a-thons, raves, talking-shops, leap-overs and choirs. The country was alive with it: stuff to cement the new nation whatever its divides.

On the edge of her desk was a small plant pot, a cluster of winter crocuses rising from the earth like slender ghosts. Ari. He understood. His mother has been gone three years and some mornings he still looked haunted. Or perhaps that was just the work. The Great Pandemonium was due in May, everything had to be ready, five years of data tracked, crunched and pored over. The wealth of a nation. She swiped at the holograph to open the various matrices, wondered what would come out on top this time. Judging by the tax tables, Joy and Consolation had proved pretty successful in filling the nation's coffers. Perhaps they would get a second term. Though she knew there'd be the usual arguments about the best terms to elect, regardless. The algorithms were so sophisticated these days, could capture even the smallest iota of emotion. Meaning the campaigns would be loud, raucous even. Her country always had been disputatious when it came to language. But generally speaking most people didn't mind. Or even think of it now, their overall contribution. They just got on with life. What mattered was being human. Humans being who they were.

She let the AI run its course, a swirl of data visualising before her. It presented like a coruscating map of light, similar to those returned by the latest universe explorer. She stared into the mass, wondered about checking the house opposite. Illegal, but still . . . She'd tracked herself, of course. A dark spot of grief, nothing to contribute these past six months. Sometimes there wasn't anything you could do.

The UBI continued its sturdy, underpinning work. More than twenty years old and still the most popular benefit in the country. They'd made an excellent decision when they tagged receipt of that to personal tracking. *A right stramash*, that was how her dad had remembered the fallout. But everyone hosted wearable tech of one sort or another by then, gave all their data away for free. So shifting it to the public rather than the private sector and making the latter pay made sense to her. The Great Easing, that was what the result became known as once the numbers were in, as though the nation had exhaled in relief, let down its collective shoulders. Nobody ever suggested getting rid of a universal basic income now.

As the data updated, she studied the winter crocuses, their translucent stems and tender lilac tips. Ari cultivated all sorts in his flat, a beautiful melange of growth. He could sell them for hard cash if he wanted. Anything could be monetised, and usually was, including the chosen terms. But Ari did it for a different reason. *Pleasure*. Something that always rode high in the polls. She understood. A country's wealth lay in what it passed on, not how much cash it could hoard, that was what her father had taught her. *You can't take it with you*, he'd said on his deathbed. *Might as well spend it while you can.*

She ate samosas for lunch, crunched data, got her reports in order, thanked Ari for the flowers. As she left, there was still a low light in the sky. When she got to her street she turned to the house opposite, slid the pot of winter crocuses onto the doorstep. She smiled as she walked away, imagined a tiny uptick on the index, perhaps even two. Tomorrow it would be dark when she woke, her father would still be dead, work would be busy. But it would be a good day.

Mary Paulson-Ellis lives in Edinburgh where she writes novels about the world of people who die with no apparent next of kin; she likes wandering in graveyards.

MICHAEL PEDERSEN

M e, I'm a thrice-weekly cross-city cultural pollinator of the Central Belt. Flummoxed? Sorry, sorry, this isnae a funding application. What I'm saying is: I live in one city (Glasgow), work in another yin (Edinburgh) and bounce between the two by the train right regularly. I travel off-peak and buy return tickets. At just 10p above the single fare it's a veritable bargain to pinball back then forth compared to a solo voyage.

Yet frequently, I – and thousands like me – must make that single trip, no return, not this spin of the moon. Despite knowing we're heading in a singular direction, I – and hunners like me – still purchase the return ticket. *Ach, it's only pennies more eh, value fur money!* The mind boggles for where the spare might end up – a penumbra in the day's forward plan. The difference is a bit more on other journeys but no over much. Remember, you can only get a *day* return on the Central Belt express.

Many get the return out of haste or indolence: it's one of the more prominent ticket choices on the home page and seeking out a single involves a few additional clicks and a clutch more seconds. Many in the train stations are rushing, sometimes forgetting that they're not coming home.

A potpourri of valid considerations come to mind (me to you) on the unallotted return coupon:

1. There's the off-chance something crops up and you might huv tae rush back. It's a 10p insurance policy.
2. Perhaps you'll bump into someone you know in the destination

station or throughout the course of your day who needs this very ticket. Such a gift would credit worthy adulation.

3. You might be a more avaricious or entrepreneurial human and fancy a whirl at haggling a sale with a stranger on the other side. Such business is for the gallus or charmed, as people can be right suspicious souls.

Me, I canter towards the machines at Edinburgh and place my spare ticket on its ledge in the hope someone finds it before making a purchase. I have both witnessed this and been on the receiving end of it. Such a find wiz a sprout of life through well-crunched frost, luck-touched, a stroke of the fiscal fortunate.

Alas, the vast majority of impetuously purchased return tickets end up orphaned – ripe and bawling, bowled into buckets or discarded on whim. All the commitment of a kiss that missed. Caught in one of Scotland's sideways gusts, many too will blow off the ledge to be minced into Hubba Bubba and splodged to the bottom of boots. A more cynical gadgie might say train-station staff are instructed to whip them off like flakes fae ice-cream cones to keep the profit margins in check.

So, let's firm this up, a furtive fox into yer lion rampant. I'm talking a big beauty of a box to harbour unwanted tickets needing put to use. I've yet to consult a box designer about how to best handle the melange of destinations on offer but know there's a bright mind out there with the perfect solution.

You pluck the ticket free from the nest, no strings attached. That said, there's the option of making a charitable donation by text or plopping some coins into one of the pots dangling around it. But, hey, the only real obligation is that yer thankful – it's a model of soundness (as Blindboy would say).

Some folks might save a little on their day-to-day journeys, others might make a day trip out of it – after aw, there'll be the odd return ticket in there for a jamboree of reasons and you can aw'wiz chance it at the other end.

An evolution of this idea sees you donating not money but time and conversation. That's taking a seat on the (newly commissioned) chatty coach – the more exuberant sibling of the quiet coach – a section of the train where people listen to and share stories on journeys with folks looking fur a bit of company. A spattering of seats, on the off-peaks, for folks keen to spread them conversational butters. For the lost, tired, bored and lonely, for storytellers wi secrets to spill. Sometimes people have faces that just don't smile very much, a well-hidden sort of friendly.

It's just train travel and not part of the central nervous system of a country coruscating towards betterment, sustainability, equality, venerability, humanitarianism, prosperity and the ethical realms we hope to roam in. But why not come together in comradery over distances travelled? And here's hoping there's something bolder, a more-ness, in there. If you can afford to, pay a little extra to help someone along their way. It's a seeping sentiment, which might well glacial-creep into your approach to all sentient beings, the work beyond.

Michael Pedersen is a prize-winning poet with his first prose book, Boy Friends *(Faber), just printed. He's a frequent traveller of trains.*

FRANK QUITELY

When I imagine the country I'd like to live in it's not so different from present-day Scotland, but there would be a few notable improvements.

I immediately imagine us finding a fairer system for owning and managing our land; sustainable ways of reforesting and rediversifying; responsible and effective ways of creating energy; new approaches to managing waste; and re-evaluating the potential of our city centres.

But these are Big Challenges.

More often I imagine a country where everyone is happier.

They're happier in themselves and with their place in the world because the work they're doing is in harmony with who and what they are.

We all know people who love the work they do.

Whether it's rearing children, driving taxis or running companies, the overwhelming majority of those who get the best results, provide the best service, and generally excel, are those who are doing work they enjoy. They're also happier, more fulfilled, and healthier in mind and body which, in turn, has a positive knock-on effect for family, friends and society in general.

We all know people like this but they're the exception rather than the rule.

Imagine if we had a system of education that had as its universal goal loving your working life.

It would start with a preschool and primary education that prepared children for life through play, active experience and storytelling.

There would be an inspiring introduction to the natural and the constructed world around us: local history; the weather, seasons, and climate; food and the food chain; mental and physical health; cooking, caring and home–life management; broad and inclusive sexual and social education; mindfulness and relating positively to others; all religions and philosophies; art, music and drama; but also the three Rs, because they're tools that help us navigate the world.

All of these strands would continue in secondary school at a more advanced level, with sciences, languages, technical and modern subjects being gradually introduced. But there would be a crucial additional approach. All suitable subjects would be additionally examined in terms of Story. We'd learn how Story has shaped our evolution from prehistory to the present day, and our education would pay particular attention to Story in religion, politics, the media and social media. It would be a system of schooling that gave the broadest introduction to life, self and other, and encourage the individual to tailor their timetable to suit their developing interests, strengths and goals.

As things stand now, there's a definite perceived hierarchy when it comes to the next stage of education. University is seen as the pinnacle of achievement, with other paths considered to be less demanding or less valuable. In my imagined country, the tertiary stage would be a stepping stone from adolescence to adulthood and would involve a wide range of further specialisation towards gainful employment that suited the skills, temperament and ambitions of the individual. A stage that, through further education, training or apprenticeship, would give the best possible grounding in their work of choice. People would emerge into the workplace with a sense of excitement and enthusiasm.

Imagine a country where people loved what they did, where they felt suited to their work, and where they all chose their own path. Such a country would make light work of those aforementioned Big Challenges.

Frank Quitely (aka Vincent Deighan) was born in Glasgow and works there still, drawing comics, illustrating things, writing stories, doing what he loves.

IAN RANKIN

I magine . . .
   Imagine: no poverty; the best healthcare; good housing available to all who need it; no racism or sexism or sectarianism.

Imagine: great education available to all; no violence or greed; safe streets; no weapons; no drugs crisis; prisons that work; clean air and clean seas and clean rivers.

Imagine: happy, contented people; less traffic congestion; wider accessibility for the disabled; more creativity; less cringe; more empathy; less anger and shouting and polarisation.

Imagine: a country with enough meaningful and satisfying jobs; a country that looks after its old and its young; a country with no graffiti or litter; a country that doesn't poison its land and its wildlife and its birdlife.

Imagine: an enlightened country; a truly democratic country; a beacon; a place of welcome, ready to move on from the errors and terrors of the past, ready to embrace the future.

Imagine all of that and more, because I'm only just scratching the surface here.

Just imagine it.

I've tried and I'll admit I've failed. But I'm happy to try, try and try again.

Ian Rankin is a novelist and creator of Detective Inspector John Rebus. He lives in Edinburgh.

EDDI READER

This morning, flying to London from Glasgow, I picked up a free newspaper. On the front page it proclaimed: 'Britons Happier When Victoria Was on the Throne'.

After cleaning projectile tea from my jacket, I read on.

The article gave the example of kids happily camping out in a London park on the eve of Queen Victoria's coronation. They had only oranges and bread to eat, but were full of joyful community glee at the celebration.

I thought that someone must be imagining things about a country that my Victorian ancestors in the East End of Glasgow never experienced. My family found limited choices in their Victorian empire: territorial war, industrial dangers, overwork, clearances, famine, infant mortality, disease, poverty, high rents, most signing their happy marriage certificates with a trembling 'X', hardly a soul living beyond the age of sixty.

Fawning to the idea of the divine right of kings didn't strike me as high on their agenda.

I was brought up with people who made do with very little and enjoyed life. But around me was an abandoned environment. We had three homes between 1960 and 1979: first, the tenements of Anderston, long since demolished; then Arden, Carnwadric, and the tribal sectarian undercurrents of southwest Scotland; and, finally, one of the sprawling council estates of Bourtreehill, Irvine, in Ayrshire. Irvine locals called us 'The Glasgow Overspill'. Those new towns of the late 1970s provided relief to the under-invested Glasgow council-housing department. The 300-year-old stone bridge over the River Irvine was removed to provide the likes of me with an ugly USA-style shopping mall. But what the planners had left of the rural old town brought me closer to the Scotland I imagined.

My family's homes were at odds with the Scotland I saw on my granny's biscuit tin. Yet that tin, with its imagery of a returning soldier standing at the edge of a sunset glen on the final mile home, somehow resonated with me: it spoke to me of home and peace.

Some summers my dad would drive us all around the Highlands and Islands on the hidden forestry roads he'd discovered welding pipelines all over the country. He'd get us all singing as we bounced over some sunny winding road. I saw glimpses of my imagined Scotland in those road trips. And I came to understand I could use folk music to try and find more of it.

Irvine, and its folk culture, saved my young musical life. The Eglinton Arms Folk Club, the Harbour Arts Centre, and the Marymass Festival gave me a deep connection to my Scottish musical culture and traditions. The community I found there led me to explore more of my native land.

Still, my imagined country seemed out of reach. I saw lack of confidence and squandered potential all around me. To get music published, or a record deal, or a book printed you had to relocate to some big Emerald City in another country far, far away. So I went looking for different perspectives and left with my new folkie friends for busking adventures in 1979. Just as Mrs Thatcher took power.

By the spring of 1981 I was in Paris.

In France I sang in the street for centimes and francs, thrilled by the community spirit. My contemporaries in France seemed highly motivated to change old orders. President Mitterrand was voted into power after years of right-wing governments. I joined those jubilant throngs celebrating in Paris well into the middle of the night. Those young Parisians imagined better. I wanted that energy for Scotland.

In 2002 I returned to live in Scotland and found a more confident country than I'd left. Five years ago, another political shift happened and I came to feel that independence for Scotland was the right direction.

Not enough people agreed with me then. But I see this changing, and we're closer to the Scotland that I imagined all my life. Confident, ready to accept that it can manage economically, that it has nothing to fear. It can support its own art, nurture its environment and society, grow the political leaders that it needs and form better alliances with its equals, including England.

When my fellow citizens of Scotland have the democratic right to pay for what we choose to pay for, invest in what we want to invest in, encourage the outside to love Scotland as we love it, then my imagined Scotland will be the reality.

The Victorian dreamers in that Emerald City far, far away can keep their bread and oranges. My imagined country doesn't have hungry, overworked, pressurised children in it. My imagined future doesn't see the past as the holy grail either.

I don't want one single Scottish child to feel they must leave Scotland to achieve anything.

Eddi Reader is an international-award-winning Glasgow singer-songwriter celebrating forty years of recording and live performing.

SEONA REID

O ne summer my partner and I were spending a few days in Applecross, a remote and beautiful peninsula on the northwest coast of Scotland. We visited the Applecross Inn and happened to sit next to three young musicians. Encouraged by those around them, they started to play. They were, we discovered, the product of the Feisean movement which provides young people with tuition in traditional music, song, dance and drama in the Gaelic tradition. As the evening drew on, buoyed by the energy of the music, we all went outside – it was a clear moonlit night – and came together in a spontaneous ceilidh, dancing Strip the Willow up and down the long street by Applecross Bay. It was a magical, if exhausting, experience. For a brief period we were an impromptu community of friends and strangers, of experienced dancers guiding absolute beginners, of different nationalities brought together by music and dance. I would love to live in a country where spontaneous ceilidhs happen not only in Applecross but across the nation in our cities, towns and villages because we recognise the joy of being united by music and dance.

Applecross happened because of the presence of three creative, confident young people and that really is my point. I want a country where every child and young person is encouraged to be creative, and can grasp that opportunity, unhindered by money, location, circumstance or background.

A few years later, I had the privilege of watching an orchestra of young people brought together by Sistema Scotland's Big Noise Programme in Raploch. Sistema works in four of Scotland's most challenged communities – Raploch in Stirling, Govanhill in Glasgow,

Torry in Aberdeen and Douglas in Dundee. Musicians and volunteers work with children from nursery age upwards, introducing those essential steps in learning an instrument – listening, concentration, rhythm, teamwork. The results are amazing, not just in the quality of music-making but also in the impact it has on the young people – increased confidence, development of academic and other skills, greater discipline, happiness, sense of belonging and fulfilment. These are not just my views, but the conclusions of the Centre for Population Health which evaluated the work.

Wind forward again and we are at a performance at the Old Fruitmarket in Glasgow as part of the Celtic Connections 2018 festival. On stage are some well-known musicians from Orkney. Then they are joined by around thirty young fiddlers who just blow the audience away. They are in their early teens and already consummate performers. We learn that they all come from one secondary school in Orkney where every pupil has the opportunity to borrow and learn an instrument. It seemed that everywhere we turned, we heard Orcadian musicians and bands: confident, talented, ambitious, building on these opportunities they had had as children. If one school can do it, why not the whole country?

And theatre too. *Like Flying* was a recent project by National Theatre of Scotland in two schools in East Ayrshire and Edinburgh in partnership with the Scottish Association for Mental Health. It was created in response to growing levels of anxiety experienced by teenagers across Scotland. Over a six-month period in each school, it invited casts of 12–14-year-olds to learn to fly – acquiring skills in aerial performance for an interactive show. The outcome? Exhilarating shows and participants who reported growing confidence, self-esteem, greater ease in making friends, and a sense of community. Parents and teachers noticed it too.

One of my favourite TED talks is by Sir Ken Robinson, a global leader in creative education. He argues powerfully that creativity lies at the root of most successful human endeavour and that creativity in our schools is as important as literacy. In the talk, he tells the story of a little girl drawing in a lesson, concentrating in a way she rarely did.

The teacher asked what she was drawing. 'God,' she replied. 'But nobody knows what God looks like,' said the teacher. 'They will in a minute,' replied the girl. Children are innately creative and will have a go if they are interested and encouraged.

We've made a start in Scotland. We're better than many places but we could do so much more. I imagine a country where *every* child, from nursery onwards, wherever they live, whatever their circumstances and cultural background, whatever community they belong to, has the opportunity – *free* – to learn an instrument, sing, make theatre, do art, be creative. These shouldn't be added extras for rich kids who can afford to buy instruments and sign up to private art classes – they are fundamental to building a society which is confident, humane, inclusive, fulfilled, happy and successful. Scotland can be that country.

Seona Reid has had a lifelong career in the arts and has been Director of the Scottish Arts Council and Glasgow School of Art. She is currently Chair of the National Theatre of Scotland, trustee of the British Council and Chair of its Scotland Advisory Committee, on the board of Wasps Artists Studios and Edinburgh International Cultural Summit Foundation and a panel member for Children's Hearings Scotland.

LESLEY RIDDOCH

Huts.
    Wee wooden huts.
    Could half a million of them sprinkled through the woodlands of Scotland really transform our health, happiness and our democracy?

Well, apart from the amount of sheer, uncomplicated fun such weekend retreats would bring to cooped-up, indoor, o'er serious then o'er drunken leisure lives, some of Scotland's most destructive habits would be usefully and completely dismantled along the way. We could become one of those countries where enjoying the countryside isn't an activity confined to the wealthy middle and upper classes.

Huts are common everywhere at wooded latitudes, from Canada through America, the Nordic and Baltic states, to Russia. Everywhere at our latitude – except Scotland.

In Norway, there are almost 500,000 huts – roughly 1 for every 10 Norwegians.

In Scotland there are about 600 – 1 for just over 9,000 Scots.

So, what happened?

The mystery of Scotland's missing huts has always bothered me – not least because I rented a stone-built bothy for seven glorious years after a series of professional accidents brought me to Glen Buchat, forty-five minutes' drive from Aberdeen.

My 'hut' was really a shepherd's house, until it was abandoned in the 1950s. It had a great roof, two bedrooms and, with its elevated location, 1,200 feet above fields of tatties, neeps and banks of heather, an amazing view. There was no electricity, road access or running water and, over the empty decades, the hut had become an animal domain.

It took years of weekend and summer stays to fix things up and learn to calm down about sharing that space: finding rabbit fur and bones under the duvet simply meant another visit from the polecat; hearing a herd of elephants dancing in clogs at night only meant the mice had returned to the attic; discovering a wedged-shut door didn't signal a secret invader but just heavy rain the night before. Cows wandered outside – part of their water trough served as my floating, makeshift fridge.

I loved the freedom and the adventure. And I knew only a handful of people who felt the same. When I was sufficiently persuaded of the merits of country life, I let go of the bothy and moved to a small house in rural Perthshire – filled immediately with my responsible, serious self and worldly possessions. My Norwegian balance of tame urban weeks and wild country weekends was over. I had become a sensible, tamed Scot.

But the experience never left me.

Why do Scots have so few huts, cabins, bolt-holes and mountain retreats compared to our neighbours? I've spent a decade researching that question – and the answer breaks my heart. During the 1920s and '30s, when working people across Europe escaped the pressures and squalor of urban life by building huts around big cities, Scots actually led the pack. But we fell behind after the wars. Norwegian efforts blossomed into a mainstream national 'cabin' culture once cars were de-rationed and incomes rose, because they had the right to build in beautiful, individual, affordable locations all over the country. But we Scots were confined to agreed communal sites, stymied by the simple fact we could never, ever, ever, ever own or rent a small patch of land. The number of huts here has halved since the Second World War, whilst the number of 'proper' houses used as holiday homes has more than doubled – making the whole idea of second homes look elitist and problematic. And, to an extent, in Scotland, they are. Here holiday homes are often large, existing houses that could (and should) be occupied by young locals, not the modest, purpose-built, forest-located wooden huts that predominate everywhere else.

There's been landowner opposition to every non-blasting-small-birds-tae-smithereens-type activity for centuries. That's why national parks happened in Scotland fifty years after England, why hydro dams happened fifty years after Norway, and why fifty years after our forebears built their pioneering and precious weekend huts, they've been demolished or stand condemned as shabby, makeshift blots on our 'splendid', constructed-as-empty landscape. Whilst a fifth of Scotland sits beyond reach or criticism as a giant grouse moor, locals, holidaymakers and outsiders must fight for the same, limited, existing housing stock.

The process of removing Scots from our own countryside is almost complete.

Foreign, wealthier visitors can outbid us for every rentable weekend cottage, humble B&Bs cost an arm and a leg, and long-term lets for locals have been turned into more profitable Airbnbs.

Is that really OK? Is it a coincidence that Scots have the fewest huts and the highest rates of problem drinking in Europe? Are we really willing to let a small number of landowners control vast tracts of our land? Or is it time to reclaim the Scottish landscape so that every family has the chance to build its ain wee woodland but'n'ben?

I know the answer I imagine.

But it's up to all of us to decide.

Lesley Riddoch is a writer, journalist and campaigner. In 2020 she published the book Huts: A Place Beyond – How to End Our Exile from Nature.

JAMES ROBERTSON

Suppose that a new, old country decided not to sing, on every public occasion, the same tired song about an ancient battle or a deity or a monarch. Suppose that this country ditched that obligation, thinking, if it's a choice between say 'God Save the Queen' and 'God Bless the Child', there really is no contest, so let's not have one.

Suppose that this was Scotland, and that its people voted for it to be a republic. What if – since they could never agree on the sentiments, let alone the tune, that would enable one song to speak for all – they agreed that the Republic of Scotland would have no national anthem?

This, in fact, is what happened. One of the decisions made by the First Citizens' Assembly (2026) was that no single song would take precedence over the others: the future would be a continuous celebration of both old song traditions and new music in different genres. Thus, instead of being stuck with one anthem that bored, alienated or puzzled half the population, those gathered on different occasions became accustomed to variety. At sporting, cultural, civic or commemorative events people might hear (and join in with) 'A Man's a Man for A' That', 'Auld Lang Syne', 'Freedom Come-All-Ye', 'Sunshine on Leith', 'Loch Lomond', 'The Flooers o' the Forest', 'Follow the Heron', 'Caledonia', 'Pick Up the Pieces', 'May You Never', 'Why Does It Always Rain on Me?', 'Hermless' . . . songs of humanity to mark human gatherings.

Organisations and institutions such as sports governing bodies, schools, universities, associations and societies were told they were free to choose whatever song or tune they thought appropriate to their ethos or to the occasion being marked; or, if they couldn't settle on one they liked, they could commission something new.

There were objections that chaos and confusion would ensue because only a handful of folk would know the words or melody of whatever song was selected for any particular event. In order to overcome this difficulty and encourage and embed knowledge of a wide range of musical works, an intensive programme of song-learning and song-writing, musical appreciation and performance was established in all schools. Music became central, not peripheral, to education – music for its own sake. The result was not chaos and confusion but an explosion of enjoyment and creativity. People, young and old, felt included and liberated; they felt good about themselves and, just as important, about those singing alongside them.

The First Citizens' Assembly also debated a national 'honours' system. An almost universal distaste was expressed for the pre-independence system, that hierarchical grading structure rooted in the long-expired British Empire. Additionally, very few people thought that those already successful in their own fields should be additionally rewarded, since they already had their prize money, cups, medals, titles and robes. But should ordinary citizens not be recognised in some way for acts of bravery, kindness and community spirit? And so a new Order of the Thistle was created. A fixed number of otherwise unrecognised individuals are inducted on St Andrew's Day every year. Nominations can be made by anybody, and a representative group of citizens is appointed each year to consider the candidates and elect the new inductees.

These were symbolic rather than structural changes. A more far-reaching move, taken to underpin the idea that all children were valued equally, was the absorption of the former private schools into the public education system. This integration took place over ten years. Surprisingly, despite dire prophecies to the contrary, this did not happen in an atmosphere of envy and revenge, nor was it resisted by the privileged few out of self-interest. Instead, it was accomplished with and for the best of motives: so that as many young people as possible had the opportunity to flourish and lead the best lives they could.

The former private schools became centres of excellence, used throughout the academic year but also as campuses for summer schools and specialist study courses. With their playing fields, gyms and swimming pools, their residential accommodation, their libraries, music, art, theatre and science facilities, they were ideally suited for these roles. Comprehensive education remains the guiding principle of the education system, but there is space for diversity and experiment and, crucially, a recognition of both special needs and special gifts among learners. The scheme has proved so successful that new campuses have had to be built in parts of the country where, for reasons of unequal wealth distribution, there had never previously been any private schools.

The cost of this investment in education has been substantial, but the consequent long-term savings in areas such as the justice system, health and social care have been even greater; and the outcome has been a kinder, healthier, happier and less divided society.

James Robertson is a novelist and poet.

ROBIN ROBERTSON

TEN THOUSAND MILES OF EDGE

Looking for the long pulse of Scotland.

Not here in the Central Belt, where most folk are;
not Scotlandland – twinned with Poundland
or Legoland, its national flower the plastic bag;
not its mapped centre, Schiehallion, with its garden
the Black Wood of Rannoch, home of my people –
but at the farthest edges, its islands and sea-coasts.

The sea protects us, the sea links us.

From the Solway Firth round the Rhinns of Galloway
past the Firth of Clyde and its closed shipyards
to the nestled isles of Bute and Arran, and round
Kintyre through the North Channel to the open sea
and Islay, home to Lagavulin, and Loch Finlaggan,
once the seat of the Lord of the Isles.

Half Scotland's catch is taken here,
from the Malin Sea to the Minches,
from the Mull of Kintyre to Cape Wrath.

To the lean wilderness of Jura: empty, knuckled
by the three Paps, with raised beaches to the west;

and north, where the tide-race funnels
into the bottleneck, the narrow gap with Scarba,
to make the monster that is Corryvreckan:
the speckled cauldron, the whirlpool, where
Orwell nearly drowned, where the sea
blisters, sliding up into hanging towers that drop
like lift-shafts, down into their own absence.

And then the garden of Colonsay and Oronsay,
safe harbour at Scalasaig, the wooded valley
of Kiloran: magnolia, maples, rhododendrons.
Mull, promontory island, Iona the bright chapel,
Staffa's pillared cave of organ pipes –
to Tiree and Coll and the Small Isles beyond.

The sea sewn by dolphins, moving north to Elgol,
where the ridged keels of the Black Cuillin
rise over Loch Coruisk's hidden glass. Skye
under its own sky, island of the MacLeods
and Dunvegan Castle, where Am Bratach Sìth,
the Fairy Flag, is held, and when unfurled
is said will multiply the men on the battlefield
and win the day for the clan, as it has done twice,
and holds one more victory yet.
In the east crook, in the Inner Sound, is Raasay,
the deep sea here is now where submarines sleep,
and the ghost of Sorley's Hallaig, where only ferns
and birches grow on the slope, below the ruins
of the cleared village where their fields had been.

West to the Western Isles, the Long Island,
sixty-five islands long – fifteen of them still alive –
over a hundred miles from Berneray to Berneray,
Renish Point to the Butt of Lewis.
Their names a litany – Mingulay, Pabbay,

Sandray, Vatersay, Eriskay — Barra of the seal-song,
South Uist, North Uist, Lewis of the Gaelic psalm:
that hypnotic drone, slow as pibroch, bleak
and rolling as this cold Atlantic swell.
The raised stones — the great circle of Callanish,
the double-skinned broch of Dun Carloway —
and the hidden stones, like the Beasts of Holm:
the skerry, just out from Stornoway harbour,
which sank the *Iolaire* on New Year's Day
with two hundred sailors, fifty yards from home.

When the seaweed harvest failed, the islanders
made offerings to Shony, the sea-god, wading
into the ocean with porridge or a cup of ale,
pouring it into the breaking waves:
throwing the produce of the land into the sea,
so the sea would throw its produce onto the land.

And now all we feed it is sewage, oil and plastic.

To the outliers: and furthest west to Hirta,
where people had lived three thousand years at least,
on seabirds and their eggs, till 1930,
when the last were taken off
and given work on the mainland, in forestry,
when not one of them had ever seen a tree.

Past the Flannan Isles, Rona, Sule Skerry,
the seal island, north of Sutherland and Cape Wrath
to the lethal Pentland Firth, to come at last
round Hoy's great cliffs of red sandstone,
the Old Man, and Rackwick Bay, to the haven
in the sound: the harbour of Stromness, gateway
to Neolithic Orkney. Within two miles,
the chambered tomb of Maeshowe, the Stones

of Stenness and the Ring of Brodgar, with the Ness
of Brodgar's temple complex being slowly released
from the ground by trowels, aligned as it is
between these two stone circles and two lochs,
hung in a basin of light.
Eynhallow, the holy island, vanishing island,
that disappears as you row towards it –
and the islands of Westray, Papa Westray, the Holm
of Papay – islands off islands off islands –
North Ronaldsay, where the sheep are kept
on the shore by a drystane dyke, and eat seaweed.

Past Fair Isle – and on up to Shetland:
the furthest north is Out Stack, north of Unst,
and furthest east in all Scotland – Bound Skerry
in the Out Skerries. See the perfect broch on Mousa,
the fulmars planing at Sumburgh and Fitful Head,
the shell-sand sweep of beach at St Ninian's ayre.

Down past the peatlands, by Helmsdale and Brora
to the Dornoch Firth and Moray Firth to
    Lossiemouth
and Hopeman beach where we huddled, sand-blown
behind windbreaks, on Scotland's cold shoulder
every summer – then round the ports of Fraserburgh
and Peterhead: whaling; fishing; then oil; then heroin.
My coast, lost like Forvie, to moving sands, like
the dunes of Balmedie to one American's greed,
and my city, Aberdeen, lost to oil – to the robber
barons and city planners. The thieves.
From the sea-village of Footdee, close-in at the wall
under the waves, to the Castlegate and the Tolbooth,
down the Spital's cobbled streets to the old town:
the melted Snow Kirk and the beauties that remain –
King's College, Dunbar's Mercat Cross,

the Chanonry to Seaton Park, with the Don
glittering below in the sun, curved
like a crozier under the gaze of St Machar.
On Sunday, south through the Mearns
and the great Highland Fault to Stonehaven bay,
to visit the grandparents: with the reward
of a Giulianotti's ice-cream cone at the end,
while *Sunset Song* played in the background
over Carron Water, under Dunnottar.
Then Crail, Pittenweem – all those pretty East Fife
fishing villages – Anstruther, Elie – to the Forth
and over it, to the great good sense of Edinburgh.
Built, like Aberdeen, on seven hills,
but great hills that still stand guard above the city.

Climbing the Nelson Monument on Calton Hill
looking out over the metalled Firth to the Kingdom;
south to the city, to the Pentlands; east to the sea;
down at the Parthenon – unfinished, barely started,
the flecked people far below, and my father
standing there, smoking, dead these twenty years.

And all that's south of here are the Marches,
the Debatable Lands, the Borders down to Berwick.
What matters here is this:
the permeable sea-membrane of land –
Scotland's ten thousand miles of edge
from the Solway Firth to the Tweed.

The sea protects us, the sea links us.

We are many people: settlers, wresting a living
from the sea – the Celtic Scots of Dalriada, the Picts,
the Norse and Normans – flying under many flags –
Saltire, Standard, Union – but quickly European,

trading for centuries across those borders,
and *internationalists*: citizens of the world.

And we peopled the world from these shores:
invented, built, explained, explored – we wrote
ourselves into history from this small country,
and our country was peopled in turn: the Irish
from famine, Jews from the pogroms, Asian,
Italian, Russian, Polish, all – welcomed, all.

We don't own the land, we tend it briefly,
and the sea protects us, and keeps us.
And the sea links us; lets us in, and lets us leave.

First presented at Message from the Skies, Edinburgh's Hogmanay
2019–20

Robin Robertson's sixth book, The Long Take *(2018), was the first poem
to be shortlisted for the Booker Prize, and won the Walter Scott Prize for
Historical Fiction, the Goldsmiths Prize for innovative fiction and the
Roehampton Poetry Prize.*

MIKE ROBINSON

When I imagine a country, it is a country with a strong sense of place – one that builds on the best of our history and traditions, nurtures the good in modern society and uses these as foundations to build towards a purposeful vision of what we could be. But it is also a country at ease in the world, leading by innovation and example, and open to learning and keen to share. A country that is willing to face up to its responsibilities and use its influence to tackle some of the critical global problems that confront us all. For me, two of the most critical are escalating climate change and the crisis in biodiversity loss.

Sustainability is simply common sense – if you continually exploit something and chip away at it, it will eventually break, sometimes catastrophically. That is true whether it is individuals, systems or society. Worryingly, it is also true of our planet. There can be no greater call to action than that, surely?

Every country develops its own narrative, often reframed to tell a new story depending on the age. Our own history contains a richness of material, of leadership and subjugation, peace and violence, inequality and reform – a palette from which we can select almost any narrative. So, what is mine?

I am both heartened by our religious tolerance, but ashamed of our sectarianism. Proud of our welcome, our stand against fascism and slavery, but embarrassed by our colonial past. I am depressed at the historical utter denuding of our own wild landscapes, but heartened by our love of wildlife. Frustrated at our role in causing climate change, but excited and inspired by our opportunity for leadership in resolving it. Yet amidst the dark and bloody struggle of history, I see small but glittering flashes of positive change, as we shed ignorance and immorality, stood against injustice and championed rights and shared freedoms. These are the seeds of gradual social and scientific enlightenment that I want to see flourish further.

But we have a great deal more to do.

Our generations have borrowed from the future, not invested in it. We have borrowed from our atmosphere, from rivers, the soil and the sea and filled them with pollution, plastics and excessive greenhouse gasses. We are borrowing financially from the future too. What right do we have to burden younger generations with such anxiety, debt and fear, without doing everything in our power to act in their best interests and, by doing so, to fill them with hope and reassurance?

We have fuelled climate change through over-consumption and wastefulness, and many of those same things have also driven inequality. We have burnt millions of years' worth of oil in four or five generations without investing in long-term infrastructure. We have designed our cities and lifestyles around cars, yet half of us don't drive. We have built houses with little or no insulation, laying the foundations of fuel poverty. We ship food halfway round the world instead of feeding people on our doorstep. We fly too much, though more than half of all flights are taken by less than 10 per cent of us and many of us take none. We have grown intolerant of nature, pushing our wildlife to the margins, to the degree that we have forgotten we are part of and dependent on nature.

I want a safe, fair, bold, resilient, intelligent, tolerant country with a reputation for thoughtful interventions, moral leadership and kindness, at home and abroad. One that acts every day as if the next generation matters and underpins everything we do with a core of sustainability. It is what our future demands. It is what our young people need from us. And it is something the whole world is striving towards.

This is new ground. We have never been sustainable. Climate change was arguably the accidental consequence of being unsustainable but we've not been able to make that excuse for forty years now. Yet we are still hamstrung by outmoded practices and stuck in Victorian thinking – much of industry is predicated on the false notion of endless growth limited only by the pace of production. If we know better now, we have yet to act comprehensively on that understanding.

We need to commit to building a future that responds to our moral and societal obligations, a future with a vision of hope and prosperity, a future that is a beacon of positive change. We will need a more defined sense of place and purpose, embracing sustainability rather than resisting or diminishing it. We need to empower people to step up to help promote and deliver action.

Above all, we need to be more ambitious.

I imagine a country that grasps and leads this challenge, not one that sticks its head in the sand despite knowing the tide is coming in. Our world is crying out for a new enlightenment. I want us to start building it here.

Mike Robinson is Chief Executive of the Royal Scottish Geographical Society.

PETER ROSS

On 16 September 2010, Benedict XVI came to Glasgow and celebrated an open-air mass, the first time a Pope had visited Scotland since 1982. The occasion drew a crowd of around 70,000, among them the Scottish press pack, on hand to record Benedict's stern words against alcohol, his encounter with a baby 'in a pink romper suit' whom he kissed through the open window of the Popemobile, and the presence of Susan Boyle, who sang 'How Great Thou Art'.

I wasn't there.

Despite being on the staff of *Scotland on Sunday*, I was allowed instead to spend the day of the Pope's visit hanging out with a group of unemployed guys who had gathered by Dalmarnock Bridge with rods and lines and bait, as they did most Thursdays, to have a drink and attempt to catch roach, dace, perch, eels, barbel, trout and – that mythic beast of the Clyde – salmon. Here, then, was a counter-narrative: instead of covering the fisher of men, I would write about the men who fish.

Almost ten years on, would it be possible for a Scottish newspaper to be so creative, some might say cavalier, with its resources? In the Scotland of my imagination, yes. My ideal country would have a media with the means – and desire – to cover the minutiae of life. That means the councils. That means the courts. But it also means the tiny moments that make up the life of a nation. The child that goes hungry because her parents haven't the money. The woman who, having converted to Islam, is making her first Ramadan fast. The men who fish. We must, of course, cover the big stories: national politics, major trials, the never-ending soap opera of fitba. But journalism also has a vital task in simply recording life as it is lived. Let us not forget to beat the drum for the humdrum.

This is not about nostalgia. When newspapers were swimming in money they did not always use it well. Our media has never been good at covering this country's ethnic mix, for instance. Coverage of people from minority faiths and cultures, when they have been noticed at all, has tended to focus on crises: racial tension and the like. In an ideal Scotland, journalists would have good contacts among these communities (even better, they would come from them) and would thus be able to report stories which did not have a race angle and were simply interesting tales of whatever sort. There is a philosophical idea here – a national newspaper ought to mirror the society it seeks to represent – but also a financial imperative: if you want to sell papers to people, write about them.

That goes beyond race and religion. Scotland's quality papers spend too much time chasing a middle-class audience which just isn't that into them any more. We also cede ground to the tabloids too easily. I have found, in many years of writing about people in working-class communities, that those people enjoy the stories when they read them. They like the same things everyone else likes: a good quote, a neat thought, vivid reporting, elegant turns of phrase. Yet the day after the story in which they appear has been published, they are back to the *Record* and *Sun*. There is an unfortunate perception that the qualities are not for them. The other day, I went into a corner shop in Stirling, near my gran's old flat, and bought *The Times*. 'That's for the brainy folk,' said the woman behind the counter. This attitude is such a shame, it's just not true, and we need to address it. If I was the editor of *The Times*, the *Herald*, the *Scotsman*, I would want it to be known that my paper is for everyone. I would want to sell copies in Scotland's towns and in the less affluent parts of the cities, not just in the former white-collar heartlands.

How? It would take work, thought, energy and, yes, money. 'Digital' has come to stand, in Scottish journalism, for a sort of inevitable slide towards a future in which people no longer buy newspapers at all. It is also used as a disingenuous excuse for disinvestment and job losses, as if digital content did not need reporters and photographers to create it. Again, I am not a nostalgist, but I have an old-fashioned view that people will read, value and pay for your product if you make it attractive enough.

And how is that attractiveness to be reckoned? Newspapers have, traditionally, been driven by certain values and qualities: speed, aggression, outrage. Those are all important. But the journalists and editors of my imagined future Scotland would bear in mind three further watchwords: beauty, compassion and love.

Peter Ross is the author of A Tomb With A View: The Stories & Glories of Graveyards.

RICKY ROSS

It's late October and as I look out my window I see Scotland at its best. Bright clear blue sky foregrounded by all the colours of autumn. On a clear day it's picture-perfect. But in reality, framing Scotland in a convenient image requires a little more nuance.

There are so many things we want our country to be. A good friend of mine returned from his first visit to the South of France and declared he wanted us all to live as if this was really the Côte d'Azur.

For the purposes of this exercise it's probably worth eliminating such climatically unlikely outcomes. However, there is a small part of France I think we could emulate more closely. An hour or so outside Paris is the small village of Trosly-Breuil, where I came very close to a model of society to which I'd gladly aspire.

In a little house there I spent an hour or so with the late Jean Vanier. Jean's community of L'Arche was founded in the early '60s when he invited two young men to share his home. The men concerned were both intellectually disabled and at that time resident in government-sponsored psychiatric hospitals. Jean Vanier described the two men, and others he encountered at that time, as 'the most oppressed people on the planet'. Inviting them to share his life launched a model of community which has since touched the lives of thousands of people.

From that encounter Jean began his vision of L'Arche: a network of 1,500 similar communities in 82 countries where all kinds of people with all manner of physical and intellectual disabilities are valued. L'Arche seems to be at odds with so many of our assumptions about how the world works. Here those who have been forgotten elsewhere are respected and cherished, happiness and joy is not limited to the wealthy, and no one is excluded.

On his ninetieth birthday, a year or so before he died, Jean made a little video in which he suggested ten rules for life. At first there's nothing earth shattering about these, but spend a little time and they begin to reveal a few deep truths about what we might be should we decide to follow them more closely. The one that still resonates for me is Rule 6: Ask people, What is your story? Jean reflected on a woman he knew who encountered a man dying of a drug overdose. In his final words the man said to her, 'You've always wanted to change me, you never wanted to meet me.' 'To meet', says Jean, 'is to listen. I need to listen to you because', he goes on, 'your story is different from my story.'

I find this comforting but also hugely challenging. Firstly, it accepts that we all have a story and our own is as important as anyone else's. But, secondly, it encourages us to think about how we encounter others. Recognising that we all come from different places – emotionally, socially, economically, intellectually, physically and culturally – has got to be a starting point to building a new country. In valuing the stories of others we might well find we start to make more sense of our own. In turn this will surely bring increased self-worth and happiness.

Scotland is beautiful. You don't need to walk very far from your doorstep to understand that. But it's only when we leave the safety of what we know and believe that we are forced to encounter others and ask the question: What is your story? The answers to that will affect how we shape education, health, employment, transport, housing and social care. We may become pleasantly surprised to find that before we go about changing anything we should listen first. Start like that and we can change everything.

Ricky Ross is lead singer and songwriter with Deacon Blue and presents Another Country *and* Sunday Soundtrack *on BBC Radio Scotland, and* New Tradition *on BBC Radio 2.*

JAMES RUNCIE

What if a country was like a festival?

Some might imagine there couldn't be anything worse. Think of Edinburgh in August and it's hard to ignore the desperate street entertainment, the relentless flyering, the productions of *Woyzeck* and *Godspell* and *Waiting for Godot*, the stand-up comedians regurgitating their sex lives, the sad clowns and challenging mime artists, the solo shows about suicidal poets where you're the only person in the audience, the shout of argument, the noise of opinion, the heavy traffic, the late nights, the unwise flirtations, the forgetting the names of old lovers, the food that you never meant to buy but were starving and you had to eat *something*, the indigestion ('Dining with Gaviscon'), the hangovers, the embarrassed apologies, the swearing blind that you'll never do it again, never ever, certainly not next year, you must be joking, *and yet* . . .

There's something exhilarating about doing things you never thought you'd do, seeing images you never imagined you could possibly see, hearing words you never thought you'd hear, thinking things you'd never thought you'd think, greeting old friends, staying up all night talking about what's important with people you've never met before, singing, laughing, dancing in the moonlight and then waking up and wondering: What was all that about?

Where else can you go to breakfast theatre, an art show, a concert and a lunchtime debate in a single morning? How else can you fit in an afternoon play, followed by poetry, spoken word, dance, a rock opera, a late-night gig and a comedy at dawn? What does it feel like to be thrown into such a crucible of creativity?

Well, it probably feels as electric, unpredictable, tiring and frightening as imagining the future of a country. You up your game. You look hard. You think deeply. You are engaged and involved with people who are doing all that they can to be at their best.

So I'd like to imagine a festival nation that is welcoming, international, diverse and full of hope, joy and an open mind: an inclusive country that challenges itself, that is prepared to think boldly and imaginatively, that embraces the awkward stranger and gladly receives unorthodox opinion; a place that is as welcoming to those who have fled repression and disaster as it is proud of those who have been born here; generous and open-minded to those who have come to make Scotland their home; new Scots and Scots by choice.

A place of curiosity, culture and invention; a land that is musical, literate, thoughtful, inventive, scientific, socially and ecologically responsible, cheerful, eager to think the best of people, humane, tolerant, forgiving and fair-minded.

What if our country was run like that?

James Runcie is a writer who appears regularly at the Edinburgh Book Festival. He lives in Fife.

SARA SHERIDAN

'Where there is a cow there is a woman and where there is a woman there is mischief.'   – St Columba, sixth century

'I can't believe I'm still protesting this shit.'
                                        – sign at the Women's March 2018

In 2018 I was commissioned by Historic Environment Scotland to imagine a different Scotland – a country where women were commemorated in statues, streets and buildings, even in the hills and valleys. One where female success and achievement was standard in exactly the same way male success feels normal in the real world. The book, originally titled on my laptop 'The Betterworld Guide', came out in 2019 as *Where Are the Women?* In researching it I studied over a thousand years of history and chose 1,200 women to include in the text. I learned a lot. That our grandmothers and their mothers going back generations were amazing. That the image of historical women as subservient and retiring is nonsense. And that gender inequality is structural and persistent. In Dundee, in the book, alongside the new V&A, I founded an imaginary institution – one that I believe we need in the real world. I called it the Museum of Misogyny.

In my imagination, the museum promotes equality for all, including BAME women, those with disabilities, working-class women and people in the LGBTQI community. As this work is of benefit to all of society (including the economy) the museum is publicly funded. It curates the misogyny of the past, holds events to educate for and incite change, funds the study of systematic and structural sexism, and pilots ways to contest and protest it as well as lobby for legislation that creates a country that we can only dream of – one where the 50 per cent of people who are normally considered a minority are genuinely equal to the 50 per cent of people who are not.

The study of history is the story of where we come from – what forms our culture. We are the sum of our experiences. Sometimes we honour our heritage and other times we transcend it but we are always formed by it. How can we understand where we are, if we don't understand where we come from? And if we don't understand where we are, how can we make interesting, ambitious and successful plans for where we're going?

In this, history is a chain. If you stop thinking of events as a series of dates, and start thinking in terms of generations, it's easier to make this connection. The suffragettes were not 100 years ago, but three or four mothers in the past, and the first women to achieve qualifications in higher education were a mere six mothers ago. Each of these generations endowed us not only with their achievements (enshrined in legislation) but the gift of their experience. They fought for change against practices that were, at the time, considered completely normal.

In the study of politics, the general view of that normality is called the Overton Window, which is the range of opinion considered acceptable in the public eye. This window can shift dramatically. Driving without seatbelts or smoking in public buildings are both issues that have become unacceptable in my own lifetime. The window moved in the late nineteenth and early twentieth century because of the work of suffragettes and the pioneers of women's education. In fact, the history of feminism is the history of such shifts. We have come a long way but we still have not created a world where you hear the word doctor or footballer or judge and you picture a woman at least half the time. This is the struggle of modern feminism – to normalise 50 per cent of the population. The cultural norms that stop us doing so are pervasive – it is the water we swim in and we are so used to it that most of the time we remain unconscious of how women are constantly othered in language, in our built environment and in the way our bodies are portrayed. Over time, popular laws and outlooks may change, but so far society has held on to its misogynistic undercurrent. It drags us unseen in a direction we do not always realise we are taking.

The reality is that we do not have equality (not even near). In the words of the sign quoted at the top of this piece, we are still protesting this shit and we need to take action to create change. In Scotland we have organisations that are collecting and collating data in their individual fields of interest, and indeed, the Scottish government has committees that consider issues from the gender pay gap to equality in education. But we also need to recognise the scale of the issue we face and effectively counter systemic misogyny by directing further study and collating everything together.

I have no doubt that misogyny belongs in a museum. I say let's build it.

Sara Sheridan writes about history and is an equality activist.

MONA SIDDIQUI

When I was an undergraduate in the 1980s studying French and Arabic, I went to Cairo for the first time as part of my year abroad. After arriving at my pre-arranged accommodation in a relatively poor suburb of the city, I had to wait outside for a while as keys and rooms were being sorted out. I stood there with my new suitcase and new expectations and looked around, anxious and curious at the dust, animals and poverty around me. A young Egyptian woman with a small child was watching me as she squatted near the doorstep of my flat. She stared at me for a while and after some time I saw her get up, find a large piece of cardboard, dust it clean and place it on the doorstep. She patted it, beckoning to me to sit down and take the weight off my feet. I smiled at her nervously, knowing that she had made a special effort for a new guest in the neighbourhood. I was neither friend nor enemy but a stranger to whom she had reached out. Later on, as I was getting settled in the flat, two young children came up and spoke to me in the local Egyptian dialect. I couldn't understand what they were saying and became slightly impatient at their repeated visits and knocking on the door. That evening, I discovered that they had been sent by their mother, the same woman, to ask if I needed anything as I was a guest in their midst; I felt ashamed and ungracious.

As children we are mostly told to be wary of strangers. There is a logic to this wariness, but my point is that many end up avoiding or fearing strangers even as adults. As we all lived with the restrictions of COVID-19 over the past two years, I realised that while I've missed seeing family, I've also missed being around strangers. Throughout most of my life, I've been at ease talking to strangers; some have shown me kindness during my travels, others have confided in me and I too have found myself sharing secrets with people whom I know I'll never see again. I have found moments of true joy and romance in many of these interactions. I think that most human beings are hardwired to want to connect with people and that the ever-increasing loneliness so many feel, despite the busyness of our lives, is testament to this need.

Empathy, hospitality and welcome are all associated with strangers and most religious traditions emphasise welcoming the stranger because there is a power in that connection. But even if, today, our lives are no longer about giving food and shelter to a random traveller, so many of our current social and political problems of suspicion, mistrust and even contempt for those we don't understand stems from our inability to empathise, to relate to someone else's life. We should teach the virtue of empathy in schools because many of us remember how cruel school playgrounds can be. Empathy is not a weakness nor soft kindness; it has a boldness which can potentially transform our own lives as well as the lives of others. Because in the end when we reach out to others in empathy, we open our minds to imagine new relationships, new friendships and new worlds.

Mona Siddiqui is Professor of Islamic and Interreligious Studies at the University of Edinburgh.

JOHN GORDON SINCLAIR

This recounting of an old anecdote lacks a number of small but significant details: the names of the main protagonists, the radio station and the title of the book referred to – all but one crucial detail and that is the essence of the sentiment expressed herein.

Some twenty years ago, I heard an interview on the radio with a contemporary philosopher who had written – or rather rewritten and updated – a work that had caused quite a stir on its first publication. It was described at the time as a 'definitive work', even though – it was pointed out – it was a 'tome of a book'.

However, according to the interviewer, the philosopher had over the intervening ten years come to contradict several of his previous hypotheses and changed his thinking on some key ideas: did he consider what he'd written in the past to have been wrong or simply misguided?

The philosopher replied to the first question simply: 'If in ten years your life experience teaches you nothing new or doesn't persuade you to reconsider some of your previously held beliefs: if you are closed to change,' he explained, 'then you might as well be dead.'

The interviewer was equally bemused by the fact that, despite the meritorious esteem in which the philosopher was held around the world, he had chosen to live in relative obscurity on a small island in French Polynesia. He had, after all, been offered fellowships at top universities around the world: both Oxford and Cambridge in England, Harvard in the United States, the Sorbonne in France, Humboldt University in Germany, with its fifty-five Nobel laureate affiliates.

Once again the interviewer was perplexed. 'You have been invited to join some of the finest institutes of learning in the world in some of the greatest cities and yet you've chosen a small, relatively inaccessible island that doesn't allow cars and where the children even have to travel to another island to go to school.' Why had he forsaken the hallowed groves of academe for some backwater island in the cultural middle of nowhere?

This time, the philosopher recounted his travels in the South Pacific island. Every islander he encountered would ask him the same question: 'Have you met the shopkeeper yet?' The shopkeeper, he learned, was the most important man on the island. 'You really must meet him before you leave,' he was told. The question was asked so often that the philosopher's curiosity was piqued: What, he wondered, made the shopkeeper so important and why was he held in such esteem? Was he rich, a wealthy landowner perhaps, or an inspirational leader? Did his shop stock particularly fine produce?

Finally, the philosopher asked the owner of the guest-house where he was staying what it was about the shopkeeper that made him so important. 'He's the nicest guy on the island – the best of all of us,' came the reply.

It was not the answer he'd been expecting. The philosopher realised that he was imposing his own notions of what was deemed to be important – wealth, property, possessions, power – on a far more advanced and rational belief system practised by the islanders.

The philosopher revealed that in that very moment he decided this was where he wanted to live.

I have told this anecdote, with all its lack of detail, several times over the years to numerous people, because it had a profound effect on me. I've searched radio archives and the internet for 'contemporary philosophers' in an effort to find a name to verify my recollections and fill in some of the blanks. I've even wondered if I might have imagined the whole episode, but – either way – it all leads to the same conclusions: firstly, any individual or society that is unable, unwilling or not permitted to change its mind is in denial of what it means to be human. If we are not allowed to learn from the past then we inevitably face a future making the same mistakes. And, secondly, this learning needs to reflect upon what our collective aspirations should be. Too often, we are measured against standards of progress, success and value – such as growth, wealth and competitiveness – that diminish ourselves, others and our environment. Like the philosopher, I want to live in a world where a person's value is based on how good a person they are and how well they treat their fellow human beings.

John Gordon Sinclair was born in Glasgow. An actor and writer, he has published three crime novels and is currently working on a fourth.

TRISHNA SINGH

In my imagined country, I picture a meal of tasty colourful dishes, spicy aromatic dishes, sweet and savoury dishes. The variety of the food represents the diverse range of people who live here, each with our own traditions and our own stories. As we sit down to share this wonderful food, we tell the stories of how it was prepared, how it was grown and harvested, and we all listen with curiosity and interest because we understand the importance of this information. Our new knowledge deepens our respect for the farmers, for the animals and for the environment that allow us to enjoy this meal.

An example of what I'm talking about is already happening in Leith, where a group of Sikh women opened Punjabi Junction, a social-enterprise café serving traditional Punjabi food to the local community. We use recipes handed down through the generations to provide a healthy alternative to fast food taken on the run.

At the heart of what we're doing is the idea of social mobility. We don't see that as simply clawing your way to the top. We believe it's about progressing stage by stage to the maximum of your potential, without ever having unreasonable or unfair barriers placed in your way.

In the case of the women of our community, two main factors contribute to their disadvantaged position: 'external' racism, emanating from the majority white community; and restrictive and dated 'internal' cultural pressures, which still affect some minority ethnic women.

Scotland's ethnic minorities experience unemployment rates between two and three times greater than white groups. For minority women there are the additional barriers experienced by all women – lack of childcare, lack of role models and lack of confidence. Sharing our food and our lives can help to change that.

In our imaginary country there is not only enough food for everyone, there is a place for everyone at the table. We finish our meal feeling enriched and satisfied both physically and emotionally. Through the act of eating together, we are better understood, better cared for, and more respected. For example, at Punjabi Junction we have become a regular meeting place for local mums. Their babies have developed a taste for our food, and we've nicknamed them the 'chapatti babies'. Small things like this help to break down cultural barriers – we have become a bridge between the Sikh/Asian and Scottish communities.

Beyond the kitchen and the table, our imagined country would keep us connected to nature. There would be trees planted in every corner of our land, filling the air with birdsong. In school children would learn about the natural world and how its wonders develop and survive. Screen time would be restricted to encourage freedom of thought and conversation across the generations as well as within our own age groups. Through the work we've done at Punjabi Junction, we've continued to embrace the wisdom, experience and goodwill of women from many different backgrounds and cultures. We have created a Sikh Sanjog – 'sanjog' means 'linking' in Punjabi – that is not divided by differences but united around shared values and respect for our diversity.

The French novelist Victor Hugo said, 'An invasion of armies can be resisted, but not an idea whose time has come.' And our time has certainly come!

We're not short of ideas either, both big and small. In our imagined country there would be water fountains all over the city so nobody goes thirsty, and to address the urgent environmental need to reduce the single-use plastic bottles that litter our streets and parks. Free public toilets would be widely available to provide for a basic human need and preserve people's dignity.

I imagine a country without unemployment, with a free health service and free care for the elderly. A country where homelessness is unthinkable. Where nobody questions our origins based on our accents or the colour of our skin. We are all human beings and we are all part of the 'tartan' that makes Scotland.

And most importantly, according to my six-year-old granddaughter Mirah, mermaids and unicorns would live freely amongst us without fear!

Trishna Singh is the Founder/Director of Sikh Sanjog, the only Sikh family-support charity in Scotland, and Punjabi Junction, the first Sikh women's social enterprise in Scotland. She has over thirty years' experience working in the voluntary sector. In recognition of her services to the community, she became the first Sikh woman in Scotland to have received an OBE in 2014. She is the Honorary Sikh Chaplain to the University of Edinburgh. She represents Sikh women on a number of committees and organisations at local and national level. In June 2022, her memoir, A Silent Voice Speaks: The Wee Indian Woman on the Bus, *will be published by Fledgling Press.*

ALI SMITH

O nce there was a small gang of kids. Well, I say small, maybe seven or eight of them, maybe twenty, maybe fifty, here they come right now, roistering round the corner with their arms linked, past the lamppost, past the waste grounds left over from bombing in the last war, past the past, past the crazy money towers of the Boris Johnson city, then right past the present because they're on their way to the future, they're pals for life forging along the pavement and they're singing this song, a simple song, it goes:

> One planet earth
> There's only one planet earth
> One planet earth
> There's only one planet earth

They don't know it because they're young, but the tune they're singing is an old one, the tune of a song called 'Guantanamera', about a place in the world that's beautiful, though nowadays cynical people have turned it into the foulest sort of prison, but that old song's words hold the place's older story of an old truthful man, he's dying, he wants before he goes to tell the story of his soul and the place he lives and how these two things, soul and place, are rooted together. He sings about the sea, and how he loves the beautiful little mountain streams, and how what's been wounded in life can come to the mountains to heal, and how all things grow, whether they're flowers or friendship or understanding, and how the way to deal with the bad times, and with the cruelty of cynical people, is to turn to the earth, cultivate its beauty, help it grow the beautiful things.

But back to the gang of kids singing and forging ahead along the pavement, because behind them, look, there's a swell of people, a swell that started as a stream and is now the size of a sea, no, maybe several seas, thousands and thousands and thousands of people, so many that they're the size of a country themselves, together they make a whole new country, no, a continent, all the people rebelling right now across the world at how this world with all its countries and continents is being treated, all the people who give a damn, people of all ages, genders, persuasions, shoe sizes, walking alongside a small gang of more than a million kids all refusing to go to school till their countries get educated about what's happening.

Then the plants and flowers that know they're threatened are pulling their roots out of the ground like they've just heard a mythical Orpheus, and they're hurrying along too, dragging dribs and drabs of earth and clean soil, sweet-smelling, all across the pavements of the city, and they've got their branches round the shoulders of those singing kids and the shoulders of those people who're giving a damn, and with them, all round them now, baying and barking and mewling and squeaking and growling and flapping like a massive Noah's ark parade, are all the creatures of the earth, air and sea likely to go extinct pretty soon too, the leopards and rhinos and orangutan and gorillas and turtles and tigers and elephants and porpoises and wild dogs and ferrets and whales and huge tunafishes with blue fins, and chimps and bonobos and penguins and dolphins and pandas and sea lions and seals and sharks and hippos and iguanas and bears, and polar bears standing on a sliver of ice, and jaguars and plovers and bison and foxes and macaws and tree kangaroos and butterflies and salmon and frogs, and right at the back the sloths, and they're all singing the song. Look up – all round them in the air above the march, invisible, evanescent, the spirits of all the already extinct species, the gone mammals and insects and fish, the dead plant-life, the burnt-black trees and creepers waving their ashy leaves, and with them all the spirits of the people and creatures who've already perished because of what's being done to where they live, and even some lifeforms from other planets are zooming down through the galaxies and joining the march, they can't not, because they know too, like the kids are singing, that there's only

> One planet earth
> There's only one planet earth
> One planet earth
> There's only one planet earth.

And those kids at the front of the great march on their way to the future spill across the borders like borders can just be dissolved, like they're not real, and they stop outside the houses of government and the banks and the offices of the huge conglomerates and industries and media giants and tech giants and oil companies, because they plan to look them straight in the eye, the politicians, and the rubbish world leaders, and the CEOs – who are all looking pretty embarrassed, pretty shifty, the smirkers and the shirkers of real responsibility – so they settle themselves down, they're not going away till this is sorted, and this story hasn't got an end because everyone in it who gives a damn is working against the kind of end that ends everything.

Seven or eight kids. A new country. With all their urgent patience they sing it again, and again, then again.

> One planet earth.
> There's only one planet earth.
> One planet earth.
> There's only one.

Ali Smith was born in Inverness in 1962 and lives in Cambridge. Her books have been translated into forty languages.

ELAINE C. SMITH

I magine a country . . .
So much to do . . . so little time . . . and small things matter . . .
Let's dream big . . .

Imagine a Scotland that thought being a snowflake was a good thing, that valued compassion, kindness, love, a good laugh, intelligence, hard work, holidays, science, clever people, literature, reasoned debate and argument that was tolerant of difference of race, sexuality, religion . . .

Actually I live in that Scotland!

On the whole, this *is* what I've experienced in the sixty or so years I've lived here.

Yes, there's·lots of negative, nasty, unkind stuff, and people who care more about wealth and personal gain than anything else, but I don't encounter that on a daily basis and never have. When I do, it always shocks and surprises me.

But that doesn't mean there aren't plenty of things that would make this an even better country . . .

Imagine a country where we know the value of a human being and not simply how much they cost us. A country that truly valued its welfare and social system, and those who work on behalf of others. Where we, the citizens, could sleep safe and sound at night, knowing that everyone who is vulnerable is truly cared for in the best facilities by the best people, and where accessing that care was straightforward. Those who are homeless, sick or mentally ill; children and young people in care; those with disabilities and learning difficulties; pensioners; and those who struggle daily just to get by: they all deserve to feel secure.

Imagine a country where we're happy to spend money on the many things we could do to make their lives better and more comfortable.

And imagine how good we would feel about ourselves knowing that those suffering the most were treated with love, compassion and true value.

Imagine a Scotland where we actually understood and valued what our taxes pay for: the social services, the bus that picks up the disabled child along the road every morning, the schools, the health service, the roads, the street lighting that lets your daughter – and your son – walk home safely at night, the rubbish collections, the galleries, the public spaces, the parks . . .

I get so frustrated when I hear people moan about council tax because it's clear that they have no real idea what we're all paying for. Imagine a Scotland where that disconnect was fixed and we understood and valued all of it as opposed to simply counting the cost.

And let's also dream of the fun and joyous things . . .

Imagine a Scotland that had a proper winter festival.

I've said many times before that in the cold dark of the year we should have a winter festival. It should kick off on St Andrew's Day (30 November). Every Christmas show, pantomime, school show, switching-on of Christmas lights, should happen across Scotland on that day. We could have some football games too, and concerts and gigs – and all done for charity! It should be covered by our media, national and local, to include those who are unable to participate in person.

St Andrew's Day would come to mean something significant, while bringing a sense of celebration, fun, joy and purpose from Lerwick to Dumfries, giving the whole country the opportunity to come together while doing something that helps others. The festival should then run right through Christmas and the new year. Towns, villages and cities could organise what they feel is right for them but still have that all-important sense of being part of something bigger. The festival should end with the celebration of sinners on Burns Night – a fitting conclusion. And then we can lie down for a couple of days!

And let's not forget to dream of the wee things . . .

When I was caught in the terrible snow a couple of years back, en route to Aberdeen on a dual carriageway, I realised that we were all stuck because there was nowhere to turn. But the lane heading in the other direction was empty and I thought, Why can't we have gates on the crash barriers that can be opened to allow vehicles to exit and turn in an emergency? That way, people wouldn't be stranded overnight in their cars. Imagine a Scotland with a transport system that would listen to wee ideas like that from ordinary citizens like me . . .

Elaine C. Smith is an actress, comedian and political activist who has worked extensively in theatre and TV for over thirty years. Her theatre work includes Calendar Girls, *playing Susan Boyle, headlining major pantomimes and touring her one-woman show, while her TV work encompasses a wide range, from* 2000 Acres of Skye *to* Rab C. Nesbitt *and* Two Doors Down, *for which she received a Scottish BAFTA award for Best Actress.*

LISA SMITH

First, my experience:

People say I have the biggest personality ever. When I meet people, I have three responses to them: 'I'm good', 'I'm fine', or 'I'm OK', but underneath I feel like screaming, 'Just go away!'

Everything used to be fine. I was working in a good job and I had moved in with my partner. But then it all changed. I had a health problem which led to me losing my job. I began drinking at the time and I was also prescribed strong pain medication. I began relying on these day-to-day and I couldn't cope. My relationship broke down and I moved out. I had no permanent home to go to after that. I had a lot of debt and it wasn't a couple of hundred quid, it was quite a lot of money.

What people don't know when they meet me is that I have lots of needs and health issues. My health can be unpredictable. I suffer from anxiety and depression, I still have a physical health problem and I am recovering from drug addiction.

I've lived in temporary accommodation in Edinburgh and it is one of the scariest things I have ever had to do. Being stuck in a place around others who have mental-health and addiction problems can be difficult. It affected my own mental health and made it worse. In that place, dealing with everyday normal tasks was just not possible for me. I couldn't manage it.

I found I had big problems getting any help or services, particularly in the evening or weekends. I would drink at night, which affected my mental health, which affected where I lived. Not having a safe space to go at nights or weekends, that was difficult.

When I went into recovery everyone thought that the problems with my mental health and addictions would be fixed, but that is not the case. It is a constant fight, fought in my own way. Mental health and its impact doesn't just affect the person themselves – it affects the children, it affects the partner, and it can affect everything in their life.

My vision:

My country is going to be boxed in, rectangular, sheltered and safe, away from hurricanes, gale-force winds, rain, snow and ice. My country is going to be a safe space.

A safe space where people can go and just sit with other people.

A safe space where if you are having a crap day, you can sit and talk to people who get what you are saying.

A safe space where there are people who get my walk, people who get my story.

A safe space where you can go and just have a juice, where you can just sit and talk and be normal. You know, just be normal.

A safe space where people are assessed on an individual level for housing, and not just looked upon as a number.

A safe space where people with mental-health problems get all the services to help them in one place.

A safe space for children, where they have a bedroom of their own, and are not living on top of their parents.

A safe space where the children are not distraught, being raised in unsuitable homes in horrible conditions.

A safe space where families can access support, somewhere safe to go, to meet other people who are in the same situation. They may have a different story, but they can still sit back and relax and talk to someone and say: 'The kids are bloody driving me mental!'

A safe space where we can all use our knowledge and our personal experience to help others.

A safe space where stigma no longer exists, whether that is stigma about mental health, addictions, homelessness, poverty or any other kind of stigma.

A safe space where I can grow and be independent.

I like my security and I like my own space. My country would be a safe space.

Lisa Smith is homeless, living in a B&B in Edinburgh. A recovering addict, she's a Shelter Scotland Time for Change peer, currently doing an IT and communication course through Access to Industry, which she hopes will allow her to turn a corner and find hope.

SUSAN STEWART

' I 'm sorry, I'm afraid I don't know . . .' is almost certainly the phrase I have used most often in my life when visiting my GP or other health professionals. Medics rightly ask, 'Do you have a family history of X, Y, Z?' But like tens of thousands of others who are adopted, I have no idea what my genetic inheritance is. I was born in 1965 and adopted as a two-week-old to loving parents who have been a stable and nurturing presence all my life. My brother was similarly adopted as a newborn some five years later and, like me, is fortunate not to have suffered serious illness or other medical conditions.

There are many facets of adoption which interest people, not least the fascination with reunions between adoptees and birth relatives; the enduring popularity of ITV's long running series *Long Lost Family* testifies to that. Yet it is estimated that only between 30–40 per cent of adopted people seek their birth parents (often when contemplating parenthood themselves). But should adopted people need to do that to discover their genetic inheritance?

Adoption nowadays is very different from the boom years of the 1950s and '60s which were characterised by 'secrecy' and the notion of a 'fresh start'. 1968 was the peak year for adoption in the UK, with over 27,500 infants adopted. Subsequent legislative changes have reflected both the welcome ending of the stigma of illegitimacy and advances in the treatment of infertility. Children who are adopted today are usually older, sometimes split from siblings, and often have a much more complex social and genetic inheritance than the healthy adopted newborns of decades ago.

The UK Government published a policy paper in September 2020 entitled 'Genome UK: The Future of Healthcare' and, whilst health is devolved, this is a strategy all four UK governments have signed up to. It notes that the UK is world-leading in fundamental research undertaken in our universities that translates into clinical practice resulting in improved outcomes for patients. An increased focus on screening and prevention – as opposed to post-diagnostic treatment – will not only improve and save lives but may, ultimately, see the elimination of some diseases. It could potentially save the NHS millions.

The emotional and physical well-being of adopted people could be transformed by the introduction of free genetic testing on the NHS for all adopted adults who wish it – and for their adult children and grandchildren. We live in a time of increasingly individualised and predictive healthcare and everyone should have the same access to the benefits of advances in genetic science.

Genetic screening can identify hereditary diseases such as sickle cell anaemia, Huntington's and cystic fibrosis, as well as pointing up a propensity to developing many common cancers such as breast and bowel cancer, and heart disease.

NHS websites list thousands of diseases which have a genetic and inherited component but entering 'genetic screening and adopted people' into their search engines provides zero results. Trawling UK and Scottish adoption advice and support group websites, I found no references to genetic screening. Nor does it seem to be high on the campaigning radar of UK adoption charities. They do hugely valuable work, much of it nowadays rightly focused on the rights and life chances of those fostered and then adopted from the care system.

Many of those affected are likely parents and grandparents already. But free genetic screening would benefit their entire families, and could influence life choices, perhaps the biggest of which is whether to have children or not. International adoption, most notably from Romania and China, has been more common in recent decades. Children often arrive here with unreliable or, in some cases, falsified information. They would undoubtedly benefit from Scotland adopting free genetic screening for adopted adults.

When my (adoptive) mum was diagnosed with breast cancer in

1998 one of the first questions her doctor asked was, 'Do you have any daughters as we'll need to get them in for tests too?' Mum and Dad, in the shock of the moment, answered yes. But it wasn't until the next day that Dad gently reminded Mum that this was not relevant to our family. My mum and dad are now in their late eighties and relatively healthy. I can only hope that my biological genetical inheritance is as good as theirs. If it comes close to matching the emotional support and non-judgemental parenting they have provided both my brother and me, I'll be all right.

This issue affects a comparatively small group of people, so the price tag would be low. But the benefits would be considerable. It's a matter of fairness and equity and one whose time has surely come.

Susan Stewart is the Director of the Open University in Scotland. She was Scotland's first diplomat to the USA and, through senior roles in media, government and higher education, has sought to champion equality for women throughout her career.

ASHLEY STORRIE

Dear Dad,

They've stopped using an alarm to wake us up – apparently it's difficult for the sleeping brain to untangle the nuance of pitch that differentiates the call for 'Shift change' from the call for 'The oxygen filtration is fucked and we're all going to die'. They play music now to avoid that moment of acute panic. Greg picked this week's music. He likes what he calls 'classic American divas', so I've been woken up by the kind of stuff Nana and Granda used to listen to, your Taylor Swifts and Beyoncés . . . Not my cup of tea, but it keeps Greg happy.

I like to wait a couple of minutes before I head down to the mess hall. I'll hang about by the window and try to work out which of the tiny lights is home. I circled it once, a tiny little ring of marker ink letting me know where I belong so I wouldn't have to pull up the chart, but it was gone the next day. It was probably Greg. He's a stress cleaner. As soon as anything goes tits up, there he is with a cloth and a microbe scanner, tutting every time he finds a speck of dust. I'll stare out and imagine you looking back up at me. We got the message from my primary school with all the wee ones waving at the camera, wishing me well, and showing the painting of me they've hung in the lunch room, and I saw you standing at the side, uncomfortable with the attention. You're a typical Scottish Da.

We're short on choice with food. Obviously we lived up to stereotype and worked through the sugary shite faster than any other crew in the history of space travel (at least that's what the papers have said). We're down to dehydrated fruit and sachets of ready-made porridge. I suggested a combination of both might be appetising and tried to cajole Greg into going halfers, but he's a masochist and enjoys the bitter crunch of a dried-out raspberry. So plain porridge it is again.

I'm heading down to the surface this afternoon to run the final checks on the hydro system. If it passes all the tests it means the first colonist ship can launch next year. There's still spaces for you and Mammy if you want them. We need teachers, and we need auld Da's to tell us we'll be all right when space dust taps against the hull and makes us scared. Just like you used to when the electric storms kept me up at night. God, I miss you, I miss home . . . I'm getting maudlin, sorry. I hope your telescope is coming on well. I'll give you a wave tonight before bed. Tell Mammy they're sending a probe with bits from home next Tuesday instead of Wednesday, and to stick me in some 'sugary shite' and some new bras . . . I already wrote her but you know what she's like, she'll have forgotten by the time she's finished reading.

I love you, Daddy,

      From your daughter in New Scotland

Ashley Storrie is a critically acclaimed stand-up, radio host and viral-video maker.

ZOË STRACHAN

Recently I was on the ferry from Berneray to Leverburgh, crossing the Sound of Harris. It can be a tricky route, apparently, but the sun was shining, the marker buoys were bobbing gently, and the Klix machine was dispensing hot brown liquid somewhat akin to coffee. A huge bird drifted past and several tourists rushed to the port side. I was half-tourist myself, taking the scenic route to do some work in Stornoway, so I ran for the door too, because a sea eagle was drifting alongside us, just for a moment or two, its feathers glowing, its vast wings beating once, twice, and away. As a Hebridean pal tweeted to me, 'Others have blackbirds or sparrows, we have neighbourhood sea eagles.' I met someone on Lismore once whose idea of a bird-feeder was pegging meat to her washing line.

Birds of prey – raptors – exert a particular pull on us. Kestrels perching like sentinels on fence posts along the motorway, the eeriness of an owl's face caught in torchlight on a country road. Red kites sky-dancing by the Firth of Clyde, peregrines nesting in an abandoned high-rise. A lucky glimpse of a hen harrier over heather and peatbog. It seems that many of my memories of the Scotland I live in come with the image of outstretched wings, the curve of a beak. The Scotland I imagine has the golden eagle as its official national bird. It isn't just protected, it's free from persecution.

When we talk about raptor persecution we're talking about who owns our country and what they do with 12–18 per cent of its land. We're talking about whether conservation means burning moorland and the mass medication of wild grouse. Whether it means setting snares and culling some animals so that you can shoot others for pleasure. When we talk about raptor persecution we're opening the can of worms of class, exposing the murkiness of money and political will. We're talking about the law and who gets away with saying 'no comment' when yet another protected bird of prey is found poisoned, trapped or shot on their watch, or on their land. In the Scotland I imagine, we haven't stopped at licensing driven game shoots, we've done away with them altogether.

My imagined Scotland is not an unreasonable place. Even if I don't eat meat or fish, people who are skilled enough can still shoot and catch small amounts of managed wild game for those that do. We see fewer pheasants because they aren't released into the wild in massive numbers any more, but if you hit one with your electric car, you're obliged to eat it yourself or deliver it to a local butcher so that someone else can. Ethical, eco-gamekeeping is the most popular modern apprenticeship, poachers are prosecuted, and people stalk deer with their cameras more often than with guns.

My imagined Scotland is still fun. If it isn't exciting enough, we can go further. We can take away the shotguns and reintroduce wolves and bears. Then those who make it back from a day in the field will have earned their dram and a story far more entertaining than the one that involved shooting 400 podgy, half-tame birds in a day. (I don't care how fast grouse can fly; it's not exactly sporting if they're driven into your gun barrel by summer-job students and fitness freaks with dogs, whistles and lurid flags.)

The Glorious Twelfth is still glorious. It's a public holiday. Some people make the Blue Peter bird-cake for their local blackbirds and sparrows, others celebrate with free travel for anyone who wants to go twitching in the countryside, or on a ferry to try to spot a sea eagle.

The Queen still comes to Balmoral, but she has stopped contesting her tax bill and shoots clay pigeons instead.

Dr Zoë Strachan is an award-winning author and Reader in Creative Writing at the University of Glasgow.

BILL SWEENEY

DRUMCHAPEL HIGH, BEGINNING OF TERM, 2035

THE HEIDIE ADDRESSES THE STAFF

Welcome back all of you and special greetings to new colleagues who have joined us this year to lead our refreshed core-subject area – 'Praxis, Poetics and Philosophy': we particularly look forward to your support for those remaining members of our former English department as they transition from those old and discredited exam-based mechanisms and acquaint themselves more closely with modern practice-based methodologies.

Last year's achievements in the essential core subjects were again outstanding: drama leading the way with last December's epic cycle of classic Davie Greig plays – who could have guessed that Year 2 students could handle the rhyming couplets of *Prudencia Hart* with such maturity and elan? But of course music and art also made their mark, especially Year 5's 'Monumental Fusion' of giant kinetic sculptures with surround-sound design, which has been delighting this summer's visitors to the Peel Glen Immersive Arts Park. Amazing how those vintage iPads were coaxed into life again (remember staring at these wee fixed screens?), and how they ran classic retro-Max/MSP patches to integrate the tourists' aesthetic reactions into the sound, colour and movement: a literally 'moving' experience. The poets and creative writers also contributed strongly: their engagement with both pre-school playgroups and the Mature

Citizens Lunch and After clubs have greatly enhanced the 'great art of living together' locally, inspiring emulation by many other schools across our modern housing-and-living schemes, even beyond Glasgow. Following this experience, and with the integration of English studies into PP&P, we hope that internal pedagogical struggles become a thing of the past and that champions of the creative approach no longer feel the need to call for separation or emancipation from what they (perhaps a little cruelly?) referred to as Gove-ite hegemony.

Of course I could go on with these listings – well recognised over the past few years by the Scottish Transcendental Education Authority when it conferred its Whole-School Collective Recognition Awards on our staff and student community – but I must stress our continued appreciation for the work of our colleagues in the 'non-core' subjects.

It is too easy for us to imagine that all arithmetical and purely analytical work can now go the way of the 'regurgitation-of-known-stuff' subject areas along with their testing regimes. We have had warning signs that handing over too much initiative to the AI bots that we now rely on for our day-to-day repetitive and non-creative tasks can occasionally have unexpected outcomes: certainly we still await an explanation of why the Culinary Arts Area Bot chose that particular dimly lit corridor to announce a fire drill in the style of Nina Simone in 'Mississippi Goddam' – we are assured that Mr Matheson is now recovering well – but it is suspected that a rogue 'humour' line of code may have been inserted by the Theatre Bot, which is now being inspected for any lingering signs of the 'Chic Murray' virus which so disrupted last year's T.S. Eliot Memorial Day.

So we will continue to argue for the 'non-core' subjects, but not only to assist with AI: we can point to many instances where their contribution has enhanced the core educational work.

Ms McNiven tells us that after the Jazz Ensemble enrolled en masse in the Mental Arithmetic Holiday Camp this July, their grasp of George Russell's *Lydian Chromatic Concept of Tonal Organisation* just clicked into place. And she expects giant steps forward at the

'All-Scotland Thelonious Monk-a-Thon' being hosted by the Tommy Smith International Jazz Institute in Wester Hailes next month. Similarly, the Gender Neutral 7-a-side Football teams benefited hugely from Mr Reid's Trigonometry Breakfast Club – they'll be showing off their innovative tangential tactics at the charity fundraising tournament for New Cathkin Park. And isn't it inspiring how the whole community has come together to help the Old Firm relocate to their eco-ground-share after Parkhead was repurposed as a library? (And good news too, that the Ozymandias Society has rescued Ibrox from the bulldozers to preserve it as a 'living ruin'.)

I also hear that our science collective are chipping in this year with a Molecular Chemistry and the Iambic Pentameter weekend – real alchemy in action – so let's stop the sidelining of the 'non-core' subjects. Let's remind ourselves that our pedagogy is based on Professor John Butt's pioneering concept of ULOs (Unintended Learning Outcomes) and remember, too, that a 'Guid Scots Education' must always be a rounded experience, embodying the essential core of the Three R's: Rhyme, Reason . . . and Rhythm!

So, good wishes to you all for the creative year to come – if there are no questions, then let's all head down to the Maxwell Geddes Holistic Audio Complex for the rest of the morning while the students organise our timetables.

Bill Sweeney is a composer and occasional clarinettist who grew up in Drumchapel, studied in Knightswood, the RSAMD and the Royal Academy of Music, and is presently a Professor of Music at the University of Glasgow.

MALACHY TALLACK

Scotland is a country whose politics have been, and continue to be, in part defined by distance: by the few hundred miles that separate us from London, and by the tensions, disappointments and misunderstandings that build within that space. For many, those miles seem longer now than ever before.

Yet Scotland has its own questions of distance to contend with. It is, after all, a lopsided country, in which people and power are concentrated in one wide band of the Central Lowlands. For those who live outside that region – particularly those who live in rural places – the relationship between geography and political agency is doubly clear. To be far from centres of power is to feel, and often to be, *without* power. It is to feel marginal.

Though there are nearly twice as many people living in rural Scotland as in the city of Edinburgh, the broad dispersal of those people means that the voice of any one community is diluted. It is hard for them to be heard. But rural communities are vulnerable, always. They are vulnerable to decisions that are made elsewhere, without such places in mind. They are vulnerable to extractive economic activity that draws wealth and resources away, without giving anything back. They are vulnerable to depopulation, and the endless pull of the cities. They are vulnerable to a mindset that sees rural problems as *local* and urban ones as *national*.

Where we centre our political imagination matters. It makes a difference. If the problems of rural Scotland are considered peripheral to the national conversation, then we will continue to recreate them, to perpetuate damage. If politics is seen as something that happens in the cities and is dispersed outward – the old, colonial model – then we are getting it wrong. And there are urgent reasons to do otherwise, to look again.

As climate change and environmental degradation become priorities, belatedly, for decision-makers, then what happens away from the cities will have to be understood, again belatedly, as a matter of significance for everyone. Land use and land ownership; agricultural practices; energy production; conservation: these are not just *local* issues, they are *global* ones. But the importance of environmental questions does not mean that answers must be found elsewhere and then imposed on rural places. That, again, is just repeating the old mistakes.

Taking seriously such questions, as surely we must, means moving beyond traditional models of power. Changing our country's relationship with its land – reducing the damage that we cause – means listening to those people, those communities, who live closest to that land. It is they who know it best, and it is they who feel themselves responsible, not just *for* their places, but *to* them.

I imagine a country in which that sense of responsibility to place, as well as to people, could help guide how politics is done. I imagine a country in which power does not flow from the centre outward – wherever you imagine that centre to be – but, rather, from the ground up. I imagine a country whose margins are no longer marginalised, and whose geographical edges are no longer edged out of political discourse. I imagine a country whose rural communities are central to its national concerns.

Malachy Tallack is a writer from Shetland, whose most recent book is The Valley at the Centre of the World.

BEN THOMSON

When we think of great Scottish food and drink, what might spring to mind are Aberdeen Angus steak, smoked wild salmon and oatcakes, porridge with a dab of heather honey, haggis, neeps and tatties, or a wee sip of a single malt. All around the world, Scotland is known as a brand that stands for high-quality, fresh, natural food.

Yet paradoxically many Scots have some of the worst diets in Europe. We eat too much sugar, salt and saturated fats, and over 65 per cent of us are overweight. We are the sick country of Western Europe, with one of the highest levels of heart disease and diabetes, and partly this is down to poor diet choices.

My vision for a brighter Scotland is simply one where we deliver on that perception of great Scottish food. That as well as producing high-quality food and drink that is respected around the world, we take pride in what we Scots eat and drink.

So how do we achieve this?

Like so many things, a change in culture starts with better education. Many of the younger generation have already absorbed this. Our 18–25-year-olds drink fewer alcoholic drinks than their parents, they eat more organic products and are more likely to have a vegetarian, pescatarian or vegan diet. The challenge is to educate the general public on better food choices while at the same time enabling everyone to eat good-quality, healthy foods at affordable prices.

However, education alone won't achieve this ambition and there are three specific ways in which government can help us both produce and eat better food and drink in Scotland.

The first is that we build our own standards for quality – the badges

'Scottish Quality Food', 'Scottish Organic' and 'Scottish Wild' should be set at a high bar and be recognised around the world. The Scotch Whisky brand has standards fixed by the Scotch Whisky Association, which has created and protected a brand that is globally respected, and we should do the same for all our food and drink in Scotland.

Second, the Scottish government already has responsibility for Scottish agriculture and may well in future have control of farm subsidies. At present these are predominantly awarded on the amount of land being farmed. In future these payments should be targeted towards food and drink production that meets the highest of standards, including a focus on organic and ethical processes. The subsidies could be used to make these foods competitively priced so that everyone is able to eat a healthy diet of locally grown and made produce.

Last, taxes should be imposed on unhealthy food and drink. The tax on fizzy drinks with excess of 5 per cent sugar introduced last year has already had an effect on changing the consumption of such drinks. Why not extend it to all sugar-based products? Over 10 per cent of the NHS budget in Scotland is spent on conditions related to type-2 diabetes, which is primarily caused by sugary diets. Better diet can not only create a healthier Scotland but also significantly reduce costs in the NHS.

Food and drink is one of the largest sectors in Scotland. Let's help it raise its game so that it's recognised as providing the best quality of Scots produce regardless of the consumer. Whether they're abroad, or one of the huge numbers of visitors who come here each year, or we Scots who live here, the standard should be equally high. The end result will be to make Scotland's diet better and create a healthier population right across the country.

Ben Thomson, CBE, FRSE, is a Scottish entrepreneur and financier who has been chair of the National Galleries of Scotland, Creative Scotland and Reform Scotland, and is currently chair of Inverleith, OMNOS and Planet Organic, as well as a visiting professor at Dundee University.

ALISON WATT

Alison Watt is an artist.

LOUISE WELSH

'BIG ROCK CANDY MOUNTAIN'

The trouble with capitalism is that for all its insistence on the labour of others, the system itself does not work. Clever economists will counter this statement with statistics and explanations of capital accumulation, competitive markets, price systems and the like. But I stick by my assertion. Capitalism is not designed to create a country in which everyone lives well. More than that, capitalism is not concerned with enabling individuals to realise their talents.

The concentration of profit, power, land and other assets in private hands, and the absolute belief in the need for wealth in order to live well, means that self-interest groups promote their own. Many of those in key roles, the people whose judgement and ability we rely on, sit shonkily on seats of power. Unfortunately a big bum on a shoogly stool is not akin to a jacket hanging from a shoogly peg. The bastards at the top clench their buttocks, brace their thighs and ride on: incompetent, entitled, oblivious.

Capitalism's obsession with profit skews values. Society pays lip-service to the injustice of nurses being paid less than bankers. We wring our hands over essential workers who cannot live within the bounds of the cities they serve, rough sleepers who punctuate our pavements, rural homeless living year-round in caravans while second homes sit unoccupied. These situations are inevitable when profit is God and people valued for what they have, rather than what they do. But they are not inevitable per se. There are possible alternatives should we choose to embrace them.

I'm writing this on a cold day at the start of winter. First frost glitters Glasgow's tenement rooftops. Minutes from my office homeless people sit wrapped in blankets on pavements, begging. Routes to homelessness are complex. They include inadequate wages, unemployment, late benefit payments, abuse, family breakdown, illness, mental health difficulties and addiction. We know that for every person we see on the street there are many more, including families with children, sofa surfing, or living in temporary or inadequate housing.

In my perfect country, property is not regarded as capital. My perfect country is a place of low rents, warm rooms, shared resources, affordable joined-up public transport, where education is free to all. My perfect country gives individuals the confidence and resources to discover their talents. In my perfect country it is distasteful to be wealthy. Individuals are respected for what they do, regardless of their job. After all, a society where refuse collectors are not appreciated is a society that has forgotten the smell of its own shit. And while we are on the subject of shit, as J.K. Galbraith points out, it is the only thing that trickles down in trickledown economics.

Is my desire for a non-capitalist country a simplistic, impossible dream?

Keep dreaming.

Keep dreaming on.

Louise Welsh writes novels, plays, short stories and opera libretti. She lives in Glasgow and is Professor of Creative Writing at the University of Glasgow.

REBEKAH
WIDDOWFIELD

Imagine a country which taps into the talents of all its people. In 2012, the Royal Society of Edinburgh published a report on women in science, entitled 'Tapping all our Talents'. They had found that female science graduates were much less likely than male graduates to pursue a career in science. But that wasn't all. Where they did go into science roles, women were under-represented in the top positions in academia, government and business. The title was a great way of drawing attention to the loss of talent that represents. But tapping all our talents is, of course, much broader than ensuring women are not lost to science. It is about making sure we harness the potential of all our nation.

And just imagine a Scotland with that level of collective capability. Imagine what we could achieve; imagine the impact it would have on our communities; imagine what it would do for our mental wellbeing if everyone was enabled to fulfil their potential.

Living in a country which harnesses the talents of all its people is an easy thing to agree with – who doesn't want to see people find their wings and fly, to develop and flourish doing something they are good at? But what does that mean in practice?

It means living in a country that fully nurtures all our children. It means giving kids access to books, music, drama and all those things that help nurture creativity and support mental wellbeing. It means not putting kids into boxes at an early age as being academic or non-academic; good or bad. It means recognising that the circumstances in which children grow up have a huge impact and ensuring that our policies and institutions address, not replicate or reinforce, social inequalities. To take one example, the Commission on Widening Access spent some time looking at the level of attainment required to be successful at university and concluded, 'Focusing purely on grades, in isolation from the context in which they are achieved, means that universities are often failing to recruit the best talent.' And if universities are sometimes missing out on that talent, isn't there a risk that the nation is too?

And it's absolutely not about everyone going to university (although everyone should have the opportunity to do so). Harnessing the talents and potential of all our nation means ensuring opportunities to learn in different ways and to learn throughout life. It means second chances, and yes, maybe third and fourth ones too.

And it means recognising and valuing different skills and talents. My gran left school at fourteen. Her reading and writing were not the greatest but as a seamstress she was phenomenal – I'm sorry to say her granddaughter did not inherit any of her talent in that regard! One of my favourite things is a beautiful tablecloth created by my gran and nanna, her mum – my gran doing the embroidery, my nanna the crocheting. So yes, we need the skills and knowledge that come from higher-level study but we need the skilled practitioners too who bring such colour and pleasure to our lives.

We know the value of diversity in the workplace and the benefits it brings in terms of performance, innovation and wellbeing. Yet how much more this matters in a country. Tapping all the talents of the population? Imagine such a country!

Dr Rebekah Widdowfield is Vice-Principal, People and Diversity at the University of St Andrews, and a board member of City of Glasgow College. At the time of writing this essay, she was Chief Executive of the Royal Society of Edinburgh, Scotland's National Academy.

RUTH WISHART

This country of mine. This shiny new independent nation-state of mine, will be encouraged to use the C-word ubiquitously. Because, at the very heart of this country, in every way, shape and form available, will be creativity.

Sir Kenneth Robinson, educational guru extraordinaire, is understandably puzzled over why governments have so much difficulty both in defining the term, and embedding it across every part of every portfolio.

However good a game politicians and policy devisers talk, walking the walk seems beyond the capabilities of many hobbled souls immobilised in the strait-jacket of structure and precedent.

Yet, says Kenneth, creativity is not some esoteric gift bestowed on only a favoured few. 'If you're human,' he observes, 'it comes with the kit.'

In this country of mine. In this shiny new independent nation-state of mine, this kit will not be vandalised by schools, nor jettisoned by politicians. This kit will be nourished, cosseted, lauded and, most crucially of all, given the free rein which allows individual imaginations to soar.

There will be a ban on aye-beenery.

There will be classrooms without walls where information is imparted to and imbued by children in wild open spaces, adventure playgrounds, museums, galleries, theatres and cinemas.

They will be exposed to every kind of music and all manner of literature. They will learn their history, and that of the wider world. They will love and respect nature and animals and spend much time with both.

There will be mud.

Our Curriculum for Excellence will be allowed to do what it said on its founding tin, to cherish lateral thought and intellectual interaction. The naughty step will be reserved for those fearful of being naughty.

Lessons will instead be projects which recognise that every pupil has skills and ideas which are of equal value. Nothing will be deemed too daft. Because 'daftness' is not infrequently the currency of genius.

And so, everyone who grows up in this shiny new independent nation-state will know they have worth; know they are valued equally.

Everyone who chooses to enter government will understand that operating creatively, being nervous of conformity, being receptive to flights of fancy, will produce quite remarkable and unexpected results. Safety first will be reserved for crossing roads, not boundaries.

And in every field of human endeavour, that innate creativity will not emerge from the kit on special occasions to be the subject of occasional admiration, lightly polished, and hastily returned to its box.

Instead it will be the beating heart of work, leisure and relationships. It will underpin essential tolerance of those whose choices differ from your own, and those who pay this shiny new independent nation-state the ultimate compliment of coming to share our homeland. Which in every essential regard will become their homeland.

This shiny new independent country of mine will understand that to be a mongrel nation, far from being a term of insult, will be the living proof that diversity is not a mere aspiration but a fact of life and daily living.

They once called Mandela's South Africa 'the rainbow nation'. It would be a grand thing if the new Scotland – this shiny new independent nation-state – earned that moniker too. (We're halfway there with the rain.)

Ruth Wishart is a journalist and broadcaster with a broad interest in the arts.

CHARLES
W.J. WITHERS

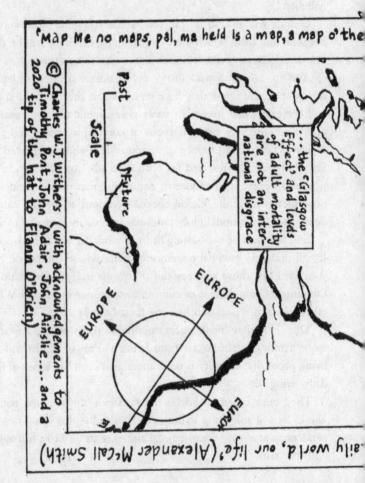

'Map Me no maps, pal, ma held is a map, a map o'the daily world, our life' (Alexander McCall Smith)

© Charles W.J Withers (with acknowledgements to 2020 Timothy Pont, John Adair, John Ainslie.... and a tip of the hat to Flann O'Brien)

Past

Scale

Future

... the 'Glasgow Effect' and levels of adult mortality are not an inter-national disgrace

EUROPE

EUROPE

EUROPE

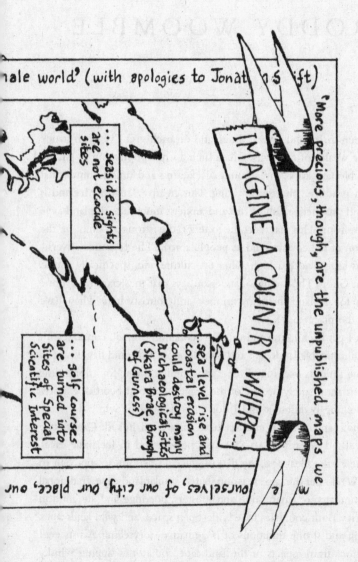

nale world' (with apologies to Jonat[h]a[n] S[w]ift)

'More precious, though, are the unpublished maps we

IMAGINE A COUNTRY WHERE...

... seaside sights
are not ecocide
sites

... golf courses
are turned into
Sites of Special
Scientific Interest

... sea-level rise and
coastal erosion
could destroy many
archaeological sites
(Skara Brae, Brough
of Gurness)

...ourselves, of our city, our place, our

Charles W. J. Withers is Professor Emeritus of Historical Geography at the University of Edinburgh and was Geographer Royal for Scotland, 2015–2022.

RODDY WOOMBLE

I've been to Iceland several times, and on each visit I've been struck by the wealth of creativity. Given such a small population in a fairly inhospitable landscape, the amount of exciting and unique music that has been produced there is amazing. The creative scene in Iceland is manic and productive, full of fire and anxiety, much like the landscape it comes from. This has become one of the strongest links in the promotion of the country and its people abroad. The Icelandic government has long placed a high value on culture and, specifically, music. President Guðni Thorlacius Jóhannesson says that musicians have 'done wonders for Iceland, bringing money and tourists here. They have made it the place to be.'

Then I get back home and think – Scotland is a small country with a fairly inhospitable landscape and a small population, and has also been producing unique, exciting, diverse and popular music for a long time too. Music must surely be one of the biggest and best Scottish exports. Yet something is different and I don't know what or why.

Icelandic and Scottish cultures have long been linked. Gaelic-style etchings dated as early as AD 800 have been found in Icelandic caves. Then there's the bleakness, the dark nights and hedonistic approach to alcohol. We border the same seas and share a similar landscape. Traditional food is similar too: langoustine and lobsters, porridge and ale, mutton and berries. Both countries have wide-open spaces and wild landscapes, with long and strong traditions of imaginative storytelling. Artists craft their visions from aspects of the landscape, sometimes sipping whisky or brennivín as a way of easing self-consciousness (amongst other things).

Making art of any sort can provide something we lack, something we weren't even aware we needed. Creativity is at the heart of what makes us human. In Iceland, they recognise this. The arts, and especially music, are a priority. They're seen as a basic human need; supported and encouraged across the board. The Icelandic government embraces the often anarchic spirit of art and artists.

Icelandic traditional music is rooted in epic poetry with diatonic melodies. 'Rímur' is its name, and it's interesting to see the influence that modern hip-hop has on many young Icelandic musicians and what they do to update it. It's as if rímur has been brought to life as something totally new – the link between the old and the new world, traditions being ripped up and put back together. But in Scotland we tend to celebrate tradition, and cleave to traditional music above more esoteric sounds.

I believe that, unlike Iceland, the arts are still marginalised in the UK. Access to them is seen as a luxury only granted to some. I was told growing up that 99.9 per cent of artists were unemployed, which wasn't inspiring! Things are better here now: Creative Scotland is a valiant funding body, and the Scottish Album of the Year awards help highlight the diversity of music released here. But it's still an uphill struggle.

By contrast, in Iceland you can leave school with a government grant to live on while you create. Art and expression are placed at higher value, and invested in, because they are for everyone. Perhaps the global success of Björk, probably the world's biggest avant-garde pop star, gave the Icelandic government the confidence to celebrate ideas others might consider strange or wild.

That confidence breeds commitment on the part of artists. Weeks, months, seasons and years might pass before a work is finished. And often the act of creating is short in comparison with the thinking and collecting that goes into it. Without concrete support, most artists compromise and do other work, which squeezes their creativity into the gaps.

I do believe the Scottish government values music and the arts but it's not enough to value tradition alone. We need to be open to supporting a wide range of creative acts and excited by the prospect.

American punk-rock musician D. Boon had a vision of a musical utopia: a band in every street. In every other garage or basement, music could be created, ideas exchanged. In my imagined country the kind of music you made would not be determined by tradition or someone else's sense of validity. Punk rock would be on the school curriculum, surrealist poetry and art would sit alongside the classical masters. The latest hip-hop records would be listened to alongside the oldest folk ballads. Ideas would be celebrated and supported, because we never know where they might lead us.

The deeply creative, eccentric collective soul of Scotland would be celebrated, nurtured and invested in for future generations to tear apart in their turn, then to reinvent as the cycle continues . . . Creativity without limits should be our goal.

Roddy Woomble is a songwriter and singer who for the past twenty-five years has fronted the rock band Idlewild.

CHRISTOPHER YOUNG

I am imagining a country in which I have just left school. I am a general trainee at Studio Scotland.

The Studio provides content for its own platform, which reaches audiences through a network of cinemas, streaming and television channels in Scotland. It also distributes this content around the world on its internet platform. The Studio is autonomous and all the key commercial and creative decisions are made by its chief of staff and key management team from its headquarters in Scotland.

Studio HQ is housed within a very large, fully equipped studio production complex in the Highlands and Islands of Scotland and all its key personnel work from there.

The Studio has a reputation for successfully delivering outstanding new work and it has a significant following at home and abroad. There is a constant demand from audiences for new productions and each department within the Studio competes for these new commissions. The Studio's popularity and success means that it can operate independently with guaranteed funding for at least the next fifteen years, all generated through a combination of its commercial activities and public funding.

Within the Studio there is a large Training Department which operates like a film and television school. This is where I will spend the next four years working alongside my fellow students, but also experienced professionals across all disciplines. In my first year I will work on a variety of film and television projects – commercial, cultural and experimental – and at the end of this year I will choose a more focused career path from a wide range of options, including all the main technical, craft- and talent-based skills needed for making all kinds of film and television, including news, drama, comedy, documentary and animation. I'll have acquired basic skills in cinematography, design, editing, performance, writing, directing and producing. In the three or four years that follow, I will develop these skills on the job and create new work both with other students and with experienced professionals working for the Studio.

New productions made by and with students within the Training Department are released on the Studio platform.

At the Studio we are encouraged to make ambitious new work, and from the start we have the opportunity to work with colleagues who have a wide range of skills and experience, ranging from beginners to award-winning professionals, all working within the Studio.

The Studio employs a large workforce of over 2,000 professionals, and the Training Department has an intake of 100 students each year. The range and variety of work that is made means that many successful students choose to continue working within the Studio having finished their training.

The Studio has satellite facilities across Scotland and many of its employees and students have the opportunity to work in different locations around the country.

Here in this imagined country I am excited at the prospect of fulfilling my dream to pursue a career in film-making, where I will be involved in making original new Scottish productions for many years to come. This is how we share the gift of imagination with everyone.

Christopher Young is a Scottish producer based in Skye and has been making films, drama and comedy for over thirty years, including the hit TV show and movie The Inbetweeners.

ACKNOWLEDGEMENTS

It won't surprise anyone who knows us to hear that the idea for this book was conceived on a summer evening in Edinburgh over a glass or two of red wine. The idea persisted in the cold light of day, and we were delighted that agent Jenny Brown and editor Francis Bickmore shared our excitement for the project and acted as patient midwives to bring it to fruition. Our first thanks go to them.

We owe a debt of gratitude to the University of Otago in Dunedin, New Zealand, where we were based as Visiting Professors when most of the work on the project was done. Thanks in particular to: Professor Liam McIlvanney and Professor Sonja Tiernan, our colleagues at the Centre for Irish and Scottish Studies; Dr Sophie Bond and colleagues from the School of Geography; the University of Otago William Evans Fellowship programme; Professor John Crump; Pro-Vice Chancellor Tony Ballantyne and his Executive Assistant Leslie Turner; and to the Trustees of the Caselberg Trust, particularly Lesley Hirst and Janet Downs, for our stay at the Caselberg Cottage on the beautiful Otago Peninsula.

Finally, and most importantly, thanks to all our contributors who gave so generously of their time and their talents to make this book a springboard for debate and conversation. This time and talent has been given without payment and instead the royalties from sales of this book will be shared between five Scottish charities whose work aims to bring a better Scotland closer: Shelter Scotland, Scottish Women's Aid, Scottish Book Trust, Refuweegee and Reforesting Scotland.

Here's to the imagined country!

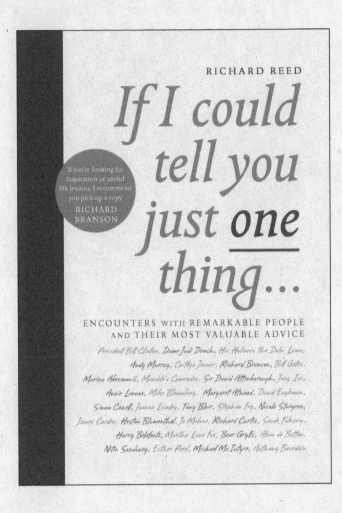

RICHARD REED

If I could tell you just *one* thing...

ENCOUNTERS WITH REMARKABLE PEOPLE
AND THEIR MOST VALUABLE ADVICE

President Bill Clinton, Dame Judi Dench, His Holiness the Dalai Lama,
Andy Murray, Caitlyn Jenner, Richard Branson, Bill Gates,
Marina Abramović, Mandela's Comrades, Sir David Attenborough, Jony Ive,
Annie Lennox, Mike Bloomberg, Margaret Atwood, David Eagleman,
Simon Cowell, Joanna Lumley, Tony Blair, Stephen Fry, Nicola Sturgeon,
James Corden, Heston Blumenthal, Jo Malone, Richard Curtis, Sandi Toksvig,
Harry Belafonte, Martha Lane Fox, Bear Grylls, Alain de Botton,
Nitin Sawhney, Esther Perel, Michael McIntyre, Anthony Bourdain

'If you're looking for inspiration or useful life lessons, I recommend you pick up a copy'
RICHARD BRANSON

'Entertaining collection of pearls of wisdom'
Times Literary Supplement

CANON‖GATE